No Name
No Number

Exploring the 11:11 phenomenon

No Name
No Number

Exploring the 11:11 phenomenon

Hilary H. Carter

AXIS MUNDI
BOOKS

Winchester, UK
Washington, USA

First published by Axis Mundi Books, 2013
Axis Mundi Books is an imprint of John Hunt Publishing Ltd., Laurel House, Station Approach,
Alresford, Hants, SO24 9JH, UK
office1@jhpbooks.net
www.johnhuntpublishing.com
www.axismundi-books.com

For distributor details and how to order please visit the 'Ordering' section on our website.

ISBN: 978 1 78099 894 7

A CIP catalogue record for this book is available from the British Library.

Design: Stuart Davies

Printed and bound by CPI Group (UK) Ltd, Croydon, CR0 4YY

We operate a distinctive and ethical publishing philosophy in all
areas of our business, from our global network of authors to
production and worldwide distribution.

CONTENTS

"In the beginning," he said, "there was only The Nothing, but a nothing with a capital N. Since it was no-thing and nothing else existed it had no name. It was hidden like the light locked in a black lump of coal. This nothing then withdrew from a part of itself so its creation could exist in freedom. This was the greatest gift – for good or ill. Then out of compassion this No-thing, this source of being scattered sparks of itself into the void it had so catastrophically created and the purpose of our creation is to redirect those divine sparks back into itself to make it whole again."

Rabbi Lionel Blue. *Thought for the Day*. BBC Radio 4. 27/2/2012

Chapter 1

The Prediction

I have to begin by telling you that if it wasn't for the number 11:11 there's no way I would have been driving into the small French town of Montignac sur Vézère on a cold, misty November morning. In fact it really is the last place on earth I would have chosen to be, even though my connection to that particular part of France had been predicted some years earlier. I could still remember the day when Catherine had given me my first ever tarot card reading. I had only just met her and I knew that she had a reputation as an outstanding psychic so I was surprised and slightly disconcerted when she turned over the final tarot card and announced, "And I can see you spending a lot of time in France in the future. You'll be in the Dordogne."

The Dordogne? She might as well have said I'd be spending time on the moon! Of all the places in the world to suggest, she had chosen the one place on earth that I vowed I would never, ever set foot in. I hated the Dordogne with a vengeance. Catherine was a remarkable and very gifted psychic so I just assumed that she was having an off day. How could I possibly have known that she had indeed predicted the future?

There are legitimate reasons for my dislike of the Dordogne as it is the very region in France where I was once attacked and almost killed by a madman. It happened when I was 21 years old. I had set off alone to travel overland from my home in England to India. My intention was to work my way through Europe and raise enough money en route to be able to survive for a few months once I arrived in India. The first stop on my long journey was at a vineyard in the Dordogne where I spent 4 weeks picking grapes. After being paid for my work in cash I booked into the youth hostel in Bordeaux. My next stop would be Italy to help with the olive harvest. However, when I arrived at Bordeaux Youth Hostel and reached into my rucksack for my hard earned money I discovered that it had all been stolen.

Alone and penniless, I was befriended by a French woman who found me work in a bar. It was a live-in position in a small village somewhere east of Bordeaux. I can't remember the name of it. Within days both the father and the son of the family had sexually attacked me. Although I was only 21, I was already well travelled. I had journeyed alone as far north as the Arctic Circle and as far south as the Greek islands and I had never encountered problems.

Following the assaults I felt frightened, unsafe and vulnerable so I packed my bags and ran away from the bar in the early hours of the morning, just before the dawn. I decided to head for my sister's home in the Netherlands. I had no money for bus fares so I hitchhiked. I knew that was a bit risky but I could think of no other way. I had hitched many times before and I had developed 2 'fail safe' strategies. Firstly, if someone I didn't like the look of stopped and offered me a lift I would ask for a destination in the opposite direction. They would then point me in the right direction.

Secondly, whenever I got into a car I would not close the passenger door properly. Then it would have to be opened and shut again. In that way I knew how to open it if I needed to make a quick getaway. This was in the days before central locking was the norm. It was this second strategy that probably saved my life.

I stuck my thumb out and within minutes a car stopped. The driver wound down the car window.

"Where are you going?" he asked in a rasping voice.

As soon as I looked at him I thought, 'No way.' All my senses shouted RED ALERT. I was staring danger in the face and I knew it. I can picture his face as though it was yesterday. He wore pebble glass spectacles, had a bulbous nose and a fat red face. He was glistening with sweat and his few remaining strands of dark hair were plastered to his head with grease. Even now, decades later, I could easily pick him out in an identity parade. The very thought of him still made me feel sick. I was heading for Tours but I didn't say that.

"Cannes," I replied, knowing that was in the opposite direction.

"Fine, get in."

That was not supposed to happen. He was supposed to tell me I was on the wrong side of the road. Momentarily thrown, I foolishly got into the car, not quite closing the door behind me. He leaned across, and pulled the black plastic handle towards him to open the door. He then closed it properly. I winced as his arm touched the front of my body and the top of his head brushed my face. He stank of alcohol and tooth decay and strong French cigarettes. I put my small rucksack on my knee as a form of protection, hugging it to me as one would hug a baby, a symbolic barrier between my body and the stranger.

He drove carelessly, turning his head regularly to look at me. My mind was racing along with my heart. Why had I got in the car? How could I have been so foolish? How was I going to get myself out of this? Each time he glanced at me his eyes scanned my body and my heart began to pound heavily in my chest. I didn't speak. I couldn't. My sense of unease was overwhelming. I had made a huge mistake by getting into the car and I had to find a way to get out. Maybe I could ask him to stop at a bar so I could use the toilet? Then I would say I no longer needed a lift and I would stay in the safety of the bar. But there were no bars in sight. I thought about opening the door and jumping out of the moving car but even though he was not driving fast I decided that was too dangerous.

Suddenly he turned off the main road and began driving through the forest. I knew I was now in even more danger. Before I had time to consider any more possible escape options, my instincts were confirmed. He was indeed a monster. He braked sharply, pulled into a clearing on the side of the road and pounced on me. I immediately went for the door handle to make a dash for safety but before I could reach it my attacker grabbed my wrist and twisted it, pushing me back against the seat and forcing my arm away from the door. He was strong, much stronger than me. His fat hairy hands started ripping at my clothes and I fought with all my might to stop him. His stinking breath was suffocating and made me feel nauseous. I fought like a cat, trying to scratch him with my nails, but that was no defence against his urge to rape me. I couldn't even scream or call out. I was in such fear that I was having difficulty breathing. All my energy was focused on fighting him off. His hands moved to my throat when I resisted his advances. They squeezed tighter and tighter on my neck as I struggled to find the black door handle with my free hand. I could feel his hot, sticky, sweaty fingers against my windpipe and I was beginning to choke. I felt death in the air. Panic rose inside me. We were miles from any houses and there was nobody around. I could feel the breath leaving my body. I was face to face with the grim reaper and I knew it. Was I going to die in a forest in the French countryside, far from friends and family?

Desperately I searched for the door handle. I was not religious but as a last resort, I called out to God. 'Please God, please, help me, I'm begging you, help me! I'll do anything you ask of me if you just get me out of this car!' I screamed silently into the ether. The plea came from the core of my being, from deep inside me, not from my mind or my mouth. In that instant I found the handle. As soon as I found it I released the catch and now it was the monster's turn to be surprised as my body fell back through the open door on to the leafy ground and, as he released his hands from my neck to steady himself, I slipped from his grasp. I twisted my body, leaped to my feet and I ran. I ran and ran, faster than I had ever run before. I didn't look back. I was running for my life, quite literally. I heard him jump out of the car in pursuit, grunting and puffing as he tried to pursue me, his heavy feet crunching on the fallen leaves as we ran through the forest, but he was fat and unfit and he couldn't catch me. I ran through the trees and across a grassy field until I came to a high metal fence, far too high to climb over, but I was young, agile and thin so I managed to squeeze under it. The ground was wet and muddy which maybe helped me to slip under so quickly. My attacker lost me for good at this point because no way would his fat belly squeeze under a gap so narrow. Even though I knew he could not follow me I kept on running and I didn't look back. Not once. I ran until I could run no more and then, scratched, soaked, bloodied, battered, traumatized, muddy and exhausted I flopped down on a bale of hay and cried. My entire body ached. I sobbed and sobbed, each sob painfully gripping my ribs like a metal vice, deep heaving sobs that spoke of a brush with death and the relief of escape. I was alive!

As I lay there on the edge of a French field, I vowed that I would never, ever return to the Dordogne. I had kept that vow until the convent appeared in my life.

Chapter 2

The French Convent

House For Sale. 94,000 euros.

The house is situated at the top of one of the most picturesque pedestrian-only streets in the historic town of Montignac sur Vézère in the Dordogne region of France. This ancient stone dwelling is built on 3 levels, in a pleasant and quiet setting offering an exceptional view of the Vézère valley. Built on a hill, the house comprises 3 rooms with separate access. It sits on a 500 square metre plot of land. Originally, it was part of an old convent.

As soon as I read the last sentence, my heart skipped a beat. I read it several times with disbelief. Another old convent? I must admit that the location sounded wonderful, although I had never heard of Montignac. I went to the bookshop and looked it up on the Michelin motoring and tourist map of France. There I found it, listed between Montier and Montigny-le-Roi: Montignac. Map reference I.11. Then I looked carefully at my map of Europe and I realized that Montignac was located at 1.1 degrees of longitude. To me, those numbers were very significant. Because of their appearance I knew that whether I liked it or not, this old convent was speaking to me in the language of numbers.

I had owned a convent once before, in Andalucía, Spain. Everything to do with the Spanish convent had mysteriously involved the number 11, 111 or 11:11 in a way that had been far beyond coincidence. Because of the traumatic events that I had experienced during my ownership of the Spanish convent, most of the original building had fallen down. After less than 2 eventful years I had sold it on as a redevelopment site. Although I didn't want to get involved in buying another old convent with all the secrets and complex history that I knew would come with it, it was no use. I couldn't run away from my destiny.

Owning the convent in Spain had taken its toll on me physically, mentally, emotionally and financially. Far from being a sacred, beautiful, atmospheric building which I could have used as a yoga centre, I had discovered a gruelling, dark, bloody history, the echoes of which were still impregnated into the walls of that ancient and historic Spanish building. After selling up and liquidating my assets I worked out that I would be able to raise a maximum of 95,000 euros to buy another property. My dream of creating a yoga and retreat centre was looking like a fading possibility. There was nothing suitable for that sort of price in southern Spain.

"Why don't you try France?" suggested my sister. "My friend has just bought a really cheap property in the Dordogne. I'm sure you'll be able to find something in that area for less than 95,000 euros."

"The Dordogne? You're joking! Forget it. I'll never go and live there. I can't stand the place. You know I hate it. That's the last place on earth I would choose to go to. I don't like France, I never have done and I never will."

But I was curious. Was my sister right? Was property in the Dordogne region of France really that cheap? I had been under the impression that French property was quite expensive. Purely out of interest, I googled 'Dordogne Property' and typed in a maximum budget of 95,000 euros.

My sister was wrong because the properties were not cheap. Only 5 properties were available in my price range. There was a small secluded barn, a building plot, a shop, a ruin and the old convent in Montignac.

Despite my personal dislike of the Dordogne I found it impossible to resist investigating the property a bit further. I couldn't stop myself. It was as if there was a force inside me driving me on. Not only was I curious but I was also very aware of the number 1's in the map reference and longitude so I simply wrote a short e-mail to the seller to ask whether the property was habitable or not. That was all. But I also set the Universe a secret challenge. 'If the seller of the convent sends the response to my e-mail at 11:11 then I will take note of that. I will then attempt to overcome my resistance to the Dordogne and I will try and find the courage to visit the convent.' That might sound like a strange ultimatum but there is a reason behind it. Let me explain.

I don't live my life in a normal way. You might have heard of the film *Yes Man* which was based on the experiences of the British comedian Danny Wallace. For a period of 6 months he decided to say yes to every opportunity that was presented to him.

There was also the novel called *The Dice Man* about a man who used the roll of a dice to make his decisions. Although not a true story, the idea of the book was based on a man (George Cockcroft) who briefly used dice to make decisions while studying psychology.

Well, I don't say yes to everything and I don't roll a dice to make my decisions but I do live according to the appearance of numbers in my everyday life. In particular I live according to the number 11:11. Whenever the 11:11 appears I use it as a sign. You could call me 'The 11:11 woman'. I really do live my life in this somewhat bizarre and unconventional way! However, it is not a random and meaningless decision, because my belief is that 11:11 is the sign of our Higher Self/Inner Divinity/God/One Consciousness or whatever term you choose to use. I believe that what we perceive as reality is in fact just a consciousness program. When the binary number 11:11 starts to appear in everyday life it indicates that your de-programming has begun. Or it might be more accurate to say that your re-programming has started. You're being re-programmed with Divine Consciousness. Think about it. Computers are programmed by the binary system of numbers so if we are living within a consciousness program then it follows that we would be programmed with the binary system too.

Not only do I think that the number 11:11 appears in your everyday life to show you the way out of illusion but I also believe it to be a fast track route. That's why I follow it. It's similar to having a direct connection to God. When 11:11 or 111 or 11 shows up it's like a finger pointing the way to go. It says, "If you're fed up messing about and you want to get off the wheel of karma and rebirth and out of illusion, just follow me. I'll bring up all your stuff so you can deal with it and I'll show you what your contract on earth is. All you have to do is to be willing to keep your mind out of any decision making process and have enough courage to take enormous leaps of faith."

I need to state the obvious here, namely that I would never take action if the number 11:11 appeared and if acting on its appearance didn't feel right. I always (and I mean always) run actions past my intuition before I act. If your intuition is not well developed then the 11:11 path cannot be trodden, although I also believe that the 11:11 will not appear in your life until you are ready. That's why it appears to some people and not to others. However, I do not run 11:11 prompted actions through my mind because I have learned that decisions based on the appearance of the 11:11 do not always make logical sense. In fact they rarely do. I have also learned that taking leaps of faith requires a large dose of courage.

Numbers are my system of reading the world. To me they are the interface between the seen and the unseen worlds. My understanding is that numbers are the language of consciousness as opposed to words which are the language of thoughts and therefore of the mind. I prefer my guidance to come directly from consciousness rather than through the programming of the mind.

In 2003, when the number 11:11 first started to appear in my life, I had no idea why it was happening. Why did I keep looking at the clock just as the digits lined up at 11:11? Why had I not glanced at the clock one minute earlier or one minute later? It's not as if I looked at the clock that often. However, number synchronicities began happening so regularly and so dramatically that I realized something very peculiar was going on, something way beyond normal. Shortly after the 11:11 began to appear to me, I decided to start my experiment, using numbers as signs to guide me just to see what would happen. I have been living in this way for 9 years and, the longer I do so, the more convinced I become that the 11:11 can be interpreted as "Act on this and you are acting in perfect alignment with Divine Will." Essentially we can either act from selfishness (our ego nature) or unselfishness (our Divine nature). Once we surrender our free will to Divine Will we become instruments of light on earth. I have found that basing decisions on the appearance of numbers is an excellent way of releasing the stranglehold of the ego. In my experience it also makes for a very interesting (although somewhat challenging, unsettling and unpredictable!) life.

I was relieved when the reply to my e-mail came through a few days later because it had not been sent at 11:11 or 11:22 or any similar time, though I did notice that it had arrived on October 31st which is Halloween. Halloween is the night of All Hallows. On A(ll) Ha(ll)ows the veil that separates the dead from the living is particularly thin. The following day is All Saints' Day, the first of November. (1.11.) It is also the Pagan festival of Samhain. (1.11.)

31st October 2006. Hi Hilary, Of course, this house needs some work to become a nice property, but it has been used by my parents as a summer house for many years. So, I confirm that this house is habitable but it will need new electricity. At this time, one room of about 35 sqm, the bathroom, WC and kitchen are fully operational. Do not hesitate to contact me again if you need further information. Yours sincerely. Bella.

Bella. Her name contained a double 'l' which I refer to as a hidden 11, but as there was no powerful 11:11 sign I decided not to do anything in a hurry. In fact I did nothing. I didn't even reply to Bella's e-mail. I simply left things as they were. Subconsciously I think I was probably hoping that if I did nothing then the convent would go away or be sold to somebody else. But deep inside I already knew that the convent would one day be mine.

All was quiet and calm until April 1st the following spring. The fact that this was April Fool's Day did not escape me. Completely out of the blue, I received an e-mail from Bella telling me that the convent had not yet been sold, so would I like to go and see it? The e-mail had been sent at 9:11. That was just enough to unsettle me because I couldn't completely dismiss it as a sign. It was not the powerful 11:11 sign that I was looking for but, as it was the date of the destruction of the Twin Towers (that huge number 11 in bricks and mortar on the New York skyline), and because 9+1+1=11, then it was enough for me to be unable to reject the convent outright.

I saw that she was suggesting May 11th as a suitable date for a viewing. Another 11, but still not the double 11:11. I sat pondering those 2 number signs. 11 and 9:11. In conjunction with the 1.1 longitude and the I.11 map reference, were they strong enough signs to act upon? If so, there should be no hesitation, so why was I hesitant? Then I casually glanced down and saw the time displayed in the corner of my laptop screen. 11:11. I drew a sharp intake of breath. That was it. There was no decision to make and there was no hesitation as it was now abundantly clear, thanks to the 11:11 number prompt, that the convent was indeed waiting for me. I did not permit my mind to affect my decision in any way. I simply decided then and there that I would buy it. In that moment I surrendered to my destiny and chose to follow Divine Will.

Chapter 3

The First Visit

I met Bella and her partner Claude on the old stone bridge in the centre of the small town of Montignac and we greeted each other in typical French style with a kiss on each cheek. Below us flowed the river Vézère, the fast flowing water that divided the town. One side of the river was fairly level and prone to flooding. The other side was steep and hilly and that's where the convent was.

"It's there," said Claude, pointing to a building not far from an old castle. I could just make out a crooked sloping roof and a patch of overgrown garden.

We climbed the steep hill and then turned off the narrow road into an even narrower passageway. This area certainly was as picturesque as the advertisement on the Internet had suggested. Stopping outside a high double gate, Bella pulled a bunch of old-fashioned keys from her bag and carefully unlocked it. It opened to reveal a steep flight of stone steps leading up towards the house. The house was exactly as I had imagined it to be: detached, small yet tall and with a deeply pitched roof, typical of the local style of architecture.

Bella, Claude and I carefully climbed the steps. I counted them: 23. It was a significant number, the number of destruction and breakdown. Each step was a different height, the stones curved and worn with age. I couldn't begin to imagine how old they were. The metal handrail was loose, having rusted away completely in parts. The garden was a good size but totally overgrown. There were cherry, plum and apple trees and a massive hazelnut tree which dominated a large part of the garden. The view was magnificent. I could see for miles down the Vézère valley, yet I could also clearly see the people crossing the old bridge in the centre of Montignac. Walking towards the front door of the property I noticed that all the garden walls were made from dry stone and I wondered where all the stone had come from.

We entered the house through the partially glazed, old, wooden maroon-painted door. It opened directly into the main living area. I was momentarily stunned by the sheer height of the place. The room was almost 4 metres high yet it was only about 5 metres by 5 metres square. The ceiling was beamed and both floor and ceiling were made of narrow, wooden planks. Bella told me the wood was chestnut. Old twisted wiring and Bakelite fittings revealed the age of the electrics. It looked somewhat dangerous, with bits of loose wire dangling here and there. The light was on even though it was a sunny day because the one tiny window above the door hardly allowed any daylight to enter. I guess it must have been a 40 watt bulb because the light hardly made an impact on the darkness. There was another smaller door that was rotten, and judging by the piles of wood dust and splinters the interior steps leading up to the door looked as if they had woodworm or dry rot. At least half of the wood had been eaten away and the rest of it was full of holes. All the glass panes in that door were broken or missing. The multi-paned window above the main door was also broken. Plaster had fallen from the walls and lay in heaps on the floor. There was a massive wooden fireplace that took up almost the whole width of the room.

"That's a typical Périgordian fireplace," Claude explained. "In the old days the family would sit inside the fireplace to keep warm."

That was it. That was the bulk of the house, just one large, high, dark room. It smelt damp and musty.

"But where is the kitchen?" I asked.

Claude led me outside once again and unlocked a door to the side of the main door. There was a tiny kitchen which led through to an even smaller shower room and toilet. This small extension had been built on to the property about 30 years earlier. It was essentially an old outside toilet with a kitchen tacked on the side. I did not relish the idea of having to get up to use the bathroom on a chilly night. My face must have shown my feelings because Claude beckoned me to follow him. Against the side wall of the house was a rickety ladder which he speedily climbed, and entered an opening into the roof space. I followed him, not quite so speedily and found myself in a potential room, exactly the same size as the room below, but even higher at the apex. As the room was not plastered I could see that the chimney breast and walls were built from beautiful pale golden stone.

"Up here you could have a bedroom," suggested Claude. "There are already 3 windows in existence so you would not have to ask permission to make an opening."

There was a tiny, metal roof window, a medium-sized opening with no glass and the 'door/window' which we had climbed through. This had no wooden frame or glass. It was a strange place to have an opening. I peered through the medium-sized window and the views were utterly spectacular, even better than from the floor below.

Climbing down the unstable ladder and back on to ground level I followed Bella as she led me through the garden. The garden was on 2 levels, a higher and a lower, separated by a rough path. There was another set of double gates at this level, hung on 2 imposing stone pillars. A beautiful long-haired tortoiseshell cat sat on top of one pillar, observing me with suspicious eyes. We stepped our way carefully back down the steep, stone steps into the lowest part of the garden and stopped outside a small stone outbuilding.

"Come and see this. In here we have a very rare medieval oven," said Claude.

He stepped inside, bending his head to do so for this building had a very low threshold.

"Come and see the old oven, made out of stone. It's really

antique. Come in, come in," he urged me.

For some reason I didn't want to enter this building, but Claude was so keen to show me the oven that I ignored my feeling of resistance and stepped inside to join him. As soon as I walked through the doorway I knew I had made a mistake. Instantly I had the feeling that I was being crushed. The pressure on my chest was enormous and I couldn't take a breath. It was such a scary feeling that I felt a sense of panic rise up inside me and, hastily pushing Claude aside, I stepped back into the garden again and breathed.

"But you didn't look at the oven!" he protested.

He looked at my face. I must have looked pale.

"What's the matter? Is it the spiders? Bella is the same. She has arachnophobia."

Bella looked at me sympathetically. I nodded in agreement, narrowing my eyes and forcing a smile. It was not arachnophobia, though I do suffer from it. It was the crushing density of psychic residue in there that my physical body couldn't handle.

"Never mind," he said. "Come and see the last room. This is the room that is the oldest part of the house. As you know, this whole site was once part of a convent. It was a teaching convent."

Claude led the way through the undergrowth and all 3 of us stepped through the ill-fitting ancient studded wooden door into the old stone room. God alone knows how old that door was. The doorway was quite low, though I could see the original stone lintel indicating that an earlier doorway had been much higher. This room, like the main room above, was lit only by a low wattage light bulb. However, no light was needed to sense the history that was seeped into every crevice of that room. It positively reeked of drama, trauma, death, life, holiness, history and prayer. It hummed with psychic activity too. I felt a strong presence in there that was unlike anything I had felt before. It was not threatening but it felt very, very ancient. I've no idea what it was. I had never felt anything that old before. It was very dark and quite difficult to see much so I took a quick photo of this room before we left.

What I could see was that this ground floor room had actually been built directly into the cliff face. The back wall was the cliff. In reality it was a cave so it was totally uninhabitable. Like the room above, it was about 5 metres square with solid stone walls on 3 sides and a magnificent, top quality dressed stone fireplace that took up almost the whole of the cave wall. It was far more impressive and commanding than the wooden fire surround in the room above. I couldn't reconcile those 2 things in my mind. A primitive cave with an exquisite fireplace? Something didn't add up.

This room, the oldest one in the house, didn't feel cramped as it was over 3 and a half metres high, the same as the room above. I wondered why it had been built so high. It's not as if our ancestors were very tall.

Water was literally running down the back wall. I didn't know where it was coming from but the dampness permeated the air. There were 2 small square windows, both so high up in the wall that it was not possible to look out of them. They were not glazed and they hardly let in any light. The depth of the opening revealed that the walls were at least 60 cms thick. This room was even darker and gloomier than the first one. On the ceiling 6 wooden beams, black with age and each in excess of 30 cms square, supported the floor of the main room above. To the right of the stunning fireplace the stone wall had been blackened by a fire and the left-hand side of the fireplace had been completely walled in with rough stones and cement. That looked suspicious, as though there was something to be hidden. I looked down at the old floor which appeared to be made mostly of bare earth with a few flagstones.

"This is the original old floor," said Claude. He bent down and pretended to lift one of the stones. "Maybe there is treasure under here!" he joked.

The flagstones looked as if they were just carefully selected stones from the hills round and about, some large and some small. Whoever had created the floor had obviously tried to find the flattest stones possible. What an unusual floor! As well as the 2 high square windows there was a graceful arched stone window which had been blocked in with stone blocks. If that could be reopened and glazed the room would be much lighter.

That was it. 3 rooms on 3 floors with 3 separate entrances, a kitchen and bathroom, one very large garden with amazing views, an outhouse with a medieval oven, a steep flight of stone steps and 2 pairs of double gates.

We left through the lower gates and walked along the path to the nearest road. The convent was in the historic part of town where there were no roads wide enough for vehicles. It was a pedestrian-only area. It was a conservation area and all the properties were listed. Just around the corner there was a stone fountain. This was the spring, constantly flowing with beautiful fresh cool water.

"Water from source," explained Claude. "Try some. Drink it. It's good. You can bring your bottles up here and fill them up." I tried the water. It was ice cold and tasted slightly sweet.

"The name of this town is Montignac and that means 'the hill down which the water flows'," explained Bella. "Any French towns that end with the letters 'ac' indicate a link with water."

I'm not sure she was right as I was later told that a town ending in 'ac' indicates the former presence of a Gallic-Roman villa. Maybe both statements are true.

There was no more to see so I said my goodbyes and promised to e-mail my thoughts about the house when I returned to England. I already knew that I was destined to become the owner of their property but I didn't reveal that fact to them there and then. As I walked up the hill towards my car I began to feel ill. My legs were like lead and I felt all clammy. I felt a desperate need to lie down so I was glad that my bed was only

10 minute's drive away. I had flown to France from England and had decided to base myself at the Tibetan Buddhist centre a few kilometres away from the town of Montignac. By the time I had driven the 10 minutes to the Buddhist centre it was obvious that I was deteriorating rapidly. I unlocked the door to my room and collapsed on the bed. I felt as though I were paralyzed. I couldn't move my head and everything ached. Oh no! That was the last thing I needed. As I lay there I tried to make sense of what was happening. I felt as if the life force had been sucked out of me and there was only an empty shell lying on the bed. I could hardly move. No way could I even lift my body enough to go for help. Nor could I summon the strength to cry out. And there was nobody I could call on my mobile for help because I was alone in France. I lay there feeling like death. I must have fallen asleep because I had a dream. Or was it a vision?

I was on the top of a hill with a friend and there was a flock of white birds feeding from the seeds in the grass. Suddenly I heard a droning noise and 3 dark birds appeared in the sky above and began to circle the hilltop. The white birds, sensing danger, tried to fly away but found themselves unable to fly. I became aware that the 3 big birds had created an 'energetic trap' of dark energy. As soon as I came to the realization that there was a trap, I woke up with a start. My heart was thumping heavily in my chest and I had broken out in a sweat.

I slept on and off all night and much of the next day, not once leaving the bed. It was over 20 hours before I was found. I had arranged to meet one of the Buddhist nuns for a country walk on the following day and when I didn't turn up she had come to search for me. She fed me hot, sweet tea, gave me massage and healing and chanted some sacred words that her Vietnamese grandmother had taught her. Gradually I began to feel slightly better.

"Have you not been sleeping?" she asked.

"Not very well."

"That's not unusual. When visitors come here to the Buddhist centre they often find that the energy is so high that they are unable to sleep. Sometimes they become ill. But we see this as positive because it is a clearing process."

She left me to sleep. Was it the energy in the Buddhist centre? Or had I caught a chill the night before when the weather was cold and wet? Maybe I had picked up a bug on the plane on the flight over to France? Was the spring water not as pure as Bella had suggested? I didn't know the answer. But I had an uncomfortable feeling that my illness might well have had something to do with that old convent.

The massage and healing helped me. When I felt well enough to drive, I transferred to a nearby hotel for a few days to recuperate in comfort. When the receptionist handed me the keys to room 111, I felt reassured. It was only a small sign but it felt as if the Universe was comforting me and reminding me that what I was experiencing was all part of a much greater picture. It was reaffirming the fact that by acting on the appearance of the 11:11 time prompt I was following Divine Will.

Once I was back in England I took to my bed and remained there like a vegetable for 2 weeks. It was another month before I began to feel anything like my old self.

When I eventually got round to downloading the photo of the cave room on to my laptop I was shocked. There was a single orb on the fireplace. It was massive. Maybe that was the ancient presence that I had sensed.

Chapter 4

Becoming the Guardian

If I could have bought the convent online I would have done so simply because it would have been easier. But I was told I had to attend the lawyer's office in person to sign the papers that would transfer ownership into my name. 6 months after viewing it for the first time, and a year after seeing it on the Internet, I was on my way to buy it. My dream had always been to create a residential yoga centre but the house was far too small to use as that. It would have to be used as an individual retreat centre or a home with a separate yoga studio. That was not what I was looking for and not what I wanted. But when the words 'I' and 'want' appear in the same sentence it strongly suggest it is the ego that is speaking. Just who is this 'I' who is wanting and not wanting? It is my ego or my lower self, and the wants, needs and desires of the ego do not have a place on the 11:11 spiritual path.

As I drove off the ferry in the French port of Dieppe I glanced down at the car milometer. Exactly 87777.7 miles. 2 days later, on the morning of 9th November 2007, I arrived at my destination. As I entered the small town of Montignac in the Dordogne region of France, the milometer read 88222.2. Not only that, the trip meter was exactly 222.2. I was pleased and reassured. These days, if I don't see such dramatic signs in my everyday world then I can start questioning my whole way of living.

I arrived in town just before 11am on Remembrance Sunday 2007. Remembrance Sunday is held on the Sunday nearest to Armistice Day so it is not a fixed date. Armistice Day is fixed. It is always held on the 11th of November. That's 11/11 at 11am.

Armistice Day is on 11 November and commemorates the armistice signed between the Allies of World War I and Germany at

Compiègne, France, for the cessation of hostilities on the Western Front of World War I, which took effect at 11 o'clock in the morning—the "11th hour of the 11th day of the 11th month" of 1918.

Wikipedia

That year Remembrance Sunday just happened to be on 9th November: 9/11. 9:11 was the time of Bella's first e-mail and it's a number that exists in the mass consciousness because of the 9/11 Twin Towers event. As I got out of the car the church bells started to ring and they rang for exactly 11 minutes. Then there was silence, absolute and complete silence, a pause of about 5 minutes. Then the bells chimed the hour. 11am. I had arrived back in Montignac and thanks to the tolling bells I knew that my appearance had been noted at some level.

The following day I met Bella at the lawyer's office as arranged. She was alone. Her relationship with Claude had ended shortly after our last meeting. She was nursing a broken heart and it showed on her delicate and sensitive face, faintly etched with the sad lines of loss and grief.

I did not understand everything about the legal procedure because although I had been attending private French classes in preparation for my move, I was still far from fluent. I asked the lawyer about the address of the property as the legal documents just referred to "The property in Rue des Jardins" and didn't say what number.

"What's the number of the house?" I asked.

"There is no number," replied the lawyer.

"I mean what number in the street is it?" I asked. Naturally I expected it to be number 11 or 111.

"The house has not been allocated a number," he said.

"No number? A house without a number? Well what's the name of the house?" I asked.

"It has no name."

No name and no number. Just a house. A house that used to be a convent…

Within the hour the papers had been signed, the monies transferred and I had a bunch of keys in my hand. 'Now the fun begins…' I thought to myself.

I had not had a survey on the property. I had seen on my first visit that the building had some rotten wood and structural issues, but that didn't matter to me. As I had been led there by the number 11:11, I knew I had to become the owner whatever the condition of the place. My mind would have said that this house was a risky or even a foolish purchase but on the 11:11 path such thoughts need to be ignored. I was not in this as a money-making venture. It was an investment, not in financial terms but in terms of my own spiritual development and in the search for some answers to the 11:11 phenomenon. As with the Spanish convent that I had once bought, I had the feeling that I was to become a Guardian rather than an 'owner'. The convent needed me as much as I needed the convent. This was only my second visit, but my first visit as Guardian.

I entered by the upper gates and had to stoop under the massive branches of the hazelnut tree to reach the edge of the garden. If I entered by the high gate I had to walk down a long flight of stone steps to reach my gate. If I took the low gate I had to climb up the 23 steps that were on my land. As I stood surveying the extensive view I immediately became uncomfortably aware of the nearby ruined tower to my left. It stood eerily above my garden. The castle was very near my property. How come I had not noticed this tower on my last visit? I had visited in early summer so maybe the leaves on the trees had hidden it from view. Now that it was November and the trees were bare, it was clear that the castle tower cast a malevolent shadow over my garden. It had a dark, forbidding presence. The small unglazed windows of this old ruin looked down on me and I felt a powerful force of evil emanating towards me. Something was clearly resenting my presence. It was as if the tower was inhabited by unseen beings of darkness. As I stood there pondering this eerie sensation, the siren on the town hall suddenly blared out. I jumped. As the siren faded, the church bells began to peal. Noon exactly! 12 tolling bells is a very significant sign. It was that moment that marked the beginning of my relationship with the castle tower.

Despite the presence of the tower, I felt a sense of excitement and anticipation as I unlocked the convent door. I couldn't believe that I had been courageous enough to buy it. Was I courageous or was I foolhardy? That I did not know. But I did know that some clearing work was needed. The residue of hundreds upon hundreds of years of history was buzzing away inside the building. Without the distraction of other people, the intensity of the energy was more apparent than during my first visit. Using my Tibetan bowl, chanting sacred mantras and burning my nag champa incense I cleared the first layer of psychic dross. My chanting resonated through the walls yet I felt a strong resistance from other levels. I soon realized that this work might take some time. There would be no quick fix.

The following day was Armistice Day in Montignac. In France this day is a national holiday. Instead of joining the rest of the town on their march through the town with the local band, I decided I would simply focus my video camera on the castle tower and just see what would happen at 11am on the 11/11. That's all. I was surprised at the result. That's one thing about my number journey I can say with confidence: I never cease to marvel at what appears in my life.

I crossed to the other side of the river so I could film the front of the tower. The river was a dominant feature of Montignac. As I crossed the bridge, I felt weak and shaky. I clambered down towards the river, intending to film from the riverbank. However, my knees began to shake uncontrollably. It was so bad that I walked back up to the road and placed my camera on the wall instead. I have never liked rivers and yet I had bought a house overlooking the river!

There was one window on the river side of the old castle tower and it had glass, unlike the windows that looked out on to my garden. I placed my camera on the wall and focused it carefully on the tower. I started filming just before 11am. Just as the hour approached, the sun reached the exact point where it was reflected in the glass of the window high in the tower. Despite the fact that it was November and the sun was not strong, the resulting flash of light was dazzling. That flash of light brought forth an immediate flash of memory.

Centuries earlier I had been held prisoner in that room in the tower. I was a young girl, not more than 14 or 15 years old. I had been quietly drawing water from the spring when I was seized by 2 men from the castle. They took me by the arms and my wooden bucket fell from my grasp. I remember thinking my father would be cross if I lost the bucket. The shock of being seized so suddenly turned my legs to jelly and I was unable to walk. They dragged me towards the gates of the castle. Those dreaded gates. I knew that very few who entered there ever left alive. We all knew that, all of the residents of the hamlet where I lived with my family. I was shoved through a studded door and dragged up a spiral stone staircase, grazing my young legs on the steps. After being thrown into a tiny room with one other woman, the door was locked. How quickly a life can change in a matter of minutes. I knew the old woman. She was the one who helped to deliver the babies.

My next memory was of being dragged towards the river. There were boats moored by the bank. I knew what was coming. I begged for mercy and protested my innocence but to no avail. I didn't even know what the charge against me was! They pulled me into the water and I remembered the feeling of my feet slipping on the muddy riverbed. They held me down and I drowned. No trial. No voice. No chance. I felt tears arise in me as this past life memory arose. Now I understood my fear of rivers. In my current life I had never felt comfortable around rivers. Not once have I ever swum in a river.

Suddenly a wind blew up out of nowhere and brought me back to the present. Hundreds of leaves began to fall from the tree behind me. I stood there as they slowly drifted towards the ground. Standing within the centre of the leaf shower I was struck by the perfection of the moment. The leaves were so reminiscent of the falling poppies that are associated with Armistice Day. I stood in silence and sent out silent prayers to those who had lost their lives in war.

Later that day I held a small ceremony in the convent to mark the start of my guardianship of the convent. Although my natural urge was to name or number the convent, I resisted. It would remain as the house with no name and no number.

On this, my second visit to Montignac, I had decided not to stay at the Tibetan Buddhist centre. Instead I had rented an up together cottage in the nearby hamlet of La Chapelle-Aubareil. Just outside my bedroom window was a church with a round aspe. 2 large bells sat on the floor just inside the door, one called Henrietta and one called Gabrielle. The ancient bells in France are named, just like people. I wondered why they were on the floor. I spoke to an old woman who lived nearby and she told me that on 11/11/1918 all the bells in France were rung to celebrate the end of the First World War. These 2 had been rung so hard that they had fallen. She also told me that all the buildings around the church were very old and had once been part of a complex of monastic buildings.

"A monastery?" I asked.

"No, a convent. All women. All the buildings here are connected by underground tunnels. The tunnels go as far as Montignac."

"How do you know?"

"Everybody knows. The information has been passed down

through the generations by word of mouth."

"But has anybody seen them?"

"Yes, of course. Some of these tunnels have been seen in my own lifetime and they link to underground dungeons. I think the dungeons are Roman. In fact the water tank in the primary school here in La Chapelle is an old dungeon. The builders simply lined it with waterproof cement and saved themselves a whole load of work by not having to dig out a new tank."

Lying by the side of the road near the one and only shop in La Chapelle was an exquisitely carved piece of stone, about 200 cms by 30 cms.

"Where has that come from?" I asked.

"That's a recent discovery. They were upgrading the pavements a few years ago and when the builders began to dig they discovered an entrance to one of the tunnels. Not only that, they found an underground oven. Knowing that if the archaeo-logical society got to hear about this discovery their pavement work would be halted, they simply closed their hole up again and said nothing. Then a local farmer found another entrance to a tunnel in his field. Again he just covered it up because he didn't want to lose his crops. The most amazing discovery in this area happened when I was a child. They were constructing a weighing scale for livestock just outside the church and when they were digging in the corner some stone sarcophaguses containing skeletons were unearthed. The more they dug the more they found. Nobody knew quite what to do with them. They stood outside the church for ages. I remember playing in them as a child. I even played with the bones."

"But they're not there now," I said.

"No, I've no idea what happened to them."

Her story reminded me of the sarcophaguses that had been discovered in the mountains in the south east of Bulgaria. They were found in the Perperikon area. Perperikon is the largest megalith ensemble in the Balkans. In 1982, shortly after the start of the archaeological excavation work, a military helicopter arrived and removed a marble sarcophagus that had been uncovered. Who knows what secrets it contained? What did the military want with a sarcophagus?

Although I became the owner of the convent in the late autumn of 2007, there was no way I could have spent that first winter there. Despite the fact that it had been advertised as a habitable holiday home, this statement could only be described as true in high summer, when it would afford shelter from the blazing midsummer sun. In reality, there was no heating, no insulation and the walls were damp. I could smell damp, rotten wood and could see active woodworm. The roof leaked and the attic was open to the elements as there was no glass in the openings in the attic. The electricity was dangerously dated and the broken glass in both the doors and the windows of the main room allowed the wind to whip through the house. The place had not been inhabited for over 50 years and in reality it was a ruin. What I also didn't realize was just how cold the weather could be in this part of France in the winter. It had plummeted to minus 15 degrees, so cold that I could not breathe the air. My month's rental on the cottage had come to an end. No way was I going to stay in the convent through the winter so I arranged for some builders to do some repair work on the roof and electrics, then I locked up the convent and left France. I would return in the spring when the temperature rose. In the meantime I needed to find somewhere to spend the winter as I was essentially homeless. This 11:11 path can be challenging to say the least but I'm sure this was simply a lesson in detachment, detaching from the need to have a habitable home. I put my belongings in the shower room as this seemed to be the most weatherproof room and headed off in search of some sun and warmth.

Chapter 5

Automatic Writing

Whilst waiting for the spring to arrive I began my research into the history of the convent. Claude had told me that my house had once been part of a teaching convent. I was obviously quite curious to discover who had established such a place. Was it the Cistercians? Or maybe the Benedictines?

My friend Patricia wrote a letter to the tourist information office in Montignac on my behalf:

Dear Madam,

My friend is a writer who is researching her next book. Please could you answer the following questions for her?

1 How many convents and monasteries are there in the town?

2 Is the castle connected in any way to the convents or monasteries?

3 Is it possible to visit the castle?

4 Who occupied the convents and monasteries? The Benedictines or others?

5 Could you confirm which order of nuns ran the convent school in Rue des Jardins?

We would appreciate your help. Many Thanks, Patricia Gallagher.

2 months later Patricia forwarded me the response:

1 There has only ever been one convent in Montignac, namely the Cordeliéres convent (aka Franciscans).

2 The castle has no link with any convent.

3 It is not possible to visit the castle as it is in private hands.

4   There has never been a Benedictine convent in Montignac.

5   There has never been a convent school in Rue des Jardins.

I was flummoxed by this information. Bella had assured me that the house had once been part of an old convent, yet I knew that the former Cordeliéres convent was on the opposite side of the river to my house. Had Bella lied? If so why? What was the truth? I would have to question her further about its history when I returned to France in the spring.

My own feeling was that it had been at some point a sacred building. The location was beautiful, the feng shui perfect, protected from behind by the hillside, sheltered in a cleft in the rocks and with far-reaching views. From my garden high on the hill I could see the town's people going about their daily business. The quality of the stone, the arched windows, the height of the rooms and the sheer awe I felt when I was within the walls all pointed towards an ecclesiastical history.

Although it wasn't easy finding out about the history of my newly acquired property, it was very easy finding out about Montignac. The town of Montignac is situated in an area of France known as 'the Black Périgord'. There are 4 Périgords and the Black is renowned as the most beautiful. It takes its name from the dark quality of the many dense oak, chestnut and pine forests. I discovered that the town was world famous because of the Lascaux Caves, known worldwide as the Sistine Chapel of prehistory. These caves were discovered by 4 teenagers in 1940 and contain some remarkable Palaeolithic cave paintings, estimated to be over 17,000 years old. It is thought that they were painted by hunter-gathering people who crushed minerals to create red, ochre, brown and black paints. The caves were closed to the public in 1963 to protect them from a fungal infection that had appeared on the paintings. Eventually, a complete life-sized copy of the caves and paintings (known as Lascaux 2) was opened nearby for visitors. In 1979 Lascaux was added to the

UNESCO World Heritage sites, along with other prehistoric sites in the Vézère valley. Courtesy of the 11:11 sign, I had landed in the heart of prehistoric man. Not only did my house have a view of the Vézère valley, but the hill directly opposite my garden was the very hill inside which these famous caves lay. I did not know why I was in Montignac but I suspected it could have something to do with the origins of mankind.

What I particularly love about using the 11:11 sign as an aid to loosening the hold of the ego is the way in which the magic appears. I, Hilary, need do nothing. The magic arises out of that space that Hilary has vacated. As soon as I had handed over the money for the French convent and my name was on the deeds, the wheels of magic began to turn.

My first book *The 11:11 Code* had generated quite a lot of interest and I was receiving regular e-mails from my readers. A reader called Andrew had e-mailed me to ask where the French convent was situated. I e-mailed back with some photos and told him it was near the Lascaux Caves.

Hi Hilary

I really enjoyed your 11:11 book. I'm a 33 man myself. I work as a therapist that may explain why it dominates my life… guess what my treatment fee is?… £33

There are 2 things that may interest you. Just before I wrote to you I got the nudge that there is sacred geometry involved with your new French project. Not within your premises themselves, but as part of a wider inter-relationship with your surrounding environment. I believe you work within the sacral chakra of your locality and therefore need to heal that particular energy in your work there.

The second point of interest concerns a free healing experience I have put on my website www.quantumk.co.uk. It is very powerful. It is based on quantum healing. Please do give it a go. It might come in useful for you.

Thanks for the photos. I didn't get any nudges (yet), but the whole area looks fantastic! It sounds like you have enough validation and plans to keep you going for a while anyway, best of luck with the project.

I took a look at Andrew's site and his Quantum K Healing experience. As K is the 11th letter of the alphabet I suspected that it would be relevant for me. The healing consisted of affirmations, visual prompts and very strange music. I later found out that this unique healing experience is based on the combination of sound, colour, fractal geometry, harmonics and symbols. It draws from the latest thinking in quantum physics to offer healing to the mind, body and soul. The 12 number sequences used in Quantum K communicate directly with our DNA, stimulating these basic building blocks of life to let go of negative programs and rebuild in line with a more positive set of instructions.

Hi Andrew

Thanks for the e-mail. We certainly seem to be on a very similar wavelength. I was fascinated by the Quantum K healing experience, especially as K is the 11th letter of the alphabet. Also, the healing experience is 23 minutes which is very significant as 23 is the number of breakdown/breakthrough.

The French convent I have bought is within walking distance of the Lascaux Caves in the Dordogne. I'm sure it will link to other sites in South West France. Do you know HOW I would work with the sacral energy? If I'm working with the sacral chakra of my locality, would that affect my own sacral chakra?

Please contact me if you have any other insights into the work I'll be doing in France.

Hi Hilary.

I quickly googled the caves and the whole area gave me a tingle and the following, shall we say, is not my fingers controlling the keyboard... You did ask about how to heal the sacral and here it is...!

This cave area is the root area of your locality and has many obvious similarities with the human condition. Imagine a colon and compare that to a damp cave like environment that is currently suffering from fungus. A mirror of our whole population I'm afraid and in great need of your healing, as is your own acquisition.

We are the land and the land is us, what we see in the landscape is a direct reflection of what should be visible in our own mirror. You are the sacral chakra for your convent and in healing yourself you will heal the land. You don't have to look any further than that, your chakra and the land chakra are linked across the dimensions and healing one heals the other. You have the potential to work outside the artificial constraints of time; you have closely linked with this area through your history so are ideally placed to heal it on a broader level.

There is also a connection here with the Divine feminine. This energy is crucial, and like it or not, you are there to bring in this energy where it is most needed. Heal the sacral chakra of your locality and the energy permeates the entire system of the country, and beyond. No small matter then... but you like responsibility so I'm sure will jump at it... indeed it is part of your agreed contract.

To do this work specifically requires use of the plants in your convent. They must not be cut but must be honoured and cultivated in appropriate places. They represent the gentle, yin, feminine, alkaline energy and will help heal the landscape while they are there and loved. You will find places where plants and flowers used to grow that need to be replanted afresh. You will know where these places are even if you cannot see them with your eyes, because you have planted flowers there before and loved doing so. You can support them with healing, water and yoga. Play the Quantum K music to them and the harmonics will lift their spirits too. They love healing sound as much as we do.

Finally, I can see a feather symbolising the bird population in the area. Birdsong will heal too, so please look after the local environment so that they can thrive. They will come to visit you to show you the rightness of your approach.

This is part of your contract as you know and the timing is perfect now to execute it. It will be a journey of great pleasure for you and a place where others may come to find the Divine feminine that lies dormant within them too. Their healing will be your healing. Your healing heals the world.

Hmmm... not sure where that all came from, Hilary, I just typed it as it came through. I think it's from my guide called Dr Philip Contreaux who used to live in Marseille a few centuries back. He specialised in this kind of thing apparently, healing spaces and people. He's come to me to help me learn the same skills. I hope it helps. I have a feeling I may have lived in the convent a couple of times too...so you'll be doing me a favour working on it!

Lots of love, Andrew

Hi Andrew

Thanks for that. Fascinating! I was giving a talk to a group of healers the other night and one of them told me I would be working with the Divine feminine energy. So that confirms what you said.

Then today I had an e-mail from somebody in Portugal who had read *The 11:11 Code* and he wrote:

"I'm only writing this e-mail to you as you may be interested in this because of what has happened to you & may trigger some memories for you. I keep getting the name Marseille & very strong French feeling."

I still find it all very intriguing as we connect as parts of the Oneness. My first guidance had come from somebody I had never met! From these e-mails and the channelled writing it seemed as if I would be working with the sacral chakra, both my own and that of the area around the convent. I did not know how this would be happening. I just had to trust that all would be revealed when the time was right. Now was not the time as I was about to head off to Turkey. It seemed a sensible choice of destination as Turkey is rich in history, not too expensive and fairly warm, my main criteria for winter living. I was still struggling to understand why the 11:11 had led me to the French convent yet it was uninhabitable so I couldn't stay there. I had to just accept that that was how it was and everything was perfect even if 'Hilary' didn't think so.

Just before I left I ordered a copy of the 'Quantum K' CD. It would be waiting for me when I returned the following spring.

Chapter 6

Rumi and the Whirling Dervishes

I arrived in Turkey in early January and although the weather by the coast was fairly mild, inland Turkey was freezing cold and quite deep in snow. So much for the warm sunshine I had been expecting! I wanted to explore the region of Cappadocia and I had chosen to do so during a particularly bad winter. In fact heavy snow had closed the road over the Taurus Mountains from the coast to inland Turkey on the very day that I chose to travel. I made it over the mountains just before it became impassable.

I had booked an organized tour of Cappadocia as this seemed the most straight forward way of getting to the places I wanted to visit. Normally I would hire a car or go by public transport but this time I opted for the easiest option. I wanted to visit the underground cities that were carved into the volcanic rock and I knew they were in inaccessible places. Because of the bad weather and the time of year, there were no tourists around except for our small group of 6 people plus the driver and the tour guide. We had the entire area to ourselves!

Cappadocia is a strange lunar landscape of hardened lava. The landscape is dotted with eerie towers created by wind erosion and it was like nowhere I had ever visited before. I had to keep reminding myself that I was still on planet earth, not on the moon. The area is famous for its underground cities. These cities, which housed as many as 20,000 people each in their heyday, had been carved into the volcanic rock by early Christians. They were incredible creations (though not very appealing to anyone who is prone to claustrophobia) and included underground churches as well as homes. The churches were very simple; just open caverns with a raised altar, beautifully decorated with fine frescoes.

Our first visit was to the subterranean city of Kaymakli. It was a kind of underground apartment building, with quite a few different levels and corridors 10 feet wide and 6.5 feet high. Doorways were closed by enormous round stones that could be 'locked' from the inside. It seemed that the builders of these high-ceilinged rooms were, for that time, exceptionally tall. We also visited an underground city beneath the town of Derinkuyu. This had 8 levels, and in spite of ventilation shafts it was completely invisible from the ground above. It felt like being in a world within a world, cut off from colour, light and the warmth of the sun. The walls, floors and ceilings were white, a chalky type of rock.

I'm not keen on being underground, though I often wonder exactly what goes on under the surface of our world, hidden from view. On a recent visit to Malta and Gozo I learned about the Maltese caves known as the Hypogeum of Hal Saflieni. In 1902, workmen digging a well discovered a complex of underground caves. When first explored, they found over 30,000 skeletons of men, women and children inside. The tunnels under the Hypogeum were sealed off for good a few decades ago after a group of 30 children and their teachers entered the caves on a field trip and disappeared without a trace. They have never been found, though for weeks after their disappearance it was said that their cries could be heard beneath the ground from various locations on the island.

Some people believe that the mysterious Hypogeum acts as a special gateway to parallel dimensions. Scientists found that frequencies between 110 to 111 hertz echo around the entire temple complex. 110 to 111 hertz stimulates key areas of the prefrontal cortex that affect mood, empathy, and social communion and can induce trancelike states.

On the second day of the Cappadocia tour our minibus pulled up on the side of a hill, scattered with the ruins of buildings which had been inhabited as recently as the 1960s. After several families were killed in an earthquake, the locals had deserted all the properties. As we got off the minibus a young man came running towards us. He was tall, skinny, filthy, unshaven and his clothes were threadbare.

"John the Baptist!" he called as he ran towards our minibus waving his arms frantically above his head. "John the Baptist church. Very old!"

All the others ignored him. He ran on ahead of us, trying to block our route, obviously desperate to earn a few liras in tips. Tourists were thin on the ground in the winter and he was obviously looking for a way to earn a bit of extra money.

He beckoned for us to follow him. "John the Baptist," he repeated. "Frescoes. Very old!"

John the Baptist. If there were ever 3 words that would make me sit up and take notice, it was those 3. I had already linked John the Baptist to the 11:11 phenomenon through Matthew 11:11.

Verily I say unto you, Among them that are born of women there hath not risen a greater than John the Baptist: notwithstanding he that is least in the kingdom of heaven is greater than he.

The very last painting that da Vinci had painted was of John the Baptist. Even now there are people who follow his teachings. They are called Mandaeans and they live on the border of Iran and Iraq.

I followed the young man. I was the only one of the group to do so. Together we scrambled up the hillside, higher and higher, past potholes that would have killed me if I'd fallen down one. I think these were the shafts that provided ventilation to the underground homes. The path was narrow, steep and dangerous. Several times I slipped on loose stones and the man caught me just before I tumbled down the hillside. This place was entirely wild and free, with no ropes, no barriers, no protection, no guards and no admission fee. Eventually we reached a rickety wooden bridge. It looked highly dangerous and for the first time on our climb I hesitated. The chances of it giving way and plunging me into the crevice below were high. Before I had the chance to consider turning back the young man grabbed me by the arm and yanked me across. He needed my money so he wasn't going to let me back out of the visit.

"Here," he said triumphantly, pointing towards a mysterious doorway, "John the Baptist church."

The church, like most of the dwellings in the area, had been carved out of the rock. Above the doorway were 3 ancient diagrams neatly inscribed into the stone. The central carving was a circle, the border of which was made from 3 concentric circles. Within the central circle was a cross with 4 branches of equal length. The centre of the cross contained a 6 petalled flower within another 3 concentric circles. On either side of this carving was a rhombus with a border of zigzags inside of which were inscribed 3 concentric circles. Within each central circle was a 6 petalled flower. The number of petals was significant. Each of our 7 chakras has petals. The 2nd chakra has 6. Maybe I was to receive some healing to my own 2nd chakra in the church. I would then be able to carry that healing back to the convent.

There was no door, just a rectangular opening in the rock face. I stepped through the open doorway in front of my guide, not knowing what to expect. It was stunning. The massive stone pillars that would not have looked out of place in a European church appeared to have been carved out of a different stone to the local stone. They actually looked like granite pillars. I have no idea how they could possibly have been transported to this place so high on the hill as they were about a metre in diameter and 3 or 4 metres tall. Although circular, they were placed on square solid stone bases. They were quite close together and were linked by massive stone arches. The overall impression was that of being inside a European cathedral, albeit much lower and less towering.

There were frescoes that had been virtually untouched for hundreds and hundreds of years although parts had flaked away through sheer age. Inside the semicircular apse at one end of the church was a carved stone bench, following the contours of the wall. I sat on the central point, on a throne-like stone seat. I guessed this was the high altar. This was unlike any church I had ever been in. I was aware that I had been granted a rare privilege.

My guide stepped outside and left me alone to soak up the atmosphere. I closed my eyes and sat in meditation for a while, then I began to chant, "AUM." The sound reverberated powerfully through the building. It was as if an acoustic vibration was set in motion and it seemed to spin round and round my head twirling me in a vortex of sound. That didn't usually happen when I chanted AUM during my yoga classes. I wondered whether the domed roof had anything to do with it. I then entered a space that I can only describe as a full emptiness. It was certainly timeless and I was only brought back into the moment by my guide shaking me by the shoulders. I could hear the repeated beeping of a car horn in the distance. My travel companions were waiting for me at the bottom of the hill. I had to go. I quickly took a few photos and headed back down the hillside. When I downloaded the pictures on to my laptop there were so many orbs that I couldn't count them.

Our next stop was Konya where we visited the shrine of Rumi, the great Sufi poet. He was a 13th century mystic and saint and in Turkey he is known as Mevlana. Just inside the doors of the shrine the words of Rumi were written on the wall.

Whoever you may be, come
Even though you may be
An infidel, a pagan, or a fire-worshipper, come
Our brotherhood is not one of despair
Even though you have broken

Your vows of repentance a hundred times, come.

Our group headed for the main shrine where the remains of
Rumi and his family are buried. I split away from them and went
exploring on my own. Within the large courtyard were several
stone buildings. I saw a half-open door and gingerly I pushed it
open to see what was inside the room. It was empty apart from a
solid stone tomb. There was nobody else around, just me and the
tomb.

Come my child. Don't be afraid. Enter. Enter. You are welcome
here.

The voice came from nowhere. Clairaudience! I'd experienced
clairaudience a few times before in my life but it still came as a
complete surprise. Who was this speaking to me? Was it the soul
that had once inhabited the bones that lay in the stone tomb in
front of me? Or could it be Rumi himself?

You can come to the shrines. You can visit the sacred
buildings. But already you know that I am everywhere and in
everything. You can find me wherever you are for I reside in
your heart. Wherever you go I am with you.

The voice was so loving, so gentle, so caring. It touched me and
it was very real. How I loved the Sufi philosophy, for it spoke of
truth, the truth of unconditional love. There was no judgment or
condemnation and forgiveness reigned supreme. The shrine was
a peaceful and sacred space.

We could not visit Konya without meeting the Whirling
Dervishes and that had been arranged for the last evening. We
met them in an underground cave. As there were so few of us it
was a particularly intimate and moving experience. We sat on
padded seats around the edge of the cave and the Dervishes

performed their circling dance known as Sema within a circular stage in the centre. To the uninitiated the dance looks just like a bunch of men spinning round and round in tall hats, but the dance is ritualistic and it has a deeper meaning. It has 7 parts and represents the mystical journey of an individual as they move away from selfishness towards union with the Divine. After reaching this state the traveller returns from this spiritual journey in order to love and serve all. Dressed in long white gowns (the ego's burial shroud) and wearing high, cone-shaped hats (the ego's tombstone), the Dervish dances for hours at a time. Each Dervish spins with his right hand reaching up to heaven to receive its blessings, the left hand down to communicate them to earth. They spin anticlockwise, slowly picking up speed and intensity until they all collapse in a sort of spiritual exaltation.

I had been curious about the Whirling Dervishes for many years and I had once decided to train myself to spin. I had gradually managed to get to the point where I could spin for over 50 revolutions without overbalancing. Except, that is, if I was in a crop circle. One summer I had walked to the centre of the crop circle that had appeared opposite Stonehenge, that ancient stone circle in Wiltshire, England and I had begun to spin. After 2 revolutions I fell flat on my back! I can only assume it was the altered energy within the circle that had caused me to fall.

I asked the leader of the Dervishes how they managed not to fall and I was told that only young men who showed the ability to spin in the early stages of spinning were accepted for training. The ones who fell easily were not accepted.

It was in Konya that I first heard about *The Knowledge Book*. This book has been channelled by a technique called the Light-Photon-Cyclone technique which is new to our planet. It is claimed that The Knowledge Book will supersede all existing sacred texts and will be relevant for the next 19 centuries. Those who study this book have a special day which they call 'Call to World Peace from the Universal Brotherhood'. When I saw the date of their special day I knew I had to make contact with them for it was the first of November: 1.11.

I e-mailed them to ask why they had chosen this day and they replied as follows;

> *Thank you contacting to us. The 1/11 was the date of the first message dictated for The Knowledge Book in the year 1981. For us this date is the Opening Program of the Planet to Peace Frequency. Since the year 1995, every year on 1st of November, we are organizing a congregation with the slogan "Call to World Peace from The Universal Brotherhood". It gives us pride and happiness to greet in this way all our brothers and sisters serving in the World Unification Project.*

As we move towards Oneness, separation will be left behind. There will not be one religion for we will have moved beyond religion. That is where The Knowledge Book comes in. The book reveals its content to you according to your level of consciousness. Time energy is loaded on to the letter frequencies. You understand the book when you read it and you receive some knowledge but it is impossible to memorize The Knowledge Book because of its link to time energy. It discloses all the secrets and facts of humanity and it explains the reasons for the paths trodden. I cannot speak here of the content for the words you are reading on this page have not been written with the Light-Photon-Cyclone technique, nor have any words on planet earth other than those in The Knowledge Book. If you feel moved to find out more there is a website called www.knowledgebook.org.

Whilst I was in Turkey I had 2 dreams about the convent. Although I was not physically in France that first winter, I already felt very connected to that old building. My first dream was about the spring that was situated adjacent to the convent. In my dream the water was flowing uphill into the spring, completely the opposite way to the normal flow. Then I realized why this was so. There was a deep empty ravine and this was rapidly filling with water; fresh, clean, blue water. Crowds of people had arrived to watch the ravine fill and there was an atmosphere of excitement and joy.

In the next dream I discovered that within one of the thick stone walls of the convent was a hidden cavity. When I looked inside the cavity I saw a fast flowing stream of clear spring water.

Were these dreams prophetic? I would have to wait and see.

All too soon my time in Turkey was over. I had explored the underground cities of Cappadocia, sat in the shrine of Mevlana (Rumi), learned about The Knowledge Book, trodden in the footsteps of the early Christians and met the Whirling Dervishes in Konya. Now it was time to return to France.

Chapter 7

The Grey Hooded Ghost

Spring had arrived in Montignac and the convent was waiting to welcome me back. I couldn't wait to see what it looked like now that the builders had installed an up-to-date electricity supply, hacked the damp plaster off the walls and replaced the rotten wooden steps. They had literally just finished work the day before I returned. I unlocked the rickety door and the first thing that hit me when I entered the convent was the smell. It smelt exactly like an old English church: musty, with a hint of cats, old hymn books and incense.

Now that the old damp plaster had gone the room was transformed. The original stonework was revealed, a beautiful pale golden stone. Underneath the old wooden fireplace an even older one had been found. It was a stone inglenook, taking up well over half of one wall. A massive chestnut beam, supported by high quality dressed stone blocks now took pride of place instead of the painted wooden mantelpiece dating from the 19th century. I could see where there had once been a doorway through the wall because the plaster had been hiding an old stone lintel which was now exposed. The floor had just been treated for woodworm and even though I had elected to use an eco product, the smell of the chemicals hung heavy in the air. The freshly pointed stonework made the air even damper than it had been before the mouldy plaster had been removed.

I quite liked the house. It was small, but it felt peaceful and quite sacred. The shower room and kitchen were in better condition than I remembered from my brief visit a few months earlier. The steps down to the original part of the convent were by now completely overgrown, slippery with moss and highly dangerous. I decided not to risk going down them. If I stumbled and fell I could lie at the bottom for weeks before being discovered. I knew nobody in town and I had no visitors. My family were accustomed to me disappearing for weeks on end without making contact so it would probably be months before anyone became worried enough to investigate my disappearance.

My dream about the water had been prophetic after all, though not in the way I had imagined. There had been a water leak in the shower room. I had put my boxes of books in there as that door was the only door that actually closed and I thought they would be safe. Now dozens of my books were ruined having absorbed the water from the flood. These were the books that I had been reading as part of my research into sacred number. I leafed through the water-damaged books trying not to get too upset. They had been sitting in water so long that they smelt ancient and evoked memories of a far distant past. Some were quite rare old theosophical texts. Others were early books on numerology that I had found in the second-hand bookshops in Tottenham Court Road, London, in the 1980s. It was times like these when I struggled. Was the destruction of these books a sign that I was getting too much in my head and that the books were not needed or was it a test of my resolve? Was I was so determined to read these books that I needed to replace them? How could I do that? Some were irreplaceable. I had no idea why this had happened. I chose to simply accept that the books were gone.

I had brought my tent with me to France because this time I intended sleeping within the convent walls rather than staying at the Tibetan Buddhist centre or renting somewhere more habitable. Setting up camp within the convent walls was not an appealing idea but the convent was my home so I needed to start living there. The sooner I was in residence the sooner I would find out the reason for me being in France. At least that's what I thought at the time. It is undeniable that the place was a ruin. I momentarily considered sleeping in the car but it was early April and the nights were still cold. I had no choice. I would just have to go ahead and set up camp in the convent. As darkness fell I went out to lock the garden gates. They wouldn't lock because they had become warped during the winter so I had to leave them open. Then I tried to close the main convent door. That wouldn't close either, never mind lock. Most of my money had been spent on the purchase and I had not yet raised enough to repair the windows and doors and install insulation. In retrospect it might have been sensible to weatherproof the place as the first step in the renovations but it was too late. I leaned a plank of wood against the door. It was draughty, but as 3 of the windows were broken and the wind was already whistling through the place it was just a case of accepting the draughts.

I pitched my tent in the middle of the room. The roof leaked and I didn't want to get wet if it rained in the night. I tried pretending that I was on a camping holiday. Before settling down for the night I hung my bag of citrine crystals above the door. I didn't want any disincarnate spirits dropping down from the threshold. That's where they tend to 'hang around' and they love residing in empty old places. I was once told that the reason that church doors were arched was to prevent this very thing happening. The house had been empty for a long time so I wasn't taking any chances. As I crawled into the tent I remembered that it was April Fool's Day and I saw the joke. I suddenly realized it was exactly a year to the day that Bella had contacted me by e-mail inviting me to visit the convent.

I switched off the light and clambered into the dark tent. This was to be my first night sleeping in the convent. I lay there trying to focus on my breathing. It was freezing cold, much colder than I could have imagined it would be and it was deadly silent. There was no passing traffic, no sounds of city life, no familiar sounds at all. Just as I was trying to get accustomed to the silence, I heard a noise. It sounded like something dropping from the ceiling.

What was it? Dust? Dying woodworm? Falling plaster? Each time I began to drift off to sleep, I heard the noise again and jumped back into waking consciousness. I could hear something scrabbling about. A bird? A mouse? Whatever it was, I was thankful that it couldn't get through the insect screen. Eventually I slept. In fact I didn't wake up until 9am the following morning. I must have been terribly tired!

The noise had indeed been stuff falling from the ceiling and the walls. When I emerged from my tent in the morning there were little piles of sand and grit and strange patches of white dust and cobwebby black stuff all over the floor and on the top of the tent. I was glad I'd had the protection of the tent. I soon learned that the slow crumbling was part and parcel of this house. Even eating a meal indoors was difficult because grit would occasionally fall into my food.

My standard of living had dropped considerably. I had no DVD player or television, no phone, no Internet, no bath, no washing machine, no bed, no sofa, no dining table, no dishwasher, no cooker, no fridge or freezer, no carpet, no curtains or blinds and no proper windows or doors! All I had was a tent with a blow-up mattress and bedding, a radio, CD player, a whole load of water-damaged books and 2 fan heaters. I tried not to think about what I had left behind. I had sold my beautiful period house in England to raise funds to pursue my 11:11 journey. The marble fireplaces, graceful wooden staircase, stained glass windows and spacious Victorian charm belonged to my past. 'Non-attachment, non-attachment,' I reminded myself. It's part of the spiritual path. I would just have to adapt to living simply.

After a delicious breakfast of slightly blackened country bread baked in a wood oven spread with local unsalted butter and fig jam, I started to clean. To say that the floor was filthy would be a huge understatement. Decades of grime were layered on to the wooden floorboards. As I got down on my hands and knees and started to scrub, it's as if I was transported back in time. I had never scrubbed a wooden floor with a scrubbing brush in my life. Could these have been the original floorboards from the days when this was a convent? As the dirt was washed away the room began to smell different. It smelt rather like incense. It was probably the oils in the wood being released. As the grime was lifted I could make out that every single board, without exception, was riddled with woodworm holes. But I'd had it treated so hopefully no more holes would appear. The gaps between the ill-fitting floorboards were packed with dirt. The floor itself was seriously uneven as the boards had been laid across the hand-fashioned wooden joists which formed the ceiling of the room below, none of which were flat and even. I didn't mind. It all added to the character of the place.

I saw the ghost on the second night. It was early evening and the sun had just set. I was sitting on the floor, leaning against the old stone wall listening to the silence when I suddenly saw it, a shadowy robed figure sweeping through the wall in the exact location where the stonework had exposed an old doorway, now sealed up. It was so unexpected, seeing a ghost, but I saw it as clear as day. I just caught sight of the side view of the figure. I couldn't tell if it was male or female as the hood of the grey robe hid the side of the face, but, whatever the gender, it was obviously going somewhere in a great hurry.

I had suspected all along that this place was haunted, but I'd been determined not to be frightened. That had been easy to say when I was living in my lovely house in England. But now I was actually camping out in the old stone building, I began to wish I was anywhere else on the planet but alone in the convent. What was strange was the way that every hair on the back of my body, from my calves to the top of my head, stood on end at the sight of that hooded figure. It was a slow, creeping sensation over which I had no conscious control.

'It's only a ghost, ghosts can't harm you,' I kept telling myself.

But I was going to have to spend the night there all alone again so I'd have to do some urgent clearing work. I lit some nag champa incense and filled the room with the smoke, paying special attention to the corners. I'd already done some clearing on my previous visit. I'd used sound and mantra along with incense. I knew at the time it had not been enough and that it would only brush the top surface of the centuries of psychic dross. I recalled a clearing ceremony that I had done at the old Spanish convent. That ceremony had somehow stirred things up on a psychic level. Maybe the same thing had happened. I knew my very presence alone would be enough to disturb the status quo here in France. I just wished I was not on my own, but I was so I simply had to be brave.

Despite my reassurances to myself, I was utterly petrified and I could not sleep. I put the radio on really loud, a French station of course. I did not even have the comfort of a voice in my own language. I put the light and the noisy fan heater on. Time slowed down. I watched the minutes pass one by one on the illuminated digital radio display panel. And each one felt like an hour. I lay there waiting for the dawn to arrive. It was one of the longest and most disturbing nights of my life.

The next day I got up with the rising sun. I tried to reason with myself. It was only a ghost. Was it malefic? No. It was totally engrossed in its own business and wasn't interested in me at all. Could it hurt me? No of course not. However, I did not like the fact that the house was haunted and I couldn't bear the thought of another night there alone. I didn't know anybody in town so I had nowhere to turn. What was I to do?

Suddenly I had a brainwave. I decided to go to the Tibetan Buddhist centre and ask for help. I set off immediately. I couldn't wait to get out of the convent. I drove along the picturesque road between Montignac and Les Eyzies to the hamlet of Le Moustier. I took the high road and paused to take in the view at the vista point as I was not in a hurry. When I pulled into the car park I was surprised to see how many cars were there. Normally there were less than a dozen at any one time. The prayer flags were fluttering gently in the soft breeze and the stupa glowed brightly in the early morning sun. How strange to find a small piece of Tibet in the heart of the Dordogne. Unusually the place was teeming with people and the office was closed. Eventually a German woman recognized me from my earlier stay and she sat down with me and listened to my story. She relayed the facts to a high Lama who was about to give some teaching, hence the crowds of people. He didn't know what to do about the ghost so he suggested I talk to a European Lama. I did. He didn't know what to do about the ghost either.

"Well we could come and do some pujas which might help. But we won't be able to come for a few days because there's so much going on at the centre this week. Or you could ask the Catholic priest in the town where you live to come and help. He could do an exorcism. Catholic priests do that sort of thing you know. Failing that, I know that you can download some special music from the Internet."

"Special music?" I asked.

"Yes, apparently this music sets up certain vibrations that can clear negative energies," he explained.

Of course! Why hadn't I thought of that? Thanks to Andrew's e-mails I had been introduced to Quantum music and I had my Quantum K CD in the car. I thanked the Lama and left.

When I returned to the house I played the CD over and over again until I went to bed. I couldn't believe the difference in the feel of the place. It really felt so much clearer. Even so, for the first week following my encounter with the ghost I slept with 2 noisy fan heaters and the main light on all night. I put my Quantum K CD on repeat, day and night for a week. The strange, discordant music worked wonders. The second week, having not seen any more ghosts, I reduced my distraction system to one fan heater, a side light and the radio. The third week, I managed to sleep with only the side light. I was thankful for the tent. There was something about that thin sheet of polyester that protected me psychologically although I had felt a bit disconcerted when I looked at the photos I had taken and saw one very large round orb sitting on my tent. Who was it? The ghost? Or the ancient entity from the room below?

Bella, the former owner of the convent, lived between Paris and Montignac. She had spent every August in Montignac since she was a child. The house I had bought had been in her family for over 50 years. Once a year the family had camped out inside the building for a month. In the early days they had used an earth toilet in a wooden hut in the garden but about 30 years ago her father had built the small extension with a shower, toilet and kitchenette, which was accessed from outside the main building. She now lived in her grandparent's holiday house when she was in town. I called in to see Bella and to tell her about my ghostly encounter. She assured me that she had never seen a ghost in all the years that she had slept there.

"What did it look like?" she asked as she poured me a cup of spine-tingling strong black coffee. She drew heavily on her cigarette and I heard her tummy rumble. Her slender figure came at a price.

"I couldn't really see its face because it was wearing a hood. I think it was a man but that's unlikely isn't it, because it was a convent for nuns, wasn't it?"

"No. It was a school. A school of religion. As Claude told you, it was a teaching convent."

"Do you know what religion? Was it Catholic?"

"Probably. I don't really know."

"Could you ask your dad if he knows what religion it was? Just out of interest I'd like to know."

Bella promised to ask her father, though she said that he was now in his 80s and was beginning to become rather forgetful. My Spanish convent had also been a school. It had been a school of illustrious studies attached to the University of Granada. How strange that I should find myself back in another religious teaching institution.

A few days after moving in I noticed a new crack had appeared in one of the walls. That was a worrying development. Bits of plaster, loose stones and lumps of dirt continued to drop from the walls and ceiling day and night. Everything was covered in grit. I had to drape old sheets and tablecloths over my new sofa. Thank God I was sleeping in the tent. I had climbed my newly acquired ladder to see if I could discover why the plaster was so loose and I was alarmed to discover that one end of the chestnut beams was completely hollow. In fact I couldn't work out how it managed to stay up there. I moved everything to the other end of the room, including the tent. If the beam was going to fall, I did not want to be sleeping or sitting underneath it when it did so, though I comforted myself with the fact that as it was hollow it wouldn't be that heavy! When I had a look into next door's garden I could see that there was a tree growing within a few inches of my wall. I went round to ask them if they could cut it down as soon as possible as the roots of the tree were growing under my house and could well have been the cause of the new crack.

I was invited into their home, which they were in the process of renovating. It was interesting to see their place. Many of their chestnut beams were rotten on the ends but they had been bracketed with substantial metal brackets. I was glad to see that repair was possible. I had already experienced the trauma of the Spanish convent falling down. I had no desire to repeat that awful experience. To have one convent fall down is unfortunate. To lose 2 would be sheer carelessness.

My neighbours' place had a similar feel to the convent and their ceilings were the same lofty height as mine. I asked them why the ceilings were so high.

"This was part of the convent school," I was told. "It was quite a complex of buildings. If you look back here," he said, pointing to the patch of land next to my wall, "you can see some of the old ruins that still remain."

There was indeed part of an arched doorway and some crumbling stone walls hiding there under the blackberry bushes. They were adjacent to my back wall. I could also see a stone trough, constantly fed by a spring. That must have been the water source for the school.

"So it was a convent school? The museum told me that there had only ever been one convent in Montignac."

"Yes, it was a school of religion. These 4 houses were all part of the school," he explained, pointing to my house, his house and 2 adjacent houses. "Mine was the school hall and between your place and your neighbour Alain's was a covered courtyard. Alain knows a lot about the convent. These buildings were abandoned long ago. Nobody cared about them. It's a shame so much of it has been lost."

I went down to the town hall to see the old town plans but they only went back as far as 1855. Even so, I could see that my house had once been joined to buildings behind mine, in front of mine and next to mine. These had all fallen down hence the incredible amount of stone in the drystone walling that was such a feature of my garden. It had obviously been salvaged from the fallen properties. My house, once simply part of a larger building, was now detached. It's unusual to have a one-roomed detached house on a 500 square metres plot of land. Quite unique!

I discovered several other interesting facts on the plans. In the maps from 1837 some of the roads had different names. The previous name of my road, Rue des Jardins (road of the gardens), was unknown. That means my convent had no name, no number and was in the road with an unknown name! The adjacent road, Rue de Napoleon, had previously been called road of the priore. Priore was not in my French/English dictionary, but I wondered whether it had the same source as the word for priory. If so, I could only assume that the road had once led to a priory. Yet the letter from the museum had made no mention of a priory on my side of the river. I was puzzled but I felt confident that all would be revealed in due course.

More than anything I wanted to know why the 11:11 sign had sent me to the heart of prehistory. I was impatient to know the answer. Why was I in Montignac? Was it only to deal with the sacral chakra of the area as Andrew had suggested? Or was there more? How long would the work take? How long would I have to stay? How would I know when it was time to leave? How would I know when the work was finished? I tried to still my mind. 'Be in the moment,' I reminded myself time and time again. It wasn't easy.

Chapter 8

The Tibetan Lama and Satyananda

"So what is it you would like to ask me?"

He was looking at me through inscrutable eyes. I was at the Tibetan Buddhist centre, which I enjoyed visiting. It was good to be able to spend time in such a clear and sacred space. The Dhagpo Kagyu Ling Buddhist Centre wasn't far from Montignac and the setting was exceptionally beautiful. It was located in a former farmhouse set on a high ridge in the midst of picturesque valleys and unspoilt forests.

I was sitting at one end of the 3 seater sofa and the Lama was sitting at the opposite end, facing me. He was dressed in the maroon robes that all the Lamas wore. It's not often one finds oneself in conversation with a Tibetan Lama so I wanted to make the most of this opportunity. The interview had been arranged earlier that day but I had not had a lot of time to think about my questions because today was the day before the new moon and everybody, myself included, had been involved in a 3 and a half hour ceremony. It was a ceremony of protection that took place once a month on the dark moon. There had been lots of chanting, droning and loud banging drums. All sorts of things were thrown about at certain points during the ceremony, stuff like rice and flower petals.

"I would like to ask about numbers. In particular I'm interested in the number 11:11. Do you know anything about this number?"

There was a pause. Quite a long pause.

"That's not what you really want to ask me. What is it you really want to ask me?"

There was another silence. Instead of being authentic and truthful (because that IS what I wanted to ask him) I said the very first thing that came into my mind.

"I would like to know who built the pyramids," I asked.

"The ancient Egyptians," he replied.

"How?"

"With ropes and pulleys like you can see in the books about the pyramids."

That was a bad start. I don't think he was right so immediately he lost some credibility in my mind. I could remember from one of my Egyptian lives that the stones had been cut with a rod that I can best describe as a laser and they had been moved by a sounding instrument that altered the force field to make them weightless.

So I tried another question.

"I have had a lot of coincidences happening in my life. I'd like to know what they mean."

"Mmmm. Coincidences?"

"Yes."

"If I walk along the road and I stand on a stone, is that a coincidence?" he asked.

What an odd thing to say. It sounded like one of those tricky Zen koans to me.

"Just standing on a stone? No, of course not," I replied.

"Why not?"

"Because I have no particular relationship with the stone."

He smiled. I had the distinct feeling that the Lama was playing with me.

"I know somebody who always dreamed of going to visit the Great Wall of China. When she eventually realized her dream at the age of 65, she was astounded to meet her long-lost sister walking along the wall too!"

"Yes. Now that IS a coincidence," I said.

"But you have not come here to ask about the pyramids and coincidences. Tell me what it is you really want to know."

I don't know why, but I did not repeat the 11:11 question.

Instead I asked:

"Do you have to give up your ego to a master in Buddhism?"

"No. The master can help you, show you how to give up your ego, but it is only you who can do the work required. It's only you who can make the changes within yourself. Nobody else can do it for you."

"I have a question about meditation. When I meditate I have my eyes closed but I put my inner gaze at the point of the third eye in the middle of my forehead. Is that how you meditate?"

"No. We meditate with the eyes half open. We recite mantras too. We have to recite them many times. We use a mala to help us to keep count."

"A mala?"

"Yes, it's like a necklace with lots of beads and as we chant we count the beads."

"How many beads does it have?"

"111."

"One, one, one?"

"Yes."

There was another silence as I tried to make sense of that fact. It crossed my mind that he was joking.

"Really?"

"Yes."

"Why 111?"

"Because we recite our mantra 108 times in 3 blocks of 36 and then there are an extra 3 beads on the mala for spacing."

"But 11 is the number I said I was having coincidences about. That was my first question, about 11:11."

He smiled and slowly nodded his head. Why on earth had he not made this connection earlier when I had asked about 11:11? I was right. He was playing games with me.

"So is the number 11:11 a recognized sign on the spiritual path?" I asked.

"I have not heard of this," he replied.

"You have not heard of the 11:11 phenomenon?"

"No," he replied. "Have you heard of Dorje Sempa mantras?"

"No, but I've heard of mantras. I have a mantra. Om Namah Shiva."

"And how many times do you chant that?" he asked.

"Oh, I just chant it as often as possible. I don't count."

"Has the number 11:11 kept appearing to you?" I asked.

"No it has not."

"Is the number 11:11 relevant to your path of Tibetan Buddhism?"

"No."

"Or 11 or 111?"

"No."

That was all I wanted to know. It was time to leave. I set the trip meter to zero as I drove out of the centre's car park. As usual I parked as near as I could to my land-locked convent in Montignac, not accessible by car. I looked at the meter as I turned off the engine. It read 11.1. That meant it was exactly 11.1 miles between my parking space in Montignac and the Dhagpo Kagyu Ling Buddhist Centre. I tried to remind myself that this was a reassuring synchronicity which confirmed that I was on track. When I did some research on the Internet following my interview with the Lama, I discovered that in Tibetan Buddhism prostrations have to be performed 111,111 times to purify the body; the Dorje Sempa mantras are recited 111,111 times to purify the speech; 111,111 Mandala offerings are made to purify the mind; and 111,111 Guruyoga recitations are said to invoke the blessing of the lineage.

The Lama was not the first spiritual teacher I had questioned in my search for an answer to the 11:11 phenomenon. I had taken the opportunity to question Satyananda the previous year, just before I sold my lovely Victorian home in England to buy the old French ruin.

I had seen the flyer in the window of the local health food

shop.

Join us in satsang with Satyananda this Saturday.

Satsang means "Meeting in Truth" – to enquire about yourself, about your true nature, finding peace and freedom within. There is no ritual or ceremony involved in a Satsang. No prior experience or religious background is necessary. All are welcome.

Satsang often starts with a brief period of silence followed by an invitation to ask questions. Individuals may participate by simply listening to and absorbing the sense of freedom and peace; others may choose to become more actively involved in a dialogue with Satyananda.

That sounded like an excellent opportunity to shed some light on the 11:11 phenomenon. I was sure that Satyananda would be able to give me some answers.

I entered the church hall. At the front of the hall was a throne-like chair, adorned with blankets and pillows. On the table next to the throne were a bottle of water and a plate of fruit along with candles and flowers. The sound system had been wired up because the occasion was to be recorded on to CD for sale after the event.

Before Satyananda appeared, we were all invited to write a question on a piece of paper and place it in the wooden bowl on the temporary altar. About 8 of us took up this offer. I wrote:

11:11. Please can you explain why this number appears on the spiritual path for many people and could you share your own experiences of this number?

I folded the sheet of notepaper and duly placed it in the bowl with the other questions. In came Satyananda and took up his position on the seat. After a short meditation he began to answer the questions. One by one he unfolded the pieces of paper, answering questions about relationships, family issues and yoga. At one point he opened a paper and put it to one side. It was my paper. Mine was the only question he did not answer!

Undaunted, I approached him after satsang.

"You didn't answer my question," I stated, looking directly into his eyes. They were very small brown eyes, but clear and kindly.

"What question was that?"

"It was about the number 11:11. I asked if you could shed any light on this number. Why did you not read out my question?"

"Ah yes. I saw this question but I didn't know what to make of it."

"It's the number that woke me up. It has been appearing everywhere in my life and it still does."

"What do you mean, everywhere in your life? Do you mean on the clock?"

"Yes, but not just the clock. It appears everywhere."

"Well maybe this is your wake-up call and the reason it appeared was simply to wake you up."

"Has this not happened to you?" I continued. "Has it not appeared in your life?"

"No. It hasn't. It is probably just in your life that the 11:11 appears."

"No. It is happening to people all over the world, not just me. I'm trying to find out why it's happening. Can you shed any light on this number for me?"

"No. I'm sorry, I can't."

I was learning that 11:11 did not seem to be a universal wake-up call. It could be that 11:11 is only a sign for certain people, probably 111,111 of us! There are many paths to Oneness. I recognize that fact. Using numbers as a guide is an unusual route to enlightenment as it is not a religion nor is it connected to any particular belief system. 11:11 is a relatively new phenomenon as it is only as old as the digital age. It is even possible that 11:11

could be the incoming mass enlightenment code and it is slowly starting to filter into the world as the new earth is being birthed. It could be the code that is bringing in a new kind of enlightenment that links to the new earth.

The day after my interview with the Lama, Bella came to visit me. She was attending English classes as she wanted to improve her English and I wanted to improve my French, so when we were together she spoke in English and I spoke in French.

Bella gave me a guided tour of my garden. It was obvious that somebody had recently been in the garden chopping things down here and there. A plum tree had been massacred and a good fifty per cent of a beautiful evergreen bush had disappeared.

"It'll be the neighbour," explained Bella. "When my father owned the house she did the same thing. She would climb over the fence and chop things down."

That's all I needed, a crazy neighbour. I had already discovered notes on my windscreen saying, "Do not park here. This place is not for your car." That was utter nonsense because the road where I parked was a public road, but some people get into ruts and don't like it when anything threatens the status quo, including such trivial things as somebody parking their car in the space that their visitors sometimes used. Already 2 of the neighbours had protested about my car. I was told that it was too big and they would 'allow' me to park if I bought a smaller car. The problem was that I could not drive directly to the house. It was in the heart of the medieval passageways, too narrow for cars. Bella suggested that I simply ignored them and parked where I liked. I took the middle course and compromised, remembering the Chinese saying that it was the brittle tree that snapped in the wind. If it was raining or if I had a lot of things to load or unload, I parked near the house. If not, I parked at the top of the hill.

Bella told me that she had spoken to her father and that he

had originally found out the history of the convent from an old man that lived in the town. She mentioned a man known as 'Le Baron' who might be able to help me though she had no idea where to find him.

"And try the history society," she suggested. "There is bound to be someone there who has the information you are seeking."

I asked again at the tourist information centre. I was always in there asking questions! I explained that I understood my convent had once been a school of religion. I was assured that there had never been such an institution. Eventually, after realizing that I was not going to fade into the ethers and nor was I going to stop asking questions, they kindly arranged for me to meet the local doctor who belonged to the local history society. Apparently he knew all there was to know about Montignac. He would be able to see me the following week.

As I walked back from the spring with my container of freshly drawn spring water, I saw a man standing on the small terrace in front of his house. It was Alain. I had been waiting to meet him because, like mine, his house had once been part of the complex of convent buildings. His place had once been joined to my house and even now our deeds showed that we shared a party wall.

"Do you live here?" I asked him.

"Yes," he replied.

"I wondered if you knew anything about the history of your house?"

"A little."

That turned out to be an understatement. Alain had been born in the very house where he still lived. He had never left Montignac. A quiet and intelligent man, he had recently retired from his work as a car mechanic, yet his true love was archaeology. He stressed that he was an amateur. I'm sure that living in this area of France had triggered his love of the past. He had been inside the original Lascaux Caves 3 times. He had also spent 5 years studying the castle and the town in great depth. He'd been in every nook and cranny of the place and had measured all the walls. That was in the days before it had been owned by the present Parisian owner. Now it was impossible to gain access to that important piece of Montignac's history. The information he had collected over the years had all been carefully documented in an old file that he took down from the shelf in his living room. His living room was small, smaller than mine, and the ceiling was much lower. The back wall was pure cave and was running with water in exactly the same way as my ground floor room. He had built a stud wall in front of most of it. The floor was solid rock. In front of the stud wall a wooden floor had been laid on top of the rock. It was really just a cave with a bit of plasterboard partitioning and suspended floor to hide that fact.

"It's so damp," he complained. "Come and look at this. I have kept some of the original floor because I think it is so beautiful."

He showed me the polished stone floor behind the stud wall partition. It was quite different to my floor. Mine looked like it was mostly earth.

"What date are these houses?" I asked.

"They date back to the 1300s, possibly earlier."

"Really? That's a lot older than I thought they were."

His fireplace was solid stone and about a third of the size of mine. I asked why his ceiling was so much lower than mine. He explained that at some point in the past somebody had converted the house from 3 stories into 4. I was glad my place had not been renovated. I much preferred the majestic high ceilings.

"I haven't looked at this for 20 years," he told me as he took down the file.

Alain showed me the maps and the plans. There was a deep well in the castle and a maze of dungeons that had been hacked out of the rocks. They dated back to Roman times. The castle had been attacked and damaged many times but in 1825 it was completely demolished except for one tower. He showed me the location of the old town walls and how our houses were outside the walls of the castle in a hamlet of less than 40 people. The records showed that in some years there were only 16 people living in the hamlet. It was called Beynaguet.

"But tell me, Alain, was your house once part of a convent?" I asked.

"Yes indeed. It was a convent school. Come and see."

He led me outside and round to the back of his house. His courtyard was small and my house towered over his as I was higher up the hill than him. This was the first time I had seen my back wall. It was well over 10 metres high and was pure stone. It looked as straight as a die. I couldn't understand how the inside wall was so curved. There was no sign of any former windows or doorways that I could see, just this one massive wall.

"I think my house used to be joined to your house," I said.

"No. It was connected but not joined. There was a large gate that led into this courtyard. We shared the courtyard. And this building to the left of my house was the school hall."

"So it was definitely a school?"

"Yes."

"A school of what? A religious school?"

"Yes, and it took children in. They boarded."

"Oh, it was a boarding school! But what sort of school? Was it Jesuit? Catholic? Benedictine?"

"This I do not know."

I was disappointed. Digging up the past was not easy. I just kept being left with more questions. How many of these houses formed the school? What had been in these buildings before it was a school? Was it a convent school? What century were we talking about? I simply couldn't understand why the tourist information office repeatedly denied its existence.

I thanked Alain and he carefully folded up his plans and maps, replacing them on the shelf where they were likely to sit for another 20 years.

The longer I was in Montignac, the louder I shouted my

question. Why had I been sent there? It was a real struggle to stay positive. I had the distinct feeling that I had bitten off more than I could chew. I was living in a semi ruin. The place had been unloved and uninhabited for such a long time that bringing it back to a habitable standard was like trying to raise someone from the dead. For the first time in my life I truly understood the term 'crumbling' when applied to a building, for that is exactly what was happening to the convent. Every morning I swept up the offerings of the house from the night before, in the form of splinters of wood, dust, plaster and various insects, both alive and dead. The stormier the weather had been, the greater the size and the amount of the offerings. The weather was unpredictable. Very strong winds arose unannounced and ended just as suddenly. Unbearable heat and humidity was usually followed by an intense electrical storm which lit up huge swathes of sky. At those times, as I lay there alone in my tent within the thick stone walls of the convent, I felt as if I was an actress playing a part in a horror film. The storms frightened me as I was unsure how sound the roof was. I had visions of the tall chimney toppling and landing on my tent. I called out silently to the Universe. "Tell me why I have been sent here. I need to know. Just tell me what I have to do and I'll do it. Then I can move on." My faith was tested because my question remained unanswered.

Chapter 9

The Prehistoric Centipede

I enjoyed exploring Montignac. I explored every single road, passage and byway of the town. I plotted all the fresh water springs and medieval wash houses (including the few that had sadly been blocked up) and I found so much of interest. What a beautiful little town it was! There had, however, been one massive planning disaster and that was the demolition of the 14th century church in the 1930s. The destruction of the old church, the leaning bell tower and the adjacent covered market had ripped the very heart from my side of town. A Gothic doorway was all that remained of the historical ecclesiastical heritage. This beautiful carved stone arch stood alone just outside the new church, a sculpture from the past, a sad reminder of what had once stood on the site. The new church was rather ugly and totally out of character with the surrounding buildings.

It was our 13th, 14th, 15th and 16th century ancestors who were responsible for the bulk of the architectural beauty that the town had inherited. Their buildings were charming, picturesque, harmoniously constructed and utterly beautiful. The ones by the river had been built on stilts to protect them from flooding. Some of the oldest properties had walls of wood and timber, and others had balconies that looked out over the river. They were beautifully kept. Colourful flower baskets hung from the walls and flowerpots sat on window sills. Beauty in all forms was high on the agenda in typically French style.

On the opposite side of town to my convent was the 'Convent of the order of St Clare'. It had been built in the 18th century and was now used to house the council offices. The tourist information office was within a former 16th century hospital. This delightful building sits adjacent to the small church of Saint

George, once the chapel that belonged to the hospital. Also on that side of town was Rue de la Pègerie, a road full of 14th century buildings that once belonged to wealthy merchants. One of these houses is thought to have belonged to Jeanne d'Albret, the mother of King Henry IV of France.

The one remaining tower of the castle was the dominant feature of Montignac. It sat high on the hill above the town on the restored ramparts. Adjacent to the tower was the chateau. This rather fancy piece of architecture had been built in the 19th century within the walls of the ruined castle. Montignac had been a very important fortress in its day, owned by the infamous counts of Périgord.

Despite the man-made beauty of many of the buildings, I was in search of the most sacred place in the town. I found it in the small park near the school. There, at the foot of the hill that houses the Lascaux Caves, I discovered a crystal clear pond bubbling with the many springs that erupt at this point. I have heard it said that where a saint falls in battle, a spring erupts. Many saints must have fallen at that place. It could have been these springs that had drawn early man to this area.

The whole area around Montignac is known locally as the Golden Triangle. It is formed between the towns of Sarlat, Brive and Périgueux. Montignac sits in the very heart of this triangle of history and prehistory. I had been guided there by the number 11:11 so it was becoming increasingly obvious that I was going to be dealing with something ancient though I still had absolutely no idea what that could be.

I had plenty of time to explore the wider area of the Périgord Noir. My first discovery was the picturesque town of Sarlat. This soon became one of my favourite places. The road from Montignac to Sarlat runs along a high ridge with spectacular and far-reaching views on both sides. I could just imagine what it must have been like riding this road on horseback not so long ago. Sarlat is 22 miles from Montignac (a master number and twice 11) and it's one of the most beautiful places I have ever seen. It looks and feels like a film set. It has the largest medieval concentration of buildings in Europe. Originally it was a pilgrimage town that grew up around a monastery with relics. This attracted lots of people. It became so big that the monastic order left. After that it fell into decline. Many of the old buildings were simply abandoned so in the 1960s a decision was made to demolish and rebuild much of Sarlat. An architect called André Malraux brought in a law that protected the historic buildings rather than demolished them. What vision and foresight! I only wish he had been around to save the old church and bell tower in Montignac in the 1930s.

During the 100-year war Sarlat served as a frontier between the zone bearing allegiance to the King of England and the zone bearing allegiance to the King of France. As a frontier it was the location of horrendous violence, especially during the persecution of the Cathars.

I met Adrian in the supermarket on my very first visit to Sarlat. I had been standing holding a courgette, looking for the scales to weigh and price it.

"Over there," a voice said in a distinct northern England accent. I turned to see a tall man pointing to the well hidden scales.

"Oh, you're English?" I asked.

"Yes, I'm English by birth but now I live in Sarlat. I have been here for over 20 years."

He explained that he was an artist and that he lived at the top of a medieval tower in the Hotel de Malville. I think that translates as hotel of the bad town. Strange name. We began chatting and within minutes we were on the subject of the Bilderberg group. He was the first person I had ever met who knew about this shadowy organisation. They are an elite group of individuals who meet once a year in great secrecy. It is said by some that the group's grand design is for a one world government with a single, global marketplace, policed by one world army, and financially regulated by one 'World (Central) Bank' using one global currency.

It was good to meet someone on my wavelength who had seen through the illusion that most people live under. He had recognized that there was a hidden agenda on earth and it didn't matter who was in power; it was the forces behind the politicians who were the ones pulling the strings. Still, there was a way out and that was by raising our individual consciousness.

Adrian was a political artist and was very knowledgeable. Over the next few weeks I bumped into him 3 times. To me that is very meaningful. When something happens 3 times I take note. It was even more significant when I later discovered that he rarely left his tower. He only ventured out on his errands once a week. The chances of me seeing him were so slim that I knew that there was a reason for our synchronistic meetings. Either he had something to teach me, I had something to teach him, or both. As I believe that numbers, signs and synchronicities are a language of consciousness, I always take note when they appear in my life.

Adrian walked the edge of genius. His catchphrase was, "It's better to burn out than to fade away." I weighed my courgette, took a note of his website address and said I would visit him in his tower sometime soon.

Although my house was situated high up on the side of the valley, I couldn't see the sun set or rise. It rose behind the Lascaux hill directly opposite the front of my house, and it set behind the hill on which I was situated, thus revealing that the convent had been built on the east/west axis like many early religious buildings. The climate in early spring was damp and misty yet when the sun did manage to break through it could be strong and really hot. Unfortunately the river valley was very prone to fog and some mornings the mists hung around for most of the day, giving an eerie feel to the town. When I ventured outside to the toilet on these misty mornings I would catch sight of the tower rising from the morning mist like the Loch Ness monster rising from the murky waters of a lake. It always made me feel uneasy.

I could also see the church tower from my garden. The chiming church bells punctuated the day at regular intervals. I didn't need a watch or a clock to mark the passing time. Every morning at 8am the bells on the church clock played a short tune. Exactly 11 hours later at 7pm the tune was played again. That meant that each day was 'officially' 11 hours long. Had anyone else in town noticed this fact? I doubt it!

It was not long after arriving back in France from Turkey that I saw the giant centipede. I was sitting indoors trying to prise apart the pages of a particularly rare and beautiful water-damaged book when I saw a movement out of the corner of my eye. What the hell was that? I turned my head and saw an enormous, ugly, black, multi-legged creature sitting on the wall. It was fat and hairy and reminded me of a prehistoric animal. I felt sick. I had never seen a creature like that. I guessed it belonged to the centipede family because it had so many legs. It was huge, as long as my hand but not as wide. Suddenly its many legs moved and it sped across the wall at the speed of light, making a scraping noise against the stone wall as it ran. It obviously had claws. I don't like spiders or insects and this was the mother of all things creepy crawly but even I could recognize that my response to this creature was way over the top. The moment it moved I screamed and headed straight for the door, grabbing my handbag on the way out. I ran as fast as I could from the convent, not even bothering to shut the door behind me. My heart was pounding in my chest and I broke out in a nervous sweat. I ran as far as the spring and got into the car and drove out of town. I just drove to nowhere in particular. I wanted to get as far away as I could and I ended up in the city of Périgueux, some 60 kilometres away. The artificial lights and bland music of the covered shopping centre calmed, distracted and soothed me. With lots of people milling around I felt safe. I stayed out until sunset. I couldn't bear the thought of returning. I even considered booking into a hotel for the night, but I knew that was crazy and that I needed to get a grip on myself and return home to sleep. I drove slowly back to Montignac and headed towards the convent with a heavy heart.

Gingerly I walked up the steps and I stood outside the front door. My stomach was churning and I was almost in tears. I couldn't understand why it upset me so much. It had triggered something deep inside me though I had no idea what or why. I eventually plucked up the courage to make a dash for the tent. Thank goodness I had an insect screen. There's no way an insect as large as that centipede could get into my tent.

When I mentioned to Bella that I had seen a huge centipede she informed me that all the cave houses in the area were infested with these creatures, and she suggested that I got a cat to keep their numbers down. That's how she coped with them. If she was right, I didn't know how I would cope with living in the convent. I needed more than a cat.

I questioned Bella about the use of the term 'cave house' and she explained that this was what houses such as ours were called. That's because they had been built directly into the cave walls. I looked more carefully at my place and realized that not only was the lower ground floor wall pure cave, but the lower part of my one habitable room was also built directly into the rock. No wonder it was so damp in my tent. Not only was I living in the heart of prehistory, but I was actually living in a cave! That's what I call a truly authentic prehistoric experience.

Chapter 10

The French Doctor

As the spring fogs lifted, my spirits began to rise. Those early weeks had been very difficult as I had tried to adjust to my new lowered living conditions. Gradually I stopped waking up in the night with the cold and damp. As the storms lessened, so did the amount of debris falling from the ceiling and chimney. I was still sleeping in the tent though. Somehow that thin sheet of polyester afforded me protection: physical, psychic and psychological. I began to quite like the house even though it continued to smell strongly of damp, musk, cats, church and school. The smell of the convent permeated everything. I constantly burned incense and scattered essential oils around the place but it made little difference. It was probably a combination of the sheer age of the place, the decades of neglect and the dampness of the rock walls. My clothes and books began to smell of the convent so wherever I went the smell went with me, hanging in my aura as if I were merely an extension of the building, identifiable by the odour.

Everything in the place was skew-whiff. The doors and windows were warped and uneven. The walls were almost a metre out of true. Unbelievably curved! The place was heaving with character but unfortunately it was also heaving with insect life. Centipedes were the least of my troubles. The change in temperature had brought about a massive increase in the number and variety of insects and other forms of wildlife. The place was literally crawling.

The views from the garden were spectacular. I would stand and gaze out across the town to the hill on the opposite side of the valley. I was standing there on the hill on one side of the river, looking across to the hill on the other side of the river. That was the hill that contained the caves of Lascaux. Every time I looked out of my kitchen window that is what I would see. I had been guided by the number 11:11 to one of the world's most important prehistoric sites. This could not possibly have been by chance; it was just that I didn't know why I had been delivered to the roots of mankind. At least the roots according to what is taught to us in school. I was open to the truth being different. What was it I had to learn? What was the reason I was in Montignac? I needed to find Le Baron. Maybe he could give me some answers.

"He's always in the bar at 6pm," said my Swiss friend Steve. Steve should know because he could often be found sitting in one of the street cafés with his 6 little Yorkshire terriers watching the world go by.

"When you next see him please tell him I'm looking for him," I asked.

"I will."

Steve was helpful and kindly. What's more, he spoke English!

"Why is he called Le Baron?" I asked.

"You'll see why when you meet him!"

I carried on searching, but he was never in the bar at 6pm when I went looking for him.

One of the most wonderful things about living life according to the 11:11 sign was that I/Hilary/my ego would never have dreamed of going to live in this small town in the French countryside. My self-limiting beliefs such as 'I only like to live near the sea' or 'I don't like France and never have done and never will do' or 'I'm looking for a place with a small garden because I don't want the upkeep of a large plot' would have prevented me living there. I'd never even heard of the Lascaux Caves before I arrived, yet here I was, living within walking distance of this incredible UNESCO World Heritage site. I met people who had looked at dozens of houses before deciding which one to buy. Some had spent years looking at the various towns and hamlets of the Dordogne before settling in the area around Montignac. For me there was no such time-consuming dilemma. My mind had nothing to do with my decision to live in Montignac. I had taken the short cut. It was purely thanks to the 11:11 sign that I was there.

"The history of Beynaguet is not important."

The doctor spoke with an air of authority that combined his maleness, his nationality and his profession. The tourist information office had done well to arrange this appointment for me as the doctor had been declared to be the most knowledgeable historian in town. It had taken a lot of persistence on my part, but now I had access to some serious local knowledge. The conversation was held in French, naturally.

"The town of Montignac was on your side of the river, within the walls of the fortified chateau. The house you can see now next to the tower is not nearly as old as the castle. It was built within the grounds of the ruined castle. The original castle has been attacked many times in the past because this part of France was often at war. Of course you realize that your house was not in Montignac don't you? You are in a hamlet called Beynaguet, just outside the fortified walls. There is nothing of importance in Beynaguet."

"Nothing at all? What about the school?" I asked.

"What school?"

"The school of religion?"

"There was no school."

"What about the convent?"

"There was no convent on your side of the river."

"But I have been told that my house had once been a teaching convent."

"Anybody who has an arched window in their property immediately jumps to the conclusion that they are living in a former convent!" he declared. "There is absolutely no way that there was a school in Beynaguet. It was a small community of peasants. They were simple uneducated people. I'm telling you there was nothing of note in Beynaguet."

I tried digesting what he was saying but it didn't feel right. I knew there were many versions of history. Written history does not always match verbal history. I was learning to run everything past my intuition.

"On my side of the river, however, there was a convent. A priory too. And this house that we are sitting in right now was once a school of catechism," he continued.

The doctor lived on the opposite side of the river to me. His spacious house was a beautiful building and it was used as his medical practice as well as his home. The floors were polished stone, the ceilings were the same height as mine and his walls had been sandblasted to reveal their golden beauty.

"I'd like to ask if you what you know about the tower that is near my place," I asked.

"That is all that remains of the castle, just the one tower and a few walls. The rest of it was destroyed in 1825. Only one tower is left of the original 12. The other 11 have gone."

"11?"

"Yes, 11 have been destroyed."

This tied in with what Alain had told me.

"And what about the bridge over the river?"

"In 1580 the original wooden bridge was burned down by Protestants. It was rebuilt but then the replacement bridge was destroyed by floods in 1620. Before the existing bridge was built in 1766–77, the only way to cross the river was by boat."

"So it took 11 years to build the current bridge?"

"Yes. It took that long because it was built by hand of course."

The bridge had been gracefully constructed from stone, with 2 arches.

"The town is divided by the river but the river was not the border between the French and the English. On the right-hand side was the medieval city of Montignac. It was fortified. Just outside the walls was the tiny hamlet of Beynaguet. At times the border ran more or less down your road. Most of the houses are

14th, 15th or 16th century houses. As you have no doubt noticed, the houses down by the river are built on stilts because flooding is a problem in that area by the riverbank. There are many old wash houses with constant running water although a few have been closed up and are now used by the fire service as a water supply. Did you know that Montignac was once a harbour?" he asked. I found that quite hard to believe as the river was so shallow, but it was true. The boats that had moored in the harbour were flat-bottomed boats and I remembered seeing them when I had been drowned in the river in a previous life.

"Many famous people have lived in Montignac. Despite the fact that it is a small town we have many famous sons including the writer Eugène Le Roy and Pierre Lachambeaudie, the writer of fables, poems and songs. He sought a peaceful transformation of society founded on justice and fraternity. Have you heard of Joseph Joubert?"

"No," I replied.

"He was a moralist. Some of his famous quotes include: *To teach is to learn twice.* And *Justice is the truth in action.*

"So even if it's not of any significance, do you know anything at all about Beynaguet?" I asked. I was rather desperately scraping the barrel for titbits. I had already discovered that 'guet' meant 'lookout' or watch (in a military sense) though I had no idea what the 'Beyna' part of Beynaguet referred to.

"There was a small chapel there but it was not important."

I was startled to hear that.

"Really? When was that?" I asked.

"Oh that was very, very old. It's difficult to find written information about it because of its age. It was probably founded in the 10th or 11th century at the very latest. It was linked to the ensualla."

I was not familiar with the word that sounded something like 'ensualla' (I have not got a clue how it is spelt!) so I took the pen from the table and began to take notes. My French was not yet fluent so I intended looking up some of the more obscure vocabulary when I got home. He immediately took the pen from my hands and wrote it down for me. Each time I tried to take notes the doctor kindly took over. The combination of his doctor's handwriting and the French way of forming letters meant I could hardly read what he had written. Despite the fact that I left with half a page of notes, all I could make out were the words 'chapel of St Thomas'. This was an exciting piece of information. I reasoned that if there was a chapel then there could have been a school attached to it.

My time was up. The doctor was a busy man and someone was knocking at the door.

"I have an appointment now," he continued. "So you must go."

The doctor did indeed know a lot about Montignac and it was very kind of him to give me both his time and knowledge. As I gathered my things together he stood up to show me to the door. I walked along the polished stone corridor with its majestic beamed ceilings and he unlocked his beautiful oak door. I left with a morsel of information and a glimmer of hope.

Leaving the doctor's beautiful home and returning to my dilapidated ruin was a sharp and uncomfortable contrast. I really needed to upgrade my living conditions. Having failed to find an available builder in the local area, I finally decided to ask a builder to come over from England to help me out. Mr Cook could turn his hand to anything and he said that he would be willing to spend 8 days working on the property. I had shown him some photos of the state of the convent before he left for France, but he was in for a shock when he first set eyes on the place. His jaw visibly dropped when I opened the gate to reveal my purchase.

"Oh, my God! Hilary. What a dump. What a state it's in."

His jaw dropped even further when he stepped inside and saw the bowing walls and the dodgy timbers. He shook his head in despair.

"You've bought the pig in the poke all right."

He might see it as a pig in the poke but it all depended on one's point of view. Who knows, maybe it was the jewel in the crown? It may not be big, it may not be up together but it was old and interesting. It could be that this house, built into the side of the cave, could be as old as mankind itself.

"If I were you I'd just put it straight back on the market, Hilary. Get rid of it. Sell it. Cut your losses. It's not worth trying to get this place back into shape. It's too far gone. What on earth made you buy it?"

How could I answer that truthfully? I readily admit that the reason for my purchase sounded crazy. 'Actually I bought it because the map reference was 1.11. and I saw 11:11 on the clock.' No, I couldn't possibly tell him. He simply wouldn't understand.

All was not doom and gloom. I silently reminded myself that where there's a will there's a way. I just had to stay positive. Let's face it, if the building had managed to remain standing for at least 800 years then I'm sure it could stand for another 800.

Mr Cook cast his expert eye over the place. It was great having someone with the knowledge, the skills and the strength to deal with what had to be dealt with.

"Are you sure you want to throw your money at this place?" he asked.

"Yes," I replied. "I don't need it to look like a stately home. I just need it to remain standing and provide me with a home."

The list of essential work was long:

- Install a wood burner so that I had heating.
- Close in the massive chimney so stuff would stop falling down the opening.
- Insulate the loft.
- Install some kitchen units.
- Brace the wall and bracket the rotting beams.

- Fit a window and a door in the main room.
- Put windows in the unglazed roof openings.
- Close in the terrace so that I could access the bathroom and kitchen without having to go outside.

In the 8 days available Mr Cook managed lots of things on the list. He was strong and capable and he worked hard. Unfortunately there was not quite enough time to close in the terrace. That meant I still had an outside toilet, but now that I had windows and a door the wind could no longer whip through the place. However, I could not stay and luxuriate in my newly upgraded accommodation. It was time to travel back to England with Mr Cook in his van because the temples of Mexico were waiting for me.

Chapter 11

The Temples of Mexico

"Why don't you come to India after you have been to Mexico? I'm going to be with Sai Baba at Christmas. You could come and stay at my apartment in Puttaparthi where his ashram is."

India! I had never made it to India. I had actually been aiming to get to India overland when my French attack took place. I had always wanted to go but marriage and family life had clipped my wings. Now for the first time in several decades I was free. There was nothing to stop me going. In fact it would be perfect to spend the winter in the Indian sun rather than at the convent. It was the ideal time to visit.

Catherine had been a devotee of the Indian Avatar Sai Baba for many years and had been given 7 personal interviews. On one occasion he had materialized a gold necklace for her which she treasured. Despite the controversy that surrounded him, Catherine had no doubts about his authenticity as an Avatar. I had heard the bad press about him and I did not share her faith.

However, Sai Baba had always intrigued me. I had first heard about him as a teenager when a book in the library had fallen from a shelf and hit me on the head. I remember opening it and wondering who this strange man in orange robes was. Then, when I was training to be a yoga teacher I had some photos of various spiritual teachers including Babaji, Sri Aurobindo, Krishnamurti, Ramana Maharshi and Sai Baba pinned up on my notice board. One day my young daughter came running into the kitchen. "Mummy, Mummy!" she cried excitedly. "The man in the picture moved. He smiled at me." When I asked her which man she pointed to the one of Sai Baba.

Now I was being given an opportunity to go and see this God man for myself. There were no strong number signs around the

Indian trip, but I had such a strong intuitive feeling that I needed to go that I accepted Catherine's invitation. The number signs of confirmation appeared later, after I had booked my flight. Catherine told me all about her new rooftop apartment just outside the ashram walls, and I started to tell her all about my convent just outside the castle walls.

"It's actually a cave. Looking carefully I can see that the convent has been built directly into the cliff face. It's a steep cliff, at least 15 metres high and..." I started.

I looked over at Catherine. She wasn't listening. She had that strange look in her eyes, as if she was gazing into the distance at something unseen. She was having a sudden and unexpected download.

"The Huguenots. Who are they? I'm getting a strong connection with Huguenots. Sorry to interrupt you like that. It's just that as soon as you mentioned the word 'cliff' I had a strong impression of Huguenots being thrown to their death off the cliff. I don't know who the Huguenots are, do you? "

"They were a religious group, members of the Protestant Reformed Church of France. They were inspired by the writings of John Calvin but they suffered a lot of persecution and were eventually driven out of France. They ended up in Protestant countries such as England, Denmark and Switzerland."

"Would they have been in Montignac?" she asked.

"Oh yes, almost certainly."

"I don't know whether the image I just had was of people being thrown to their deaths or whether they were dead bodies being thrown over the cliff," said Catherine, "but there were so many of them. It must have been a massacre or something. Have you any idea what year that would be?"

"There were several periods. In particular the 16th and 17th centuries. And you're probably right because there was a massacre in the 16th century. Tens of thousands of them were killed."

There was a pause. I could picture what it must have been like and it was a disturbing image.

"The Cathars. There's a link with the Cathars. Who were they?"

"Another religious group. They were pacifists. They believed that there were 2 worlds, the spiritual world, reigned over by God, and the evil, material world governed by Satan. They believed that in order to go to heaven, the soul had to be pure so they renounced worldly pleasures. They were tolerant of other religions, and believed in the equality of the sexes. As you can imagine, they weren't very popular with the Catholic Church! I know they were in the Dordogne, but I don't know whether they were in Montignac or not."

"That doesn't matter. You'll be healing some Cathar stuff in the area. Now I'm getting an image of a wheel and you are the hub at the centre of the wheel. You are being activated as a prism of light."

"How does that happen? How do I get activated?" I asked

"You are being given keys to activate you. They are in various places around the world. I know you've been invited to Mexico. I can tell you that this invitation is led by spirit. The person who has invited you has been strongly guided to do so."

"How do I get these keys you mention? Who gives them to me?"

"All you have to do is visit the places. You are carrying within you all that is needed for the work. As you visit these ancient sites you will be collecting keys in the form of energy and you will become like a portable prism, allowing the light to work through you to prepare the grid for 2012 and beyond. You're like a generator but you're not on full power yet. Visiting these places will allow the power to be turned up in time for when you return to the convent. I'm getting that this is a lengthy journey. How long is it?"

"The tour of the temples is 11 days. Not that long. But I've noticed that the 111 degree line of longitude runs right through Mexico, so I have decided that I will travel this line all the way from Mexico to Canada."

"You need to do that. You need to travel the line. You've been guided to do that as part of your activation process. You'll be healing and clearing the etheric web of the earth as you travel. As the lines get cleared they're able to be reactivated by the Christ Consciousness grid. This work can only be done on the physical plane. It can't be done from a higher level or by remote healing.

The etheric grids connect with strategic vortex points on the earth. The etheric grid has been perforated through the negative behaviour of man. That's how the etheric web, the spiral webbing of light, of Christ consciousness, got deactivated in the first place. This disconnection started way back, hundreds of thousands of years ago. That's probably why you've been sent to the heart of prehistory, back almost to the beginning of time. This etheric 'webbing' is like wounds in the subtle body of the earth. You already know you can get rips and tears in your aura, and earth is no different as she is a living entity."

Catherine was confirming what I had already suspected, that my task in the heart of prehistoric France involved ancient times.

"For the earth to move forward we have created a 'story'. There are thousands of lightworkers on the planet right now. We are the only ones who can dissolve the story, dissolve the dream that we think of as reality. This is an important point so I'm stressing it. This work can only be done on a physical level whilst in the physical body. A realignment will take place in the mass consciousness as we move into unity consciousness. We've done it many times before. En masse, we hold the light as the earth shifts into the 5th dimension. That'll happen in 2012. The earth will pause. During that time it will shed its skin, just like a snake sheds it skin. Then the shift will take place. Life will continue as before and all this," said Catherine, waving her hand to indicate our 'normal' physical universe, "will be forgotten. We won't even remember it."

"We won't remember it? So what's the point of having this physical experience?" I asked.

She remained silent. It would be a few weeks before she was sent a download to answer that for me.

"So what are you doing after you've travelled the 111 degree line?" she asked.

"I'm going to stop off in New York for a week."

"Will you visit the 9/11 site?"

"I might do."

"I think you need to as part of the clearing process. Make a point of going there."

I took note of what Catherine said.

"And lastly, but certainly not least, you must do the Template ceremonies in Glastonbury," she stated firmly. "There are 7 ceremonies and you need to do them all. I have done the first 6 already but I'll be joining you for the 7th one because that is the last one and it has just been transmitted. The first 4 are happening this week and the other 3 will be held in November."

These dates for the Template were to be held during the 4 days before my flight to Mexico. The last 3 were to be held in the week after my return from Mexico and before my flight to India. I saw what was happening. Despite the fact that I was only going to be in England for such a short time, the Templates were happening on the days I would be there. To me that was confirmation that I needed to do them. They would have to be crammed into my busy schedule but it felt right to do them. It would also be a good opportunity to spend some time in Glastonbury, which is thought to be the heart chakra of the earth.

The Template ceremonies took place under the shadow of Glastonbury Tor and involved the use of spinning geometric shapes. The Template ceremonies are to assist us in integrating the acceleration of electromagnetic download by reconnecting our biocircuits. They are intended to move us on from a fear-based paradigm. I didn't feel any different after doing the Templates but I guessed the new energies would take time to be absorbed and assimilated to the extent that they would change my energy field.

I was looking forward to my Mexico trip. Mike Handcock, a New Zealand-based entrepreneur, presenter, author and a self-confessed global gypsy, had picked up my book *The 11:11 Code* in Kuala Lumpur. I wonder if he had spotted the K of Kuala (11th letter of the alphabet) and the fact that Kuala Lumpur has 11 letters…?

"I couldn't even see what it was about," he explained. "It was wrapped in cling film so it was impossible to flip through and read a bit before I bought it. However, for some reason I was just compelled to buy the book. There was no question about it. I'm quite an intuitive person so I bought it."

In the same way that convents find me, I know that my book *The 11:11 Code* finds people and can act as a trigger to open them up to light. It could have been a very different story.

It was April 19th, the evening before the full moon in Scorpio and the week before *The 11:11 Code* was due to be released. The text message from Sarah was brief:

Call me as soon as you get this msg. Urgent.

Sarah had been to see me a few days earlier, and had subsequently been to see another friend called Maria. The following day, Maria was in her garden when she became overwhelmed by a feeling of darkness. It seemed to engulf her and she felt her chakras close up as a form of protection. She was so concerned that she phoned her psychic friend called Edward. Edward immediately identified that Maria was under psychic attack.

"But where's it coming from?" asked Maria.

"Who have you seen recently?" asked Edward.

"Sarah."

"No, it's not her. It's coming through Sarah though."

Maria began to list the names of people either she or Sarah had seen in the previous few days. When she reached 'Hilary' he stopped her.

"Yes, it's Hilary. Who is she?"

Maria explained that I was an author who had written a book about the number 11:11 which is a spiritual code that could lead Humanity towards their true Divine purpose on earth. The book had just been printed and was due for distribution the following week.

"The dark forces do not want this book to be a catalyst for change in people," he explained to Maria. "There is a black occultist hanging around Hilary. He is trying to weave a spell on the book but he cannot penetrate Hilary's energy field because her spiritual practises give her protection. The occultist that is trying to break through Hilary's energy is looking for a way in to get to the book. His attempts to do that have affected Sarah's energy, and then yours in turn. I'll work on clearing you both, then you must contact Hilary and get her to call me. It's urgent. It can't wait."

I could see what was happening. It was exactly what had happened when I was clearing the convent in Spain, namely that the Universe was sending me the people I needed to help me with the work that I facilitate. I was doing nothing yet I was being guided to people who were working for the light. I was not working alone. I was also being reminded how necessary it was to keep my aura strong, clear and protected through certain spiritual practises such as censing, chanting, fasting, yoga and right diet. Fortunately I had been going through a particularly disciplined phase. My practices had been strong and regular so the black magician had been unable to penetrate my energy field.

I duly phoned Edward. It was the morning of the full moon. He was a dowser and had been dowsing for over 30 years.

"Hilary, I'm so glad we have managed to make contact before

the mass release of your book. It mustn't go out until the dark energy is cleared; otherwise it could have the opposite effect and instead of leading people towards the light it could lead people away from the light. It's a powerful book and the dark forces will do their utmost to stop the message of the book being sent out into the world."

He explained that the source of the darkness was coming from both France and Spain. The occultist was a member of an underground order intent on blocking the earth's ascension. Edward could block the spell but he needed a copy of the book in his hands to do so. He would perform a ritual using one copy and once it had been cleared then the entire print run (and all future copies) would be completely clear and impermeable to any future attempts to distort the message of light.

This episode made me acutely aware of the existence of forces that operate from a different perspective. I was so thankful that I had been following good practice during that time. In particular I knew that my mantra Om Namah Shiva was an extremely powerful form of protection.

So Mike Handcock might have thought that he had found *The 11:11 Code* but the truth was that it had found him. After reading it he wrote to my publisher to invite me to co-host a tour of the ancient temples of Mexico. Naturally I did not hesitate to accept his invitation. I'd never been to Mexico. Mike had been guided to invite me because I needed to visit the temples to collect the keys. I didn't tell him that was the reason. There was no need for him to know.

People had come from all over the world to join this tour. They were from South Africa, India, Australia, Malaysia and New Zealand. There was only one other English person on the tour. At dinner on the first night I was chatting to her, and asked her which part of England she came from.

"Bristol," she replied.

"I went to school in Bristol," I replied. "But it was a very small school so you might not have heard of it. It's called Redland High."

She paused.

"I have heard of it. My daughter goes to Redland High."

That's a bit of a coincidence and it was not unusual for me to encounter such synchronicity, but there was more. I told her that I had to travel miles to school each day because I lived on the opposite side of the city to the school.

"Where did you live?" she asked.

"Knowle," I replied. "Do you know it?"

"Yes, I know it very well. Even though I live in Redland my family actually came from Knowle. In fact my grandparents lived there until quite recently."

"Whereabouts?" I asked. Before she answered I just knew what she was going to say.

"Calder Road, right opposite the police station."

"That's where I lived," I replied. Yes, I too had lived in Calder Road. As the 6th largest city in England there were thousands of roads I could have lived in, but I had spent 10 years living a few doors away from her grandparents. That neat synchronicity was a confirmation sign. It demonstrated to me that I was in the right place at the right time.

The temple tour started in Mexico City which, at 2240 metres above sea level, is one of the highest cities in the world. More interesting is the fact that it is located at 19.26 north of the equator, very near the important 19.5 degrees.

19.5 degrees north and south are the latitudes where the apex points of a star tetrahedron within a sphere will contact that sphere's surface when one apex is positioned at the north or south pole. This particular degree has also been linked to Cydonia on Mars as well as with ancient structures here on earth, including the pyramids at Giza, the huge stone circle in Avebury in Wiltshire and the sun and moon pyramids at Teotihuacan that we were about to visit.

It was during our visit to the pyramids at Teotihuacan that I was guided to perform a ritual ceremony with the group to reopen an energy gate. This group of seemingly random individuals from different parts of the globe was made up of the people who had responded to the 'Rock Your Life' invitation to tour the Mexican Temples. What many of them did not realize was that they were not a random group of tourists but part of a soul group who had chosen before incarnation to help with this work. In fact many of the original applicants for the tour had dropped out because of a health scare. Swine flu had suddenly appeared in Mexico so some people cancelled. This was the Universe weeding out those who were still operating from a level of fear that would have interfered with the clearing work. Those who had passed the swine flu 'fear initiation test' were the resulting group.

The Teotihuacan Pyramids are a short distance north of Mexico City, and it was on the pyramid of the moon that the first key was collected as a group of us gathered in a circle. I felt the spiralling energy encircling my body and intertwining with my energy field as I stood at the top of the pyramid. I loved the fact that direct access to the site was permitted, unlike places like Stonehenge where barriers prevent physical contact with the stones. If I couldn't have accessed the apex of the moon pyramid I wouldn't have been able to collect the key.

Cholula was next on the agenda. It was approached by a long underground tunnel that was completely blocked by stagnant energy. Not only do I have a personal dislike of tunnels because of a past life trauma in a tunnel, but to walk through the congealed darkness at Cholula was not a pleasant experience. One of the group picked up on this atmosphere and was very reluctant to enter, but her reluctance helped me because I focused on her fear rather than my own. It was an extremely long walk, in excess of 800 metres, but we chanted our way through (Om Namah Shiva) and managed to clear a pathway of energy. It was enough to allow a trickle of light through those dark stone passageways. That trickle would increase over time until it became a river of light. As you give, so you receive, and I knew that I was collecting the second of my keys here.

In Oaxaca we stayed in a boutique hotel. As we disembarked from the bus, Mike joked that I needed to put my chequebook away, for the hotel we were staying in was a former convent. We were shown to our rooms and had about an hour to get ready before we went out for dinner. However, after less than 15 minutes, everybody gradually reappeared by the pool. No fewer than 6 of the group had either sensed a presence or had felt uneasy in the rooms they had been allocated. A lot of clearing took place whilst our group was in residence!

Monte Albán was the most powerfully charged site of the tour and I had difficulty breathing at that site. My chest was unusually tight. When this happens it always indicates to me a strong past life connection with the place. The rain clouds hung dark and low in the sky but a gap in the clouds allowed the rays of the sun through, lighting up the massive stones of the pyramids. The setting was dramatic and this key came in the form of sound. It happened as I looked into a glass cabinet containing exactly 11 skulls. I can best describe the sound as an electrical buzz that surrounded my own skull.

We arrived at Chichén Itzá on September 22nd, the day of the autumnal equinox. It was inevitable that this was to be the most important day of the tour for it is one of the 4 most sacred days of the year. The longest day (summer solstice), the shortest day (winter solstice), and the 2 days of equal length (the equinoxes) are beyond religion.

It was amazingly quiet at Chichén Itzá considering that we were there on the day of the equinox but I guess that most people would choose to visit later in the day when the 'serpent show' would be happening. Twice each year, during the spring (March 20th or 21st) and autumnal (September 21st or 22nd) equinoxes, the position of the sun casts a shadow that makes the form of a serpent on the steps leading to the top of the El Castillo pyramid. Thousands turn up to see this biannual event. On reflection, the morning of the equinox could well be the quietest time of the year to visit!

As soon as we entered the site I knew that there was some major work to be done. I also knew exactly where it had to be done. I double-checked the location with Keith, one of the other tour hosts. He agreed. Keith and I would be doing this work together. We had worked together many other times before in other incarnations so we had this connection that transcended time and space.

I first met Keith in this life at a hotel in Mexico City. It was the hotel where the group had arranged to gather for the first meeting. I had never met any of them before and the only person I might have recognized was Mike as I had seen his photo. As I stood at reception I saw a man approaching the desk. I had no idea who he was. I looked at him and he looked at me.

"Who are you?" he asked.

"Who are you?" I replied.

We began to spiral around each other in a dance-like movement, looking each other in the eye and smiling. We spun around and around in a physical and energetic interplay. I have never greeted/been greeted by any other human being in that way before. It was simply a case of instant recognition. I recognized Mike too. We had been together in many lives, more recently as husband and wife and the love I felt for him was as strong as ever. True love never dies. It appears as the love between friends, parent and child, siblings, lovers, work mates and so on. That is how we can experience love at first sight, except it's not 'first sight' at all. It is the true love that survives through all incarnations.

Before we gathered the group together at Chichén Itzá I began to clear the area using incense. I wanted the area to be as clear as possible before creating the circle. Within seconds of my incense sticks being lit, a security guard came rushing over.

"Stop! No fire allowed."

"It's not fire," I explained. "It's just smoke. Incense smoke."

I smiled sweetly and carried on clearing the area, wafting the thick incense smoke high and low.

"You must stop," insisted the guard.

I ignored him. This is totally out of character for me because I am usually quite law abiding, but the work had to be done and nothing and nobody was going to stop me. If they wanted me to stop they would have to drag me away screaming. When he realized that I was a 'disobedient tourist' he went off in search of backup help. While he was gone I finished the cleansing and Keith and I quickly gathered the group together and all joined hands in a circle. Out of the corner of my eye I saw the guard return with another man but by now the incense had done its work and the sticks were no longer smoking. He could not stop me from making a circle. I don't think that holding hands in a circle was against any rule in his rule book. After consolidating the safe and protective surrounding by chanting AUM, I entered the centre of the circle and with Lemurian sealing spells I opened a channel that had been purposely closed many hundreds of years ago. It had been closed to protect this very important site. Although a lot of my work can be done without other physical beings, in this instance, because of the depth and importance of the work, a group of people was needed.

We ended the ceremony by singing *All You Need is Love* by John Lennon. I felt a sense of satisfaction. The site had been activated in time for 10/10/10.

There are 12 triple dates of power leading up to the earth's ascension, which is when we take a shift in consciousness. They are: 01/01/01, 02/02/02, 03/03/03, 04/04/04, 05/05/05, 06/06/06, 07/07/07, 08/08/08, 09/09/09, 10/10/10, 11/11/11 and finally 12/12/12. 9 days after 12/12/12 is the 2012 winter solstice and the now famous ending of the Mayan calendar. The next day 22/12/12 could be called the official beginning of the Golden Age. 22122012.

Chapter 12

The 111 Degrees of Longitude

The temple tour over, it was time to travel the 111 degree line of longitude. This line had been brought to my attention when I looked at my map to find out the exact location of Mexico City. I had noticed that the 111 line went right through Canada, the USA and Mexico. I felt it needed to be travelled for 2 reasons. Firstly as an experiment: would the number 11 appear more often than it usually did whilst I was physically on the 111 line? Secondly, I thought it needed clearing though I wasn't sure why or how that could be done. I also had a strong feeling that I needed to start in the north and end in the south, in Mexico. It was rather inconvenient as it meant I had to fly from Mexico to Canada to get to the beginning of the line. I also made the decision to travel by public transport rather than being cocooned in a hire car. That way I would be more open to meeting people and I would have less control over my exact route. I could leave the details of my journey to sort themselves out.

Public transport in Canada and the USA was scant. In fact it was the worst public transport system I had ever encountered, but I had made my decision not to hire a car and I was sticking to it. I had wanted to start my 111 journey at the town of Suffield in Alberta as the longitude there is exactly 111.11. However, that was not possible as not only did the Greyhound buses not stop there, but Suffield is a military base not open to the public. It is a major centre for the military, used by both British and Canadian forces. Right on the 111.11 longitude!

I had no choice but to pick up the bus in Calgary and travel through to Medicine Hat in order to cross the line. At the start of my journey I took some money from the ATM at Calgary bus station and noticed that my withdrawal had taken place at exactly 11:33:33am. A good start!

I took a few photos through the window as the Greyhound bus crossed the 111.11 line of longitude. I took a few more as we entered Medicine Hat. I couldn't believe it when I downloaded them on to my computer because every single photo contained a very distinct number 11. It was clearly visible and the fact that the 11 was there on every single photo was indisputable. At first I was utterly dumbfounded. How could this be so? Where had the number 11's come from? Were they drifting through from another dimension?

Having reflected long and hard, I eventually managed to work out how this had happened. The Greyhound bus had a number on the front: 1146. The angle of the sun at that particular time of day had cast a backward reflection of this number on to the window on my side of the bus. The 4 and the 6 had been in shadow so only the 11 had been reflected and because the numeral 1 looks the same upside down and back to front, the reflection appeared to me as a perfect number 11. Even though I had managed to get my mind to solve the mystery of this 11 appearance and I now had a logical explanation, the sequence of events that had ultimately manifested as the appearance of the 11 on my photos was, to me, pure magic in action.

It took a good few hours to get from Calgary to Medicine Hat and it had been my intention to stay over in Medicine Hat for one night and then take the bus south to Great Falls the following morning. However, the Greyhound bus services had been cut so drastically that there were no buses going south. Instead of driving a mere 407 (4+7=11) kilometres directly to Great Falls I would have to travel west to Vancouver and then take the bus from Vancouver to Great Falls, a journey of 2 and a half days. In a car it would be a few hours. Undeterred, I thought I would simply hire a car for this part of the journey. But that too proved impossible because one-way car hire from Canada to the USA was not permitted. Trains did not go south either. I even considered taking a taxi but there was no taxi company in the town! I was well and truly stranded. I did not know what to do. I could only assume that there must be a reason for me to be held in Medicine Hat.

I had booked into a motel near the bus station and it was the receptionist who told me of the origins of the name Medicine Hat. Apparently a young Blackfoot set out to save his tribe from starvation one very cold winter and he made his way to the breathing hole with his wife and their dog. This was a sacred place to the Native Americans where the water spirits went to breathe. When the young couple reached the river a giant serpent rose up from the breathing hole and demanded the sacrifice of the wife in return for a special hat that would endow the wearer with great hunting prowess. The Blackfoot tried to fool the serpent into taking his dog instead of his wife but the serpent wasn't fooled so reluctantly he threw his wife into frozen water. He was then told to spend the night on the small island of Strathcona and in the morning he found his hat at the base of the great cliff. The breathing hole remains open to this day.

Upon hearing this story I knew that the breathing hole was the place where my 111 journey was to officially begin. As soon as I made that decision things began to flow. All I had to do was find it. I walked out of the motel to begin my search and the very first person I asked not only knew where it was but offered to drive me there.

I stood on the stony riverbank and noticed a pile of shells and white feathers. I knew that I was being shown the location of the ceremony. As I gathered my ritual belongings together a massive bird flew by so close I felt the waft of its wings: a blessing from the bird tribe. I lit the incense, rang my bell, said some prayers and chanted some mantras. I could sense the water spirits encircling the area, joining in this important ritual. I was not alone!

Finally I threw an amethyst crystal into the breathing hole, knowing that by doing so I was anchoring a thread of light in that sacred spot. As it landed in the water a white feather fell from the sky above. I picked it up and put it in my pocket. I walked away and I felt a thin strand of silver light coming out of the back of my heart chakra. I could physically feel it. It was like a spider's web, a silver line of thread. This is what I was to carry through to Mexico. It would start as a thread of light but over the decades it would widen into a river of light.

Now the crystal had been planted and my work was done I could be released from Medicine Hat. When I arrived back at the motel I mentioned to the receptionist that I was stranded. He called his friend who offered to drive me as far as the Canada/USA border in return for petrol money. From the border I could then take a bus south.

The next morning his friend arrived to collect me. He turned up in a massive 4 wheel drive truck with an equally massive crack right across the windscreen. Frank was a redneck through and through. He drank 25 beers a day, smoked 40 cigarettes and spent his life hunting and fishing. He killed his own deer for meat, chopped them up and barbecued them. He had spent his whole life in Medicine Hat and he knew the area very well. We began chatting about the strange place names nearby such as Milk River, Many Berries and Writing on Stone.

"Writing on Stone? Why is it called that?" I asked.

"Because there are lots of stones there inscribed with strange hieroglyphs."

My curiosity was aroused so Frank said we could make a detour to Writing on Stone. This place was sacred and I could feel it. As we stepped out of the truck 2 hawks appeared in the sky and began circling above me. What did they want? They were trying to tell me something. What? Was I to do some clearing?

The strange rocky landscape of Writing on Stone was unlike anywhere I had ever been. Petroglyphs and pictographs had been carved into the sandstone by the Blackfoot Indians as long as 3,500 years ago. The wind there was strong and wild. It gathered pace as it blew across the flat prairies. Frank told me that last year there had been a tornado and many homes were destroyed. The wind made it very difficult to light a fire so I used my body as a windshield and eventually managed to get a small fire going. I lit the incense from the fire and performed a ceremony to the 4 directions and the 5 elements.

Then we made an offering into the river because Frank said that you have to offer tobacco to the river. It was touching to see this big, tough he-man honouring the river in this way.

Eventually we arrived at Sweetgrass which is a very small border crossing, and Frank dropped me off. There was nothing there except a small shop and the border office crossing post. I was starving but the shop would not serve me as I had no license plate. How could I have a license plate if I had no car? At least I could see from a timetable pinned to the wall that there was a local bus heading south from the other side of the border at 4:45pm. By now it was 12:45pm. Only 4 hours to wait in the biting wind…

I walked up to the border and handed in my passport, feeling very conspicuous as I was the only pedestrian. I think I must have been the first person ever to cross that border by foot. I pulled my suitcase along behind me. I don't know what had possessed me to bring a suitcase and not a backpack. The guard took one look at me and with a startled expression he took my passport and sent me into the office to wait for an interview. I looked at my fellow detainees. There was a black man clutching a wad of diplomas, an elderly woman in floods of tears and a young couple struggling to contain their 2 boisterous children. Eventually my name was announced and I was called to the counter by a large, uniformed man. I use the term 'man' loosely. Machine might have been more fitting as he was enveloped in so many layers of conditioning.

"Where are you going?" he asked abruptly.

"Great Falls," I replied

"How are you getting there?"

"By bus."

"There is no bus."

"Yes there is. It leaves at 4:45pm. It runs as far as Shelby then I will get a bus from Shelby to Great Falls."

"There is no bus."

"There is. At 4:45pm."

"You have not planned this at all have you?" he sneered, looking at me with contempt. "There is no bus to Shelby."

What could I say? That he could walk a few metres to the shop and look at the bus timetable for himself? That I couldn't possibly plan a trip like this because I act in the moment according to what the outer universe puts in my path? I would then have to try to explain to him that I was researching the number 11. No. He would probably have me locked up. I remained silent. He looked at me with his steely brown eyes and I gazed back through one soft green eye. The other eye wouldn't open. I had been bitten on the eyelid at Writing on Stone and my eye had started to swell up. I admit I must have looked like a bit of a dodgy character. The gale force wind had blown my long hair into a haystack and it was all knotted and sticking out at the sides. I had an angry red rash on my hand, an allergic reaction from my metal bracelet, and I could smell the incense on my clothes from leaning over the ceremonial fire so I smelt very musky.

"Where are you staying in the US?"

"Hotels, motels. I have not booked ahead as I don't know how long this trip will take."

"Why should we let you in? You're nothing more than a hitch-hiker."

"No, I'm not a hitchhiker. I'm travelling by public transport."

"Huh!" He looked at me with contempt. "No, I'm not letting you in. You cannot enter the USA."

"Okay," I replied nonplussed. I was in complete surrender. If I was not allowed into 'the motherland' then that would all be part of the grand plan.

"Sit down," he demanded, pointing to the row of seats by the window.

I knew not to argue back. That would only allow him to steal my energy. I sat down and remained seated for several hours whilst he disappeared into the back room. Maybe he had gone for a long late lunch? When he eventually returned I was called forward; he said that he had changed his mind and that he would let me in after all. He charged me 6 dollars and handed me a receipt that said "Sweetgrass MT Port # 33310". 333. I registered the reappearance of that number.

I don't know why he had changed his mind and I don't know what he had been doing in those hours. Maybe he had looked at my website and had seen that part of my journey was linked to Veterans Day/Armistice Day and that as I travelled I would be sending out prayers and healing to those who had fallen in war. Anyhow, less than half an hour later I was sitting on the small local bus on my way to Shelby. The only other passengers were 5 border guards in their uniforms. So much for the bus that didn't exist...

I asked the driver to drop me at any hotel in Shelby and he pulled up outside a 1960s motel. I hadn't picked this hotel. This hotel had picked me. Not that there was much choice as Shelby was a very small town. I intended having a good night's sleep and heading down to Great Falls the following morning.

Shelby looked just like a film set. There was only one main road and it looked exactly like the 'Cowboy and Indian' films I had watched as a child. There was even a Wells Fargo! But there were no buses south, not for 3 days. This was ridiculous. My impatience welled up and I decided I would go against my inner knowing and hire a car. There were no hire car companies in town. Maybe I'd be extravagant and get a taxi? There were no taxi companies in town. Once more I was stranded. All I needed to do was to find out why.

I had plenty of time to explore the town. I visited the tourist information and I was given a gift pack. That was rather a nice touch. I opened it to find an interesting mixture of some information leaflets, a healthy cereal bar, a packet of chewing gum and 3 tampons.

My visit to the local museum triggered a past life memory because I saw my beautiful moccasins sitting in a glass cabinet. Remembering them so clearly made me realize why reincarnations of Tibetan Lamas are tested on their ability to recognize objects from their previous incarnation. My grandmother had made the moccasins for me. I was a young girl Native American and my mother had died so I lived with my grandmother whom I loved dearly. She was teaching me all about the herbs and plants that could be used for medicine. She was a medicine woman and that is what I was learning to be.

Despite the fact that I was exhausted, I hardly slept that first night. The second night was just as bad. I mentioned it to the hotel receptionist and asked if I could change rooms.

"If you're at all sensitive I don't think it'll make any difference if you change rooms. There's a vortex in this hotel," she said.

"Pardon?" I replied. Had I misheard her? "A vortex? What do you mean?"

"A vortex of negative energy," she replied.

It turned out that the receptionist was an Empath and she was the co-ordinator for an international Empath website. She explained that there had been a massacre in Shelby on January 23rd 1870 and the psychic residue still remained. That was an understatement. It was here that the greatest slaughter of Native Americans ever made by US troops took place. Major Eugene Baker commanded 6 companies of US soldiers. They killed virtually all of the defenceless women, children, and old people in the winter village of Heavy Runner despite the fact that the chief of this tribe had good relations with the white man. Astoundingly, there isn't a single book in print today about this major historical tragedy. Nor is there any memorial on or near the site to mark this dreadful massacre. A small group of the descendants of the massacre victims gather every January to remember what happened in exactly the same way that we remember the war dead on November 11th.

For now, the unmarked mass grave of more than 200 Native Americans still lies somewhere under the black silt of the Marias River flats. Amongst those bodies lies a young woman who was learning the secrets of Native American medicine from her grandmother. No wonder I had been sent to clear the vortex.

The receptionist also told me that the local farmers were up in arms because so many areas were being fenced by the military. Nobody knew what was going on in these fenced in areas and the locals were becoming increasingly concerned about this secrecy.

I cleared the vortex that day and the following morning, after a good night's sleep, the bus arrived at the motel door to collect me. It was a tiny shuttle bus that was mainly used for transporting disabled people to the nearest hospital at the town of Great Falls. There were only 3 of us on the bus: the driver, me and a disabled man in a wheelchair.

My decision to travel by bus certainly opened my eyes to parts of American society that I might not have encountered had I travelled by car. Having been dropped by the disabled bus at Great Falls transit station in order to pick up my Trailways bus, I sat in the waiting room and observed my fellow passengers. There was a Native American couple with a tiny baby tightly strapped to a cradle board with strips of leather. When the baby cried it took mother about 10 minutes to unravel her to feed her. By the time the baby was untied it was hysterical with hunger. I saw the wildest man I had ever seen in my life. He had crazy eyes, matted hair and a waist-length beard. He was absolutely filthy and his smell filled the waiting room. There was an obese woman who took up 2 full seats yet still her fat hung over the edge. There was also a completely bald woman and a man with breasts.

To get from Great Falls to Salt Lake City meant picking up a bus at a town called Butte and then taking an overnight bus south. There was no other way I could do that leg of the journey. I would miss all the scenery and I wouldn't be able to meet people. Not only that but I had to transfer to another bus during the night. There was a 2 hour wait for the second bus. As I entered the waiting room I glanced at the clock. It was exactly 11:11pm and there was a plaque informing us that we were on Route 66. As I stood there taking in the fact that it was 11:11, the clock on the wall stopped dead. I saw it stop in front of my eyes. The second hand was jammed at 11 seconds to the hour. It remained like that until I boarded the second bus at 1.11.am. I was pleased. A strong sign!

The bus from Salt Lake City to Cedar City took me slightly off the 111 line of longitude towards the 112 longitude. I saw no signs as I travelled through the Capitol Reef National Park; but when I stopped in Cedar City and walked to the hotel opposite the bus stop I was given room 111 so I knew I was being told that it was okay to have deviated. The hotel spelt my name wrong with a double 'l' which I refer to as a hidden 11 sign. Having checked in I went online and noticed that Google had been spelt Googlle. Goog(11)e? I had never seen it spelt like that before – or since for that matter.

Cedar City to Flagstaff is less than 200 miles due south but once again there was no direct bus. The only way to get there by public transport was via Las Vegas. Las Vegas! That's not a place that I would willingly choose to visit so I didn't know what to do. Was I to hire a car or just accept that I was being diverted from the 111 line for a reason? I was tired and my intuition was not firing on all cylinders so I wandered over to the bus stop to check out the bus times. There was a man doing the same thing. We got talking and I was surprised to discover that he was English. Not only that, he was a number 66 man. He was travelling Route 66 by bicycle. He was doing the journey in stages, storing the bike with local people between each leg. Having just cycled 300 kms he was heading for Las Vegas to play poker. He was really into numbers, and as a talented poker player he was off to win some money. We travelled together and he booked us into Circus Circus, a monster of a hotel. Although I'm not a gambler I thought I would try betting on the number 11 on the roulette wheel. I lost. My English friend won hundreds of dollars that night at the poker table. He had a secret method of playing poker but he would not reveal it to me!

My next stop was Tucson, Arizona. When I got off the bus I walked to the hotel that was the nearest to the bus station, booked a room and was handed the receipt. The Days Inn address was 222 South Freeway. The post code was 85745=29=11. Phone number 5207917511=38=11 and Fax number 5206223481=33. I was given room 221. I had checked in at 10.20. I was obviously still on track.

I had arrived in the week of the multicultural festival and Tucson was buzzing with activity. The Aztec dancers were riveting. An enormous amount of energy was created by the persistent drum beats and the dancers. The leader ended the dance by leaning over a burning flame, his bare chest directly in the flames. I needed to speak to this man. I thought I'd follow him after his performance, but I quickly lost sight of him amongst the crowds. I didn't panic. If the Universe wanted me to talk to him, he would be brought to me. 10 minutes later I saw him standing alone by the side of the road. He was a short, stocky man with long grey hair hanging halfway down his back. He was still wearing his impressive headdress made of feathers. I approached and stood opposite him.

"Hello," I said, "I saw your performance earlier and I just wanted to ask you a question."

He looked at me kindly and curiously.

"And what question is that?"

"Well, I know that you are an Aztec Indian and I just wondered what your people thought about 2012."

"Ahh, 2012 and the end of the calendar, is that it?"

"Yes. I wondered whether the Aztec Indians foresaw the end of the world."

He turned the question on me.

"What do you think will happen?"

"I'm not sure, though I thought maybe the earth would be destroyed by fire."

"What sort of fire?"

"Just fire, you know what fire looks like."

"What sort of fire?" he repeated.

"Well if a comet hit the earth or something and set it on fire."

"What sort of fire?" he repeated for a third time. I was looking directly at him. His liquid brown eyes were like deep pools of water and I was drawn into their depth. For a few moments they merged with mine and it was as if we were one pair of eyes. He was definitely transmitting to me in some way. Suddenly I had a shift in understanding. Of course! It was the Plutonic fire!

Some years earlier I had been working as a consultant psychological astrologer. Carl, the husband of a friend of mine, had come to see me in a really distressed state. His wife had left him and had gone to live with another man, taking their young son with her. Carl was devastated for he simply had not seen this coming. Some years earlier he had a powerful vision during a deep meditation session. In this vision he had seen his wife and son destroyed in a fire. He had been so distraught by this vision that he had refused to have a second child with his wife as he did not want 2 children to die in what he assumed would be a house fire. Ironically, it was this refusal to have a second child that had been partly to blame for his wife leaving. I remember looking at his chart and seeing a powerful aspect from the planet Pluto to his Venus, his relationship planet.

"Carl," I had gently explained, "it's Pluto. This is the planet of destruction and renewal. When you had your vision it was not LITERALLY a fire that took your family away. It's Pluto destroying the status quo, that's all. The key words for Pluto are destruction and renewal and the symbolism is that of a phoenix arising out of the ashes." That is exactly what happened in his marriage. Carl and his wife were eventually reconciled and the relationship was renewed and strengthened. That's the fire that the Aztec Indian was trying to explain to me. It's the fire of trans-formation. I felt so optimistic about the future of our earth after this exchange.

I had finally ended my 111 journey between San Carlos and Guaymas in Sonora. It was so lovely to cross the American border and find myself back in vibrant, hot, colourful Mexico. It was a complete and welcome contrast to America. I booked myself into a hotel for a week to recover from my road trip and to relax. As I pulled my suitcase through the gates of Hotel Creston I saw a lorry parked outside. FUGAS 222.22.22 was emblazoned on the side in bold, bright colours.

I thought it was strange the way that everything in my hotel room was inscribed with my initials, H.C. But then I realized that it was because the name of my hotel was Hotel Creston. I reckoned I was staying exactly on the 111.11 line of longitude, though it was difficult finding a detailed map of the area to confirm this fact. I needed a map that showed the lines of longitude and latitude. I took the local bus to Guaymas in search of an ordnance survey map. I searched high and low but I couldn't find one anywhere. I need not have worried, for on the bus on my way back to San Carlos I found myself sitting next to a Mexican cartographer. Not only that, but he had in his hands the most up-to-date map of the area that he had just collected from the printers. It was hot off the presses. What incredible cosmic grace. Not surprisingly, this man knew every inch of the local area. I grilled him for information. I was looking for a sacred place where I could formally seal my 111 journey with a ceremony. Originally I had hoped to take a boat out to the tiny island of Socorro because this island, like Suffield in Canada, was exactly on the 111.11 longitude. However, when I went to the marina to enquire about taking a boat out there I was told it was not possible.

"But anything is possible," I insisted. "Why do you say it cannot be done?"

The answer surprised me.

"Because it is a military base. It belongs to the navy."

2 military bases on the 111.11? Suffield and Socorro Island? That was too much of a coincidence. But I reminded myself that occultists of both black and white magic know the power of numbers. Manuel opened up the map, fresh off the press, and showed me where my hotel was. He knew exactly where I was to go.

"This area is desert," he explained, indicating a large area on the map. "But there's an oasis where there are springs and water-falls. It's not accessible by road. You must walk to find it."

It was due north of my hotel and I could see from the lines of longitude that were clearly marked on the map that it was located at exactly 111.11, the same as the hotel I was staying in. Perfect. I had found my ceremonial site. Manuel handed me the map. He placed it in my hands and then gently placed his own hands over mine. It felt like a blessing.

"It's a gift for you," he said, looking directly into my green eyes with his beautiful deep brown eyes.

"Thank you," I replied. As I thanked him I also silently thanked the Universe. The more I surrendered to the number 11:11, the more gratitude I felt towards everyone and everything. I truly had been transported into a new way of being that gifted me magical moments like that.

Getting out into the desert without a car was not easy so I

invited a guest from the hotel to join me on my trek. She had a car so she could drive us to the edge of the desert. Even with a detailed map it was not easy to find. We followed the dry riverbed, a rugged, rocky route. Eventually it became impassable so we climbed up the steep sides of the riverbank and headed down a path in the direction of the oasis. The path went on and on and the hotter we became, the less we spoke. The sun burned down on us relentlessly and there was no shade. I have experienced high temperatures before but I have never experienced anywhere as hot as that Mexican desert. At one point we saw a cowboy on a white horse. It was so surreal that I took a photo of him to confirm that he was not a mirage. I was on the verge of hallucinating and I honestly thought I might collapse from heat exhaustion.

In retrospect it might have been better to have undertaken this journey in the evening, but I had decided that 11am was the perfect time to have the ending ceremony. Just as we were about to give up ever finding it, we saw it in the distance, slightly in a dip. We could just see the tops of green trees.

I had never been to an oasis before. Here on the 111.11 line was a little piece of paradise. It marked the end of my 111 journey. The silver thread that had been placed in the breathing hole in the river at Medicine Hat was now anchored at the other end in a Mexican oasis. Don't ask me what time that happened (other than it was way past 11am!) because I have no idea. I never thought to look at my watch. I remember hardly anything beyond the moment when I saw the trees of the oasis. I certainly remember nothing of the journey back to the hotel.

Just before I left Mexico I had another e-mail from Catherine. She wanted to warn me that she had been quite ill but that she was recovering and would be well enough to go to India. Following a serious, mysterious and unnamed illness that had almost resulted in her death, she had vacated her physical body and she wanted me to know that now her body was inhabited by a being of immense power. In other words, she had had a walk-in.

I had picked up this e-mail at the Internet café in Guaymas, Mexico. On the bus on the way back to Hotel Creston, I was reflecting on this sudden turn of events. A walk-in? I had heard of this happening before. The author Lobsang Rampa claimed that he was a Tibetan lama who had taken over the body of a man (a plumber) in England, and had started writing books about esoteric subjects. Could it have happened to Catherine? I just didn't know what to make of it until I looked out of the bus window. 'Walk-ins welcome' said the sign outside the hotel we were passing. That was very synchronistic. Maybe it was true.

Chapter 13

Ground Zero

I had finished the 111 degrees of longitude trip, and I was heading for New York before flying back to London. It was there that I picked up an e-mail from Catherine. Before I set off for Mexico I had asked her what the point of having this physical experience was and she had not answered me.

What's the point of having this experience? Answer: to wake up from the dream we have lived for so long thinking it was our reality, our life. Identifying with form, our partners, relationships, jobs etc. giving it all so much emotional energy. Now as preparation for the shift takes place we are so much more detached. We know we are multidimensional beings of light, we own our innate Divinity, we remember we are here as the midwives for mother earth as she goes through her transition. We hold the light and anchor it within our heart, the cosmic heart to which every living aspect of creation is aligned. We are not concerned about the increasing negativity happening on the earth as we realize it is a great purification taking place hence the natural disasters as mother earth purges herself of this negativity.

The collective consciousness is being purified hence all the negative happenings on our planet. In our personal lives too everything that does not serve our highest Divine purpose is coming up for transformation. This shift is happening within us to align with the planet as she makes her shift. Every other planet in the solar system is also moving forward, this shift is a galactic one!

21st December 2012 is when the earth moves into the sign of Aquarius through the procession of the equinoxes, this happens approx once every 26,000 years. This time though the earth begins to point towards the centre of the galaxy as it rotates, rather than away from it as it did before. This is what will enable the change in consciousness to take place.

Wow, Hilary, that just got channelled, it feels really exciting. Hope Mexico is going well.

Catherine 15/09/09

Rather than cocooning myself in a hotel in New York, the 11th state of America, I stayed in a loft in Brooklyn. I took the opportunity to visit Ground Zero. I simply stood at the site as an activated prism of light. Hundreds of people were thronging around but as I stood there I had the sensation of stepping out of time. Unusually I had not taken note of my time of arrival but when I felt I was ready to leave I glanced at my watch and it was 12:12. I don't know why, but at that minute my attention was drawn straight to the colon that separated those 2x12's.

I have spent over 7 years investigating the 11:11 and it was not until I arrived at Ground Zero that my attention was brought to the colon that separates hours from the minutes on my phone. I had only ever looked at the numerals and all of a sudden I realized that right in front of my very eyes all those years had been the colon. It shocked me how the obvious can be screaming in our face and we don't see it because we are not aware enough or we are stuck in the way we act or perceive things, seeing the familiar in a familiar way rather than with fresh eyes. My rut was looking at number prompts like 11:11 or 12:12 and never questioning the colon. Once my awareness had been brought to the colon a whole load of stuff came up.

What is the meaning of a colon? There are several meanings.

In the body the colon is the last part of the digestive system where water and salt are extracted from the solid wastes before being expelled from the body. The fact that the colon in the physical body is linked to the second chakra did not escape me for I knew that I was working on the second chakra in France.

It is also a punctuation mark (:) used to precede a list of items, a quotation, or an expansion or explanation. It is also used in various technical contexts, for example a statement of proportion between 2 numbers, or to separate hours from minutes (and minutes from seconds) on digital clocks.

The colon is sometimes used in computer programming for various purposes. It can also be used to represent a sound, e.g. ::Click::, though sounds can also be denoted by an asterisk or other punctuation marks.

The most intriguing use of the colon is the way in which it is commonly used in texting. It is written like this: :) or :-) to represent the eyes within a smiling face. This is a very new use of the colon which has only become widespread since everyone started owning mobile phones.

Although I take particular notice of the repeated number 1 when it appears as 1,11,111,1111, 11.11, 1.11, 11.1 and so on, the greatest and most powerful appearance is definitely when it manifests as 11:11. That colon in between the 2x11's has the most dramatic visual impact and seems to carry deeper messages and offers the greatest catalyst for change. If I see that the time is 11 minutes past 11 on a regular non-digital clock the impact has much less effect.

There's another interesting phenomenon regarding the colon that I happened upon whilst writing this chapter. Try typing bracket followed by colon followed by bracket and see what happens!

Zero is the symbol of void. Ground Zero. How did it come to be known as that? Of all the numbers in existence zero is probably the most misunderstood. In fact I'm not sure that zero could be understood. The source of the zero in our numbering system is hotly disputed with some claiming that it was invented by Hindus in the 9th century and others pointing out the fact that much older civilizations such as the Mayans used zero. In the Mayan system of writing numbers a dot represents the number 1 and a horizontal dash represents the number 5. Number 11 is represented by a dot placed centrally above 2 horizontal lines. If we turn that vertically it becomes 11·.

It is therefore one number 11 and one dot which is exactly half of the powerful 11:11 time prompt.

The 11 also appears on the pause button. Look at the pause button on any of your electrical equipment and you'll see what I mean. Those 2 straight lines are what we press whenever we want to pause a moving image or sound. Therefore 11:11 could be called pause/pause. I wondered whether this could relate to the pause in the earth's rotation.

Within numerology I interpret the zero as full circle. When I see the zero in my everyday life I see it representing something coming to an end or to completion.

Of all the letters in the alphabet there are only 3 that could be misread as numbers in the decimal system: a capital I, a lower case L and the letter O. The letters I and L can be read as a number 1 and the letter O can be read as zero. On the keyboard the letter O is adjacent to the number zero and the letter L is adjacent to I. The L is sandwiched between the colon and the letter K, the 11th letter of the alphabet. The colon key is diagonally adjacent to the O and next to the L. 1 and 0 both belong to the binary system which is the number system that is composed of only those 2 numbers.

Zero belongs to the binary system of numbers which is made up only of 1's and 0's. One and zero. One is one but is zero nothing? It can't be, because it holds equal energy to one within the binary system. Without the zero the binary system wouldn't exist! And if it's called zero, it is named. How can we name something that doesn't exist? We can't.

Therefore as zero exists, zero is not nothing. If zero is not nothing it is something. We use zero to represent nothing but nothingness cannot exist as we have just seen that nothing is something. If nothing is something, then something is nothing. We can go on ad infinitum between those 2 statements. Isn't that what matter is, the interplay between those two, between 0 and 1? From that interplay all numbers arise. There is a relationship between 1 and 0. That brings us to the Fibonacci number sequence. The first two numbers in the Fibonacci sequence are 0 and 1, and each subsequent number is the sum of the previous two where we add the last 2 digits together.

0+1=1
1+1=2
1+2=3
2+3=5
3+5=8
5+8=13
8+13=21 and so on.

From the binary numbers 1 and 0 all other numbers arise. It's a really interesting number sequence that is linked to the spiral and to the golden ratio.

We can count things that do not appear to exist.

"There are 0 (zero) apples in the bowl."

But as we have seen, 0 (zero) exists so the apples in the bowl both exist and don't exist.

If nothingness cannot exist then even if the universe didn't exist it would still exist. It would be a universe which has always existed and has never existed, both at the same time. A universe with no beginning or an end. Try and get your head around that! And this arose from a visit to Ground Zero...

The only thing that doesn't exist is nameless and cannot be named. No Name=No existence. What about No Number? No Number=No existence? That is not possible for all numbers exist so:

No Name= No existence.
No Number= Existence.

No Name and No Number are therefore in constant interplay like the 0 and 1 within the binary system. The mirror image within the 11:11 is maybe a representation of these facts within the physical universe.

Chapter 14

Adrian's Theory of Everything

Although I was not in France during these months I was able to continue researching the history of the area around Montignac on the Internet. I discovered that the history of my part of France was particularly long and brutal. Montignac was a walled town and who knows what must have gone on inside those walls. As my house was literally just outside the walls of Montignac I doubt whether my place would have escaped unscathed. Whoever lived in the castle would have been able to see everything that was going on in the convent.

Bella e-mailed me to say that she had spoken to her father who confirmed that the house was a former 'école de bonnes soeurs'. That translates as school of the good sisters. I wondered whether they wore the same grey robes as the ghost. She said that it was in existence hundreds of years ago, probably around the year 1400 at the very latest.

I was amazed and delighted. At last some decent information! And this would certainly tie in with Alain's estimate of the house being 14th century. Intuitively, this felt right, for the house had a distinctly female feel to it.

I kept in touch with my artist friend in Sarlat by e-mail. As I had suspected early on, my artist in the tower did have something to teach me. Having checked out his website I saw that Adrian had come up with something called: "MY AMAZINGLY POPULAR THEORY OF EVERYTHING". Adrian had thought long and hard about human existence and had condensed his findings into a few pages of A4. Even so, having read his theory, I needed to simplify it even more. So I e-mailed him. His responses to my comments are in italics.

I have read your theory – very interesting.

Cool!

So, to simplify EVEN FURTHER your simplified version of EVERYTHING IN THE UNIVERSE, are you saying that…

Everything exists in a container that we call space. Space has no dimensions.

Empty space has no dimensions, like before the Big Bang happened.

The first dimension is a line, an infinite number of points arranged next to each other. This is the mineral world that exists with no awareness.

The mineral world is the first level of existence which coresponds to a one dimensional consciousness.

The second dimension is a surface or plane. The 2 dimensional world exists at 90 degrees in relation to the first dimension. This is the dimension of plants which again have no awareness but which do demonstrate instinct.

Yes. Plants are a dimensional leap above the mineral world. Maybe they are dimly aware, but personally I doubt it. Some scientists say they react to human thoughts directed at them, so I cannot say for sure what they are capable of.

The third dimension runs at 90 degrees to the 2nd dimension. Animals exist in 3rd dimension awareness and they perceive the universe as flat. That's because they perceive 2 dimensions in space and the third dimension as time.

In some way, animals are a dimensional leap below that of humans, maybe it's our capability to be aware of our own existence and project our thoughts way into the future (even though most of us forget these abilities and live our lives in a slumber-like absence! lol).

Humans exist in the 4th dimension, with awareness AND consciousness.

On a good day! Lol.

Humans perceive 3 dimensions in space (length, width and height). The 4th dimension we call time.

In the 5th dimension the restrictions of time are removed/risen above.

An infinite number of points make a line. An infinite number of parallel lines at 90 deg to the direction of the line make a surface. An infinite number of parallel surfaces, at 90 deg to the direction of the surface, make a solid. An infinite number of parallel solids, at 90 deg to the direction of the solid, makes a 4 dimensional solid. Time, therefore, runs at 90 deg to our 3 dimensional world of space.

We can therefore assume that the 5th dimension follows the same pattern and runs at 90 deg to the 4th. The 5th dimension is the world of multiverses.

Have I got that right?

Yes.

To simplify the dimensions to one sentence would be:

Rocks live in 1 dimension, plants live in 2 dimensions, animals live in 3 dimensions, humans live in 4 dimensions and in the coming new age super-humans will be living in the 5th dimension.

Hi Adrian,

Do you think that when we die we move to the 5th dimension (albeit temporarily) which is why psychics can foresee the future as the 5th is beyond time. And when we mere mortals step through the time frame and access lives both past and future here in this world like I do sometimes, are we accessing the 5th dimension?

Hi Hilary,

The 4th dimension is like one guitar string of past, present and future, but the 5th dimension is an infinite number of guitar strings with infinite possibilities in other universes, a much higher place! Maybe one guitar string is also made up of an infinite number of fibres that contact each other so closely that we slip in and out of one *fibre and back again without the slightest notion that we have changed our destiny through an action (or inaction), but we stay in the same guitar string of time and space. 'Heaven' would be a place where we can look at the guitar string from outside it, but as it stretches out away from our fixed point of view, future and past events would disappear beyond a heavenly horizon, so we would have to move (if we still had a body) in order to see further... However, I recently read a fascinating book (in French) by Régis Dutheil, a professor in quantum physics, entitled L'homme super-*lumineux, *in which he says that there are 2 universes separated by the barrier formed by the speed of light. We are made of energy that exists under the speed of light, and so it has matter made of atoms (a sub-luminous universe), but "heaven" (or the world above) is made of energy where there are no limits caused by "matter"; the energy is open in this super-luminous universe. There is no time or space and so all information including that in the past and future will be available to the "bodiless beings" that live there.*

Being in touch with Adrian was a reminder of my life in the convent. Although I was many miles from the convent, the energy of that old building felt as if it were with me. Of course I struggled with the fact that I had been led to the convent by the 11:11 sign and then I had to leave it because it was barely habitable. Sometimes I questioned the point of me buying it. I had to remind myself that for every situation there was a big picture and at that moment in time I could not see the big picture. I just had to keep faith that one day all would be revealed. I also had to remind myself not to be attached to an outcome and that possibly there was nothing to reveal. It could be that my lesson was to learn not to have expectations about an outcome! I needed to stop questioning and live each day.

Chapter 15

Goa

Had Catherine really had a walk-in? That question can't be answered with any degree of certainty. What I do know (and what can be proved) is that she had been taken to the brink of death and back again. Something had happened during that experience. It may be that previously unused parts of her brain had become activated. It could be that she had, in a sense, been reborn. Or she could indeed have been taken over by a different being and had experienced a walk-in. I was keeping an open mind on the matter.

I was back in Glastonbury for the final Template ceremony which was to be held in the Assembly rooms. I looked around the hall for Catherine. I hadn't seen her since before she had the walk-in. Then I spotted her. There was no doubt about it, she looked different. She still spoke like Catherine and was recognizable as Catherine but she had a different 'feel' to her. It was rather like looking at an identical twin and not being 100% sure which twin it was. She had still not fully recovered from her illness and was not very mobile.

"Do you think you're going to be well enough to go to India?" I asked.

"Oh yes, I'll be fine. Besides which it'll be good for me to spend time in such a warm climate. I have a lovely rooftop terrace at my apartment and I'll be able to relax in the sun. That'll be the best medicine for me."

"Well, if you're sure. I don't want to end up having to look after you."

I hadn't noticed the 'I' and the 'want' in that sentence when I spoke it. They would come back to haunt me many times over the following weeks.

Not long after the template ceremonies in Glastonbury I met up with Catherine at Heathrow Airport. We had arranged to meet 2 hours before our flight to India. She was in a wheelchair. I was taken aback. I hadn't realized that her physical problems had deteriorated to such an extent in such a short time. She assured me that she'd only agreed to the wheelchair to save her having to stand in the airport queues for hours as her hip was too painful to bear her weight for long. I was to be her carer for the flight and, although I didn't realize it at the time, that would be my role for a further 2 months whilst we were together in India. The very thing I hadn't wanted to happen was happening.

The flight to Bangalore was flight 119. That came to 11. I was in seat 31A and the gate closed at 13:30. Those numbers looked good to me. Not only that, we had been upgraded. That was a good start.

We arrived in Bangalore early the next morning. Within an hour of settling into our hotel I was fast asleep. It had only been a few days since the final Template ceremony in Glastonbury and I was exhausted which is why I fell asleep so quickly. It was not a restful sleep because I had a bad dream. Actually, although I call it a dream it was much more than that as it was almost physical in nature.

I was at my friend Sue's house and I looked out of her window and saw the full moon through the trees. After I pointed it out to her she told me to sit down at the table with the others. It was a round table and I didn't particularly take note of who else was sitting there. There were about 8 or 9 others. I sat down and seconds later everybody leaped on top of me and I was being suffocated. I could clearly feel the roughness of the woollen garment of the body immediately on top of me. I thought that maybe this was their idea of a joke but it was my worst nightmare to be suffocated like this. I began to cry in the hope that they would realize that it was not funny because I was so short of breath that I was about to die.

I woke up very suddenly. I was lying on my back and the

bedclothes were nowhere near my face. I was shaking like a leaf. I told Catherine about my dream. Immediately she knew what it was about.

"It's the Template. It has brought up all the stuff about the moon. Think how often you have gazed at the moon, especially when it is full. That astral dream experience you describe was clearing the darkness you have accrued over all these years. Do you see that? And the table was round, just like the moon."

That struck a chord with me. I recall reading a book called *Who Built the Moon?* by Christopher Knight and Alan Butler. They explain how the moon does not follow the known rules of astrophysics. They found neat number patterns concerning the moon and its relationship to the earth. For example, the Moon revolves at exactly one hundredth of the speed that the Earth turns on its axis and the Moon is exactly 400 times smaller than the Sun and exactly 400 times closer to the Earth. Experts now say that life on earth is only possible because the Moon is exactly what and where it is.

The Template explains the planetary alignment of December Solstice 2012 as a portal through which the galactic photon wave will enter, searching for "world-bridgers". World-bridgers are those humans who have fully reconnected their biocircuitry. As such, they are able to receive and transmit light.

When a critical mass of conscious entities makes this adjustment, a new resonant global field of accelerated collective coherence creates the quantum leap required for planetary transcendence.

I interpret the term "conscious entities" as those who have released the hold of the ego, surrendered their lives to their Divine Consciousness and awakened their dormant junk DNA. 11:11 seems to be an external sign to indicate that the DNA is changing.

Whenever we were together in those first days in India,

Catherine channelled messages for me. Some of the information coming through was very practical, such as telling me to increase my intake of fruit and vegetables. Other messages were deeper, such as the following one.

It may appear that there is a personal Hilary and Catherine within the play of consciousness, hence free will. In fact there are only a thousand aspects of the Divine One God who is waking up and finding Itself within the dream play of consciousness. Everybody is acting out different roles on different levels of evolution as they awaken to the fact that there is only the One (the script-writer, the orchestrator). The choreographer of this grand drama (all happening simultaneously within the cosmic law of cause and effect set in motion since the first moment of eternity, the now) when the script was enacted, played out and over and now plays out through time and space.

Life is the evolution of separate particles of God evolving through this cosmic play to know and find itself all at the same time – simultaneously – the source finding itself.

The Atma is the primordial energy and there is only one Atma. We don't have individual souls. No one has a soul because no one is personified as they are the primordial energy of creation.

We are thoughts in the mind of God which means God thought He'd split himself into a thousand parts but in fact He'd done nothing because Big Bang theory is part of the illusion and it's what created and perpetuated Maya.

Phew! I had to agree that her channellings were getting deep…

We had flown into Bangalore and after a few days recovering from our jet lag we set off for Palolem in Goa. Palolem is a laidback resort on the edge of the Indian Ocean. Rather than heading straight for Sai Baba's ashram Catherine felt it would be better for her health to be by the sea and she would be able to have treatment from Nigel, her favourite acupuncturist. She was struggling to walk because of the pain in her spine, hip and pelvis and she was in constant agony. She took to her bed in Goa and, as there was nobody else to step up to the task, I was the one who looked after her. This was not easy.

Having collected and delivered her breakfast to her one morning as usual, she ordered me to sit down whilst she dictated a list of errands for me. I had e-mails to send on her behalf, fruit and yoghurts to go and buy and phone calls to make.

"And you must phone Sarah at exactly 1:30pm because that's 7pm in England and that's a good time to catch her."

My shackles rose. She had pressed a button. That was right in the middle of the day when I had planned to be having lunch in a beachside café.

"Okay, I'll ring her at some point today."

"No, Hilary, you must ring her at 1:30pm exactly because her family won't be home at that time so she will be able to speak without distractions."

"Listen, I'll try and call her today but I'm not going to say an exact time because I might be doing something else at 1:30pm." My voice was tinged with annoyance.

"There's an energy in this," she replied immediately. "There's a block. What's it about? It must be coming from you. It must be your stuff because I no longer have any stuff."

"1:30pm is right in the middle of the day," I explained. "I was hoping to be on the beach."

"There are phones on the beach."

"Well I might be having my lunch."

I had stepped into defensive mode. The truth was that I had been tied down with family life for the past 20 years. Now I had tasted freedom and after barely a year of my new lifestyle I felt as if Catherine was taking it away again. I was not in a state of total surrender. I also tried to remind myself that maybe it was no longer my friend Catherine in this body before my eyes and I was talking to the walk-in.

"I prefer to go with the flow, Catherine. I will aim to make the call at 1:30pm but if I'm not able to then I'll do it as soon as possible after that."

Catherine acquiesced.

I rang Sarah and gave her the following message, written in capital letters on a crumpled piece of paper by Catherine:

PLEASE CAN YOU CONTINUE TO SEND HEALING FOR THE NEXT 2 DAYS AS APPROPRIATE FOR CATHERINE AS SHE STILL CANNOT WALK MORE THAN A FEW STEPS ON HER CRUTCHES. HER ILIO-SACRAL IS STILL OUT AND HER RIGHT HIP IS STILL PAINFUL. THE NEXT 2 DAYS ARE CRITICAL AS WE FLY TO SAI BABA ON MONDAY. PLEASE HELP.

We were staying in a small guesthouse. There were only 12 rooms. The 11:11 sign was not appearing but the French woman in the room above me came from Montignac, a notable synchronicity. Catherine's channellings kept on coming.

Although you are not in the French convent you are working on clearing it in preparation for your eventual return. As you travel the earth you are clearing the parts of the earth grid that directly affect the convent. France has a cruel and brutal history. Pure evil reigned for hundreds of years. Of all the cruel Counts, history recalls that the most cruel of all were those in the castle of Montignac. This work is not a task for the fainthearted. That is why you have been sent. Although you are carrying an abnormal amount of sensitivity, you are also extraordinarily brave.

I wasn't sure I agreed with that last statement. There were times (like when I saw the ghost) when I was petrified. Even the giant centipede had scared me. Yet I recognized that although I was sometimes afraid, I was not afraid of fear. It was this fact that gave me the courage to walk the 11:11 path. I was also capable of taking huge leaps of faith.

Chapter 16

The Transmission

Although she had formerly been a tarot reader, a channeller and a stage psychic, since the walk-in Catherine's way of working had changed. She now claimed to be channelling very high energies. During the transmissions an energy transfer would take place between her and the recipient. She was only channelling for selected people and there was a charge for her messages or 'transmissions' as she called them. Despite the fact that I was slaving away as her unpaid nursemaid, she expected me to pay for my transmission. I was not impressed.

"It's okay, Catherine, I don't want a transmission, thanks."

She was aghast.

"You need one. Don't you realize what a privileged position you are in? I have a direct connection to these incredibly high energies and you don't want to hear the message? Are you crazy?"

Eventually I succumbed. It was my curiosity that got the better of me as usual.

Catherine requested that I book myself in for a series of Shirodhara sessions at the local Ayurvedic centre during the following week. This is an ancient Ayurvedic treatment that works on the pineal gland, on the third eye. Catherine wanted me to have the last one just before my transmission. She explained that my energies would be wide open directly after the treatment and therefore I'd be more receptive to receiving and assimilating the high energies.

The Ayurvedic centre was a half hour walk from the lodging house. I set off down the path through the coconut grove. The ground was littered with fallen coconuts. It must have been a windy night. A family of wild pigs was shuffling about in the dust, the babies squealing loudly each time mum shoved them sharply with her snout. I heard yelping and saw 2 puppies play fighting on a grassy mound. There was no sign of a mother so I wondered whether they had been abandoned. At the end of the path there were a few wooden shacks and from there I stepped on to the magnificent beach. If this beach wasn't listed as one of the top 10 in the world then I'd be surprised. No permanent structures were permitted to be built within about 100 metres of the beach. In practice this meant that at the start of each season, all the bars, cafés and dwelling places had to be built from scratch. The building materials used were very basic: logs, wood and rush matting. The buildings were therefore in total harmony with the environment and many had a view of the sea.

The beach itself was lined with coconut trees and looked out on to Monkey Island, a mysterious place inhabited by many poisonous snakes and of course plenty of monkeys. At low tide it was possible to walk across to the island and from the other side dolphins could usually be seen frolicking in the sea. But today I turned left on the beach and walked barefoot in the warm, shallow water at the water's edge, avoiding the groups of cows as I walked. A 3-legged dog almost knocked me into the water as it ran to escape 2 mongrels, their tails held high in dominance. I carefully avoided standing on any of the small crabs scuttling along the sand. At the end of this stretch of beach was the estuary and I turned and walked along the path and up towards the centre.

I removed my sandals and entered the straw hut where my oil treatment was to happen. The room contained a high teak bench with a carved hollow for my head. Above the bench was a metal bowl suspended from a wooden beam. There was a hole in the centre of the bowl with a string hanging from it, so that when the bowl was filled with warm coconut and sesame oil, the flow of oil could be controlled. I lay naked on the bench, covered only with a small cotton cloth. The young Indian girl in charge of my treatment tied a twisted cotton band around my head, just above my eyebrows and she covered my eyes with 2 small, damp cloths. Then it began, a trickle of warm buttermilk oil on the centre of my forehead. The girl set the bowl in motion. Because of the height of the wooden beam from which it was suspended, the bowl swung slowly. From right to left, from left to right it swung, trickling oil across my forehead as it moved. I followed the path of the oil with my inner eye, much as one might follow the to and fro of the ball during a tennis match. A CD was playing quietly in the background. Om, Om, Om, Om, Om, Om, Om, Om, Om, Om, Om... No music, just a constant low chant. As the oil trickled from my head into my long hair, the girl massaged it into my scalp, squeezing out the excess oil and allowing it to flow into the hole in the hollow on the bench so that it could be reused. The treatment was long. The bench was hard. The oil was going to and fro and it felt as though the upper part of my skull was being separated from the top of my head.

The CD came to an end at the same time as the treatment. As I lay there all I could hear was the sound of the monkeys in the trees and the soft breeze brushing the palms. My breath was slow and soft. Bliss! When it came to standing up I was a little unsteady on my feet so I walked back to the guesthouse slowly. I was still in an Alpha state when I arrived at Catherine's room for my transmission.

Catherine was, at this time, completely bed-bound again. Even with help she couldn't manage to hobble across the lane to the vegetarian café. She was extremely wary of being in the company of other people whilst in this state. She knew that her energy field was wide open as the walk-in was still adjusting to her physical body. She had to keep herself in a safe energetic space whilst in this state.

"Pull up the chair and sit next to me," she said. "We both need to face the window. Uncross your legs and put both feet on the floor. Now hold my hands."

I did as I was told and she began with a prayer, invoking angels, ascended masters, Sai Baba, Babaji, Jesus and even Merlin. She asked for an inter-dimensional doorway to open and for the highest frequency of light possible to enter. Then we waited. Nothing happened.

"This is very strange. Normally the energy comes in immediately."

We waited. Still nothing. Catherine looked genuinely puzzled.

"I don't know what's going on. This isn't what usually happens. Maybe we can ask a question. Do you have any questions you want to ask? Don't forget that it's not Catherine you're asking, it's the high frequency energies that are working through Catherine's physical vehicle that will answer your questions."

"I do have some questions. I've written them down and they're in my bag."

I pulled out my notebook. I had a long list of questions. If Catherine really did have a direct line to these high energies I was going to make the most of this opportunity. Not surprisingly, my first question concerned 11:11.

"Why am I having this 11:11 experience?"

There was no response. Just silence. My question hung in the air in the same way that heavy incense smoke hangs. Suddenly I began to feel strange, as though I was a white marble statue sitting there on a green plastic chair in a second-grade guesthouse in an Indian coconut grove.

"I'm getting energy now," said Catherine. I sensed a hint of relief in her voice as this stuff that was happening was new to her too. She was on a learning curve.

"I've got Babaji coming in now. He's coming in really strong."

I felt it. I really did. I felt an incredible down-pouring of light. It was like being in a power shower but instead of water coming out of the shower head, it was light. I'd never experienced anything quite like that. I wasn't frightened. There was no sense of danger. Then I had weird sensation in my third eye that felt like fire. It felt as though my third eye had been cut open with a red hot knife. I remember wondering whether this had anything to do with my treatment but this burning cut was vertical and the oil during my treatment had dripped horizontally. Catherine had remained silent whilst the light was pouring down but now she spoke.

"Babaji is telling me that he has been working on your energy and raising your vibration. He is here now. He has been waiting for you for a long time. He's taking me back to the early 1800s and you are with him in a beautiful garden full of flowers. You're about 4 years old and he knows you as Little Flower. You're somewhere in the Himalayas," she said, emphasizing the third syllable of the name Himalayas in the way that most people do.

"Oh, sorry. That's Himalayas," she said, correctly emphasizing the second syllable. She sounded taken aback. She shook her head. "I've never had that happen before, being told off like that! Now he is ready for your questions."

Apparently Babaji had corrected her pronunciation. I repeated my 11:11 question. This time the response was swift.

"The places you are being guided to through the appearance of the 11:11 are the sites where the vortexes of energy need to be cleared in preparation for anchoring in the energy for the ascension of the earth. If any part of the grid is blocked it's going to affect the flow of energy to other vortexes, just like in acupuncture. If you have a block in a meridian channel it stops the flow of energy."

"Why 11:11?"

"The 11:11 represents 2 rods of light, male and female. One comes down from above, the other rises from below. They represent positive and negative in perfect harmony. The places you are being guided to by the number 11 are the location points of vortexes of energy that are needed to anchor energy in preparation for the ascension of the earth. The line-up in outer space is such that as the stars align with their space on earth, everything falls into place. It's coming from outer space, this powerful light. If the grid is clear enough to allow it to 'click' into the grid then the earth will not have to tilt. If the grid is not clear enough, the tilt will have to take place."

"So the places I am being sent to are vortexes of energy?"

"Yes. Vortexes. Or you could call them portals. They are where the grid of light locks into place on the earth. The light will imprint in geometric designs. You will discover alignments between the ancient sites. This is the secret the Knights Templar had. They had the secret of the imprint. That's why they aligned their churches to hold the energy, holding the light in the correct alignment. These mathematical shapes and angles are the most efficient way of holding the maximum amount of light. They knew the secrets would be revealed in the end days."

"Where had they got the knowledge from?"

"It has been passed down through the ages. The Templars had this knowledge and they used sacred geometry and symbols in their ceremonies and rituals."

"So if the channels and portals are clear then the transition will be smooth and gentle?"

"Yes."

"Will there be earth changes?"

"You're coming from the mind. Only the mind wants to know the answer to that. He's telling you to be in the moment and not to project forward for you need to be in the place of no-thought to end this play of consciousness."

"What is consciousness?" I asked.

"Now you are being shown a blank cinema screen. There's only light on the screen. This is pure consciousness. Nothing is happening. Now there is a film on the screen. The pure consciousness is watching the film and the film is watching the pure consciousness. Up until now the actors in the film have not realized that they are acting out a film script. They have become so engrossed in their roles that they think they are the characters they are playing! A few have realized but now word is getting round and more and more of the actors are waking up to the truth, the truth being that they're the light of pure consciousness on the screen. Next question."

"I'm writing a book. Do I need to write this book or is it coming from ego?"

"As I have just explained, we are in a dream, in a film, in a play. Call it the play of consciousness if you like. If it's written in the play that you write the book then your book will be written. If it's not in the script then it won't be written."

"Do we have free will?"

"The ultimate answer is no."

"What direction will my life take after this trip to India?"

"You are using your mind again. Can you see that? You must be vigilant and not project forward with the mind. You're thinking about the future. He's pressing this point home. Stop using the mind to create thought forms. That's the way out of the dream."

"Yes, but he said I could ask questions!" I protested.

"I know. He said that so he could show you, using the questions you ask, how you are using your mind. This is very important, Hilary. He is stressing this point. TO GET OUT OF THE DREAM STOP CREATING THOUGHT FORMS."

She spoke slowly and firmly. I was getting the message.

"Is Babaji in the dream or not?" I asked.

"All is illusion. Babaji is part of the illusion."

"Did existence start with the Big Bang?"

"The Big Bang is part of the illusion."

"Now I want to ask if I need to continue teaching TaiYoga as a way of raising consciousness."

"If it's written in the script it will happen. If it isn't written, it won't happen. Be in the moment with it. Allow consciousness to flow through you and act with the flow. Next question."

"When we return to One Consciousness will we still have separate bodies?"

"Are the drops of the ocean separate? Next question."

"I try not to come from fear so how can I lose my fear of spiders?"

"Understand that they are part of the One and see them as such. Send them love when you see them. You can also pray for help on that issue."

"Are the past lives I have accessed a personal memory or a collective memory?"

"There is a string running through all lives from birth to death through individual particles of light. This string is a transmitter of energy and also a recorder of events, the Akashic records, hence the evolution of the particles of light."

"I think there might be something hidden under the floor of the convent. Am I right? Do I need to dig up the floor and find something?"

"Render unto Caesar that which is Caesar's."

I think that meant no.

"What do you mean?"

"Next question."

"I have been guided to this convent in France and I don't know why. Please tell me the reason."

"You have already been given as much information as you need at this point in time. All will be revealed in due course. Be patient. You are on track."

"From my understanding, Catherine is now an enlightened being. Enlightened beings such as Jesus could walk on water and things like that. Will Catherine be able to walk on water in the future?"

"Irrelevant. Next question."

Catherine's responses were coming through so immediately that there is no way they could have been going through her mind. There was no pause between the end of my question and her answer.

"You are Higher energies that have entered Catherine's body. Where have you come from?"

"We neither come nor go. We just are," was the immediate answer.

"Is there anything you would like to tell me that I have not asked?"

"Babaji has prepared for you a body of light and when you are ready for it you will become that body of light. He wants you to know that you will not be disloyal to him if you allow other teachers to enter your life. He is reminding you that we are all part of the same consciousness. Does that make sense to you?"

"Yes. And I still don't really understand 11:11. Can you ask if there is anything else he can say to help me to really understand the significance of the number 11:11 appearing in my everyday life?"

"The number 11 contains all. It represents the Source. It is the sound current from which all existence springs. When it appears it is infinite energy appearing. Look at the number 11. It is a numeric representation of perfect alignment. When it appears it is demonstrating to you that you are in perfect alignment with Divine Will. You say you do not understand the 11:11 but you do. I see this by your actions. When you base your decisions on the 11:11 you act in truth. The truth flows from you. You are in the process of moving beyond duality. That's why it appears."

"Thank you. Does he want to give me any other messages?"

"Reality is a consciousness program. Human DNA is triggered at specific times to wake us up. 11:11 is a consciousness code and when the 11:11 shows itself in our physical world it indicates that our DNA is being re-programmed into the new consciousness that is rapidly manifesting in humans all over the planet. Everything that has been hidden now has to come up for transformation. It has to be brought to light."

"Now the energy is weakening. It's drawing away. I think the transmission is ending... it's getting weaker..."

Suddenly there was a power cut and the lights went out with a loud bang, a suitably dramatic ending to my revealing transmission.

I returned to my room and lay on the bed, trying to make sense of what had just happened. Did Catherine really have a direct line to the great Babaji, the eternal yogi? I wasn't sure. I certainly couldn't understand why he had said that we didn't have free will. I had always been of the opinion that we did.

The one thing that kept my mind open to the possibility that she was accessing Babaji was the way she had been corrected when she had pronounced the wrong syllable in the word 'Himalayas'. I could not explain or rationalize that. There is no way that correction could have come from her mind and I saw how visibly taken aback she had been when it happened.

My mind began to wander and I remembered the chocolate cake I'd seen in the organic café that morning. Maybe I could go and have some cake and tea later on? Then I remembered Babaji's words. A thought had arisen in my mind and I was projecting into the future. So I let the thought go and brought my attention to the breath for I was finding that was the easiest way to stay in the moment: breathe in, breathe out. And chant my mantra. Om Namah Shiva. This was the mantra I had chosen for myself. I had been dating a guy who practised transcendental meditation. Each day he spent at least 15 minutes chanting. I had asked him how I could get a mantra but when he told me you had to pay a small fortune for one I decided I'd just choose my own. I always play music softly in the background when I'm teaching yoga and I had a CD of various different chants. I picked Om Namah Shiva at random, not realizing that it was linked with Babaji in any way. I chanted (and still do!) a lot. As I wash up, as I cook, as I drive, as I walk and at night I chant myself to sleep with my inner gaze at the third eye point. I even chant in my sleep!

About a year after I started chanting Om Namah Shiva, Babaji entered my life. I was at a festival and I noticed that one of the marquees was offering free chai, a sweet spiced Indian tea. I went along in the afternoon for my chai but when I arrived everybody was singing so I sat down and joined them. At the front of the tent, on a small altar, was a picture of a young Indian man. As soon as I looked at the photo tears began to pour down my face. I was really embarrassed to be in floods of tears so I looked away. After regaining my composure I looked again and once more the tears started. At that time I had no idea that the man in the picture was Babaji, the immortal yogi of the Himalayas. He is the yogi written about in the famous book *Autobiography of a Yogi* by Paramahansa Yogananda.

Later that day there was a concert being held as part of the festival so I went along. There was a group of about half a dozen musicians on the stage and I joined the audience who were all sitting on the floor. We were asked to close our eyes for a few moments before the music began. I closed my eyes and sat quietly waiting. Then it started, the soft sound of an Indian harmonium. As soon as I heard the first note my tears began again. They poured down my face from behind my closed eyes. I simply couldn't understand what was happening. I was being touched in a way that I had never been touched before. Something deep inside me was being triggered. I later discovered that the group was called Goma and they had a strong connection with Babaji. One of the members had spent time with Babaji in His physical form in His ashram in the foothills of the Himalayas in India.

In order to focus people's minds on God, Babaji taught people to repeat the ancient mantra OM NAMAH SHIVA. It means 'I surrender to /bow to/take refuge in God'. Constant repetition of a mantra (called japa) opens one's heart and mind to God, and stops (or at least reduces) the internal chatter of the mind.

Babaji once said: "The mind can be purified only by japa. This is the only medicine for the disease of the mind. While your mind and heart are impure, how can God live in your heart? The water to clean your heart is the Name of God. So teach everyone to repeat the name of God everywhere."

As I lay quietly chanting my mantra I saw a spider sitting on my leg. My normal response would have been to run for the door but, with Babaji's words fresh in my mind from my transmission, I didn't run. 'Send it love, send it love,' I told myself. At that point it jumped on to my chest in one huge leap. A jumping spider? That was simply too much to handle. I screamed and leaped from the bed, waving my arms frantically as I tried to brush it from my chest. In my panic I squashed it and a greyish green sludge oozed out of its body all over my dress. It was obvious that I still had some way to go to deal with my insect issue.

Chapter 17

The Role of the Carer

The words coming through Catherine over the following weeks were not words that existed within Catherine's vocabulary. Her downloads would be littered with phrases that she didn't understand.

"What's an acronym?" she asked me.

"What does encapsulation of the cellular structure mean?"

"The King's pyramid has the same ratio as the skeletal system."

"Mars has the same ratio as zero point."

Catherine is not unintelligent but the profundity of the stuff coming through her did suggest to me that she was indeed accessing some higher energy. It was interesting (if somewhat unsettling) watching her as she struggled to adjust to the new person she had become. Or should that be the new person was struggling to adjust to living in Catherine's physical body? This was new territory for both of us and it required an open mind and a great deal of flexibility to cope with what was happening. We were both on unfamiliar ground.

The alarm clock roused me from a deep, exhausted sleep at 6am. I woke to the sound of chattering monkeys and squawking birds. I could hear the rhythmic swish of the brush as the young cleaning girl swept the courtyard. It was a daily ritual, 7 days a week. The young Scandinavian child in the room next door was crying, a thin pitiful wail that suggested debilitating illness. A bell was ringing in the distance. It was probably the fish man selling his wares. The hum of activity from the nearby main road could clearly be heard, as could the laughter of happy children playing amongst the trees. Palolem was a beautiful place to be. I only wished I had more time and freedom to be able to enjoy it.

As usual I was up early to take Catherine to a medical appointment. I could have done with a lie in because I was definitely running out of steam and patience. This self-surrender thing was challenging to say the least.

Having found a rickshaw to take her to the Ayurvedic doctor, then waited outside with her stuff while she had a treatment, found a rickshaw to return her to the guesthouse, arranged for her lunch to be delivered to her room and having mixed her medicine and checked that she had everything she needed, I retreated to my room with a sigh of relief.

"Catherine, I need 2 hours to myself. I will come back later to check on you."

I had 2 hours in which to relax from her demands and get some writing done. I also had to eat lunch during this time, but 2 hours alone was better than nothing. I sat down at my laptop and started writing. I'd just got into the groove when there was a knock at the door. It was Catherine. She had managed to hobble the few metres from her room to mine because she wanted some of the channelled notes from yesterday.

"I'll give them to you later."

"I need them now because I've got energy."

"You can't have them now because they're in my notebook and I'm using it."

"Well tear out the page from your notebook."

I sighed in annoyance. She was pressing a button. I really felt that her demand was unreasonable. Wanting it now, and right now? This was MY time. 2 hours, that's all I had asked for.

"You'll have to wait."

I closed the door and returned to my writing. But now I was annoyed and disturbed and I'd lost the flow. Being Catherine's carer was not easy.

What constitutes a patient?

A patient is dependent upon the carer for care. The patient has a role to play as much as the carer has a role to play. Both patient and carer are human beings. Just as a carer needs to be empathetic and to try and put herself into the patient's shoes, so the patient needs to try to imagine what it must be like to be in the carer's shoes.

Caring is a demanding role, even with a model patient. It is physically, mentally and emotionally demanding. It is unreasonable for the patient to expect 24 hour care. The carer needs time alone to unwind and do nothing or do something, whether it's a lunch break, a coffee break or just a 'space' break. Each carer will have different needs just as each patient will have different needs. The patient needs to respect this and understand that, medical emergencies excepted, these periods of space are necessary for the carer to be able to adequately cope with her role. Even in hospitals and hospices the role of care is shared. The patient is being supported by the carer. Who is supporting the carer? That is a question for the patient to reflect on and so to keep the requests and demands for help to the minimum required, leaving space for the carer to offer more if she feels able to give more.

Leaving my writing I set off in search for lunch. Crossing the road towards the restaurant I was nearly knocked over by a young lilac-robed Indian with a shaved head as he rode by on a Honda 500. As I waited for my vegetarian thali an elephant ambled past, led by an orange-robed sadhu. The sadhu headed in my direction and asked for some money. I asked to take his photo, a fair exchange.

The thali was delivered on a silver tray. There were 8 small stainless steel bowls, each containing a different food. I had chopped tomato, onion and cabbage, hot lime pickle, white fluffy rice, yellow dhal, lightly seasoned greens, live yoghurt, spiced green lentils, a chapatti and a poppadum. There was also a bowl of rose-coloured water. I drank it, only to discover that it was heavily laced with chilli. My mouth tingled for half an hour and I felt the chilli burning its way uncomfortably through my body for the rest of the day.

Whilst I was enjoying my lunch, I was blissfully unaware that Catherine was lying in bed having another download.

"Plans have changed," she stated when I returned to her room to check on her. "We might be going to Sai Baba on Monday as planned but we might not."

I couldn't believe what I was hearing. I groaned inwardly because I knew what that change of plan would mean. More endless phone calls on crackly Indian phone lines, cancelling the taxi, the flight, the hotel transfer, the hotel rooms and the transport to ashram in Puttaparthi. More phone calls requesting healing from people who were already healing her through distant healing and more days spent looking after her. As I sat there I thought about everything involved. Normally I would have become quite angry but I decided there and then that I would simply try and surrender to what was happening. I would attempt to change my pattern. I just thought that whoever it was that was inhabiting Catherine's body was just being as awkward and difficult as possible. I had to stop seeing the walk-in as my old friend Catherine or I knew I wouldn't last the course. It helped to remind myself of the teachings of Babaji, the immortal yogi of the Himalayas.

Sometimes we are sent a present in the form of a sentient being whose behaviour irritates us into learning a new lesson or perspective about life. Observe events and how they are connected to your life. We are here to learn from these events. They are not haphazard. They are synchronously connected to form the fabric of our path to the Higher Self.

"I don't need to reflect on it," I said. "I'll go with it, whatever you decide." I honestly was trying very hard to be on the path of self-surrender.

Although I could not see it at the time, what was really happening was that Catherine was bringing all my ego stuff up to be dealt with. All the things that annoyed me, all my expectations, judgements, likes and dislikes, wants, needs and attachments were my buttons and Catherine was managing to press every single one. That was no mean feat because, believe me, I had plenty of buttons. For as long as I had an ego I would have buttons that could be pressed. I just couldn't believe how many buttons I had. There seemed to be no end. It would be some months later, long after my return to France, before I would understand what had really been going on during the Indian trip.

I was beginning to seriously question what was going on. I knew I couldn't take her demands any more. I'm fairly patient but I'm not a saint, and nursing and supporting Catherine required sainthood. Yes she had a lot of knowledge and wisdom, and she genuinely thought that she had had a walk-in, but I was still not convinced. Anyway, I was physically, mentally and emotionally exhausted and I told her that I would not sleep in her apartment under the recently-erected mobile phone aerial. She felt really let down and she told me so.

During these difficult weeks as I struggled with my ego, I often consoled myself with the comforting thought that I could opt out of this journey at any time. I had never promised to be joined to Catherine at the hip. I could simply have said I had had enough, was going my own way and goodbye. Yet there was an invisible force keeping me there, just for one more week, just for one more day. There were enough miracles and magic to keep me interested and intrigued enough to want to know more. I was hanging on by a thread and that thread, strange as it sounds, was the fact that she had changed the pronunciation of HimalAYas to HimALayas during my reading.

At 7:30pm on Sunday evening, the day before the original flight, Catherine made a complete about-turn and decided that we would be flying as per the original plan. Then, just as I was coming to terms with the fact that our original plan would be going ahead, plans changed yet again! Yes, we would be going to the Sai Baba ashram but we would stay in Bangalore for a few days en route as Catherine wanted to make an appointment at a private hospital to try and find a diagnosis for her condition. The osteopath had diagnosed an autoimmune disorder but she didn't know why it was so painful for her to walk.

The path to realization that Catherine had chosen to follow was very different to my own. She channelled spirits, ascended masters, Sai Baba, Babaji, Quan Yin, Merlin and so on. She was a dedicated devotee of Sai Baba and she did not experience the appearance of the 11:11 in the way that I did. My path was that of following signs and using synchronicity, especially around the appearance of the number 11:11 as a way of guiding me back to Source/God/Oneness. I knew it wasn't a simple case of either/or but could these 2 paths be combined? All the ascension stuff that took off in the 1980s was, in my opinion, all part of the illusion, as were all these guides, helpers and angels. I'm not saying that they don't exist on other dimensions or in parallel universes, but I'm only using the word 'exist' there in a very loose way, for if all is illusion then NOTHING exists, including us. Is the 11:11 actually a route through all i(ll)usion? Is the 11:11 sign a direct connection to Oneness? Babaji was supposedly working through Catherine yet even in his channelling he said that he was part of the illusion.

At this stage I'd been in India for almost a month and 11:11 had not appeared at all. I hoped the lack of signs did not indicate that I had gone off track. Maybe the 11:11 been replaced by the path of blind faith and Catherine was teaching me to let go of my ego by being so difficult that I either broke down or surrendered. I was confused and I realized I was walking a bit close to the edge of sanity. I stepped up my yoga practice and breathing exercises to enable me to cope.

Chapter 18

Puttaparthi: Sai Baba

Puttaparthi, the home town of Sai Baba, was a noisy, dirty, bustling town and much bigger than I had expected. There was construction going on everywhere. More and more apartments were being constructed, each block higher than the next one. These new apartments had all mod cons yet the sand and cement were delivered by bullock carts and the scaffolding was made from bamboo, held in place with string. Some of this scaffolding was 10 stories high. In the early days when Catherine had first visited Sai Baba the town was much smaller, as were the crowds surrounding Sai Baba.

The accommodation within the sprawling ashram varied. At one end of the scale were very basic (and very large) wooden huts with outside taps. Each devotee was allocated a sleeping space on the floor.

Then there were the single sex dorms with up to 10 beds. These were cramped and untidy with people's clothes, laundry, possessions and bags all taking up the already limited space. Top of the range were modern self-contained apartments that were owned by the wealthier devotees though they were only permitted to stay in them for a maximum of 2 months in each year. The rest of the time they were available to those fortunate enough to be allocated one.

I chose to stay in a guesthouse just outside the walls of the ashram because I needed some time alone. It was a very basic room and it was running with ants but at least I had some space. On the first day I was there I handed my clothes in to be washed as there was nowhere for me to wash them. That afternoon as I walked down by the river I saw my linen trousers hanging on a washing line, having been washed in the filthy river water. My clothes were returned to me later that day. Each item was neatly marked with a number 11 in blue biro which wouldn't wash off. That meant I was walking around with visible 11's all over my clothing. I thought that was a rather unusual appearance of the 11!

Fortunately for me, Catherine had bumped into an old friend called Gillian. Gillian was great company and she helped me to care for Catherine. I moved out of the guesthouse when Gillian and I found ourselves a lovely rooftop apartment. Catherine couldn't reach us as we were up 6 flights of stairs in an apartment block with no lift. No way could she climb the stairs in her condition.

It was good to get some space. I could reflect on things more easily from a distance and that helped to keep my mind clear. What was going on? I had heard that India was always a challenging place to be, especially on a first visit, and that was certainly proving true for me. I don't know what had possessed me to decide to stay for almost 6 months on my very first visit to India. I had plunged in at the deep end and was at risk of drowning.

I also couldn't decide whether Catherine had experienced a walk-in or not, and there was no way of proving it. It was clear that she was channelling very high energies now. And was Sai Baba a God incarnate or was he a false prophet?

Catherine had bought an apartment near Sai Baba's ashram because her intention had been to spend the rest of her life living next to the ashram and her beloved spiritual master.

"But he might die and then what?" I said. "Will you still stay near the ashram then?"

"I know when he will die. He has predicted his own death. He said he will leave the physical form when he is 96 so I will have more than 10 years in his presence."

None of us knew at that point in time that less than 2 years after our visit Sai Baba would be dead. We would be with him for his last but one Christmas.

"I thought you said he'd live until the age of 96?" I said to Catherine after his death.

"That is how most of us had interpreted Baba's words. But we were counting in solar years. If you count in lunar years he did indeed die at the age of 96."

I lay in bed on that first night within a few metres of where Sai Baba was sleeping. Could I feel any energy? No. Did I feel as though I was in a high energy location? Not particularly. Did I feel different or did I feel I was in a special place? Not really.

But that first night I did have a dream. I dreamed that a crocodile was under the water and was trying to jump out and get me. Then when I woke up my mind was like pure, still white light. It was utterly calm and peaceful. I could normally only reach this state when I combined fasting with meditation and even then it was rare to reach such a state. I took note.

For the first week I didn't go to darshan to see Sai Baba. I was too busy with choir practice as Gillian and I had joined the choir at Catherine's suggestion. She said that would be the only way we would get anywhere near him. Tens of thousands of people visited his ashram these days. When Catherine had first started visiting there had only been hundreds and over the years she had been granted 7 personal interviews.

During choir rehearsals I heard a lot of stories about Sai Baba as I was surrounded by devotees. I was well aware that they might have been biased. Even so, there were some incredible tales told by educated, seemingly sane people.

An American school teacher told me that she had come to the ashram with her friend and that Sai Baba had materialised her friend a diamond ring. When her friend was making her will she was deciding how to divide her estate between her 2 daughters, as her younger daughter had been a loyal, loving and supportive help to her during her life whilst her older daughter had more or less abandoned her. So she spoke to them and asked them what they thought she should do. The older daughter wanted the ring. The younger daughter wanted the house so that is what was decided. As soon as she died, the older daughter went to the jewellers to get the ring valued. As soon as she handed it over, it shattered into smithereens.

Another devotee was given a gold watch, apparently materialized by Sai Baba. Sai Baba asked him if he liked it as he was not looking delighted with the gift. The devotee replied that he liked it very much but as it was such an expensive watch he wondered how he would get it through customs without a receipt. Minutes later Sai Baba waved his hand in the air and handed over a receipt from a well-known store, all correctly printed and dated for that day. Some weeks later, the devotee went to the store concerned and asked the assistant if he remembered selling the ring. The assistant said he remembered it well as the purchaser was wearing orange robes and had a mass of afro hair.

I also met a man who told me that his friend had been suffering from sexual dysfunction. During a personal interview Sai Baba had massaged oil into his genitals to trigger the healing process. Stories of sexual misconduct surrounded Sai Baba and this was one of the reasons for my uncertainty of his status as Avatar. Yet after the massage the young man did indeed heal and was able to function sexually for the first time in his life. If Sai Baba had massaged his friend's arm or his foot to heal those parts of the young man's body, nobody would have batted an eyelid.

At last the big day had arrived and I would see Sai Baba for the first time. It was Christmas Eve and we assembled at 2pm outside the great hall. We were all dressed in our white, cotton Punjabi suits that were sold at the ashram shop and we wore flower garlands in our hair. By the time everyone was seated it was after 4:30pm. I was near the front row, on the side, giving me a clear view of the entrance through which Sai Baba was to enter. Gillian was directly behind me. I had no idea what to expect, but somehow deep down I knew that this would be a test. I wanted to see if I was affected in any way by being in his presence.

Suddenly I became aware of a shift in energy. I actually felt an energy entering the hall. The tinsel began to blow in the breeze, as if moved by an invisible force. Then Sai Baba entered. He was in a wheelchair, dressed in orange robes, with thinning afro hair. He looked frail and old yet he had a powerful presence. I had seen his picture all over Puttaparthi. Now I was looking at the man himself. I couldn't keep my eyes off him. My first thought was, 'At last, after so long.' I had known of his existence since my teens and I had finally made it to his ashram. He was wheeled slowly along by a male devotee. An Indian woman in the front row handed him a letter which he took. I was looking at him closely, looking for a sign that would prove to me that he was more than just a human being. All eyes were fixed on Baba. He was now only a few metres away from me. Slowly he turned his head in my direction and looked directly at me. He was STARING at me. His eyes were locked on to mine. As he was wheeled past, still he looked, turning back slightly to keep the eye contact. He had picked me out of the crowd, out of tens of thousands of people. I don't know how long it was, but it was long enough for me to realize that something had happened in that long moment. He definitely had powers greater than an average human being. The strange thing is that Gillian had exactly the same experience as me.

"His eyes locked on to mine," she told me later.

"No, they locked on to mine," I insisted. I was 100% sure of that fact. Eventually we came to the conclusion that he had indeed locked on to both pairs of eyes. Being Sai Baba, he was able to do things that were beyond our comprehension. Apparently a transmission of energy takes place when a spiritual master looks into your eyes. I must have been granted a particularly large dose of energy. Mind you, I needed it!

It was 11th January: 11.1.10. Because of the 4x1's in the date I was taking particular note of what was unfolding on that day. I woke early and walked up to the German bakery café for my fruit porridge, a 5 minute walk. Already the beggars were lined up by the sides of the road, sitting in the dust with their arms outstretched. "SaiRam ma, SaiRam. Maa, maa," called the wizened old women from their pitch on the pavement outside the ashram. There were at least a dozen of them sitting there every day. Their voices followed me down the road. I had to be careful where I walked in case I tripped over one of them. One beggar had no legs, a tiny body and an oversized head. He used to sit on the pavement outside the German bakery calling out for help. His voice was high pitched yet gruff. The tall skinny beggar stood outside the supermarket. He had deformed hands and no fingers which he thrust in my face each time I passed him. Then there were the children who had been taught to pull people at the elbow, putting their hand up toward their mouth as if they were eating. "Food, maa, food." They were extremely persistent. If I ever stopped at a stall to buy some fruit, I would soon be joined by beggar children tugging at my sleeve asking for apples or bananas.

As usual there was a long wait for my porridge in the German bakery so I glanced through the morning paper whilst I was waiting. An article caught my eye. It was written by the famous Vietnamese Zen Buddhist monk Thich Nhat Hanh. It was on page 11. In conjunction with the 1's in the date I realized there must be an important message for me.

Although it was a fairly long article, one part leaped out at me.

The world outside is our consciousness, it is us. It is not something separate and distinct. The object and the subject of perception are one. Without subject, there is no object. Without object there is no subject. They manifest at the same time. Consciousness only lasts a millisecond. Then, because moments of consciousness succeed each other continuously, you have the impression that consciousness is something that lasts. But the notion of a permanent consciousness is illusion, not reality. Consciousness is only a flash.

That tied in with what Babaji had said, that all is illusion. Yet it didn't explain why or how the number 11 kept appearing in my life. It could be that the more I surrendered to Divine Will, the more it appeared and as such it was the number of enlightenment. Yet there have been many enlightened beings who have made no mention of the 11:11 phenomenon. That brought me back to the idea that 11:11 could be the number of mass enlightenment. Using the number 11:11 as a guide would not have been possible before the digital age. Stone Age man had no clocks. As recently as the 1980s digital clocks, mobile phones or computers were not household objects. The digital era is relatively recent, as is the 11:11 phenomenon. Could this be the route to enlightenment of the future? I believe it could be.

Apart from the message in the newspaper, I knew that Thich Nhat Hanh lived in France in a place called Plum Village. It was located in the Dordogne, not too far from Montignac. Yet again I was being prompted to remember that, despite the fact I was so far away from France, the convent was with me and in no way had a disconnection between me and that old building taken place.

For some reason I couldn't get the town of Pondicherry out of my mind. I had such a strong feeling that I had to go there. I mentioned it to Catherine. She was dismissive. "You'd just be wasting your time. I've been and there's nothing of interest. I was very disappointed and I think you will be too."

But that was only an opinion, someone else's opinion. I don't live my life by other people's opinions. I live my life according to synchronicities, intuition and the number 11. I knew that Pondicherry was a French colonial town situated by the sea, not too far from Sai Baba's ashram. It had 11 letters in its name too. When I looked on the map to see exactly where it was I noticed that it was between the 10th and 12th lines of latitude. Then I experienced that strange sensation in my body which happens when I experience a 'knowing'. I knew that I was being guided to travel the 11th line of latitude from the east coast of India, right across to Kerala on the west coast. Not only that, this was a journey that I had to take alone.

As the date was 11.1.10 I knew that this 'knowing' needed to be followed by action. Was I to continue my journey with Catherine or was I to follow my guidance and leave her? It was clear that there was no choice to make for I had surrendered to following the number 11. It was time to leave Catherine. I had been with her for several months, supporting her in all sorts of ways whilst she was in a wheelchair and on crutches. She had finally been diagnosed as suffering from a fractured sacrum. No wonder she had been in so much pain. With correct treatment she was now able to walk unaided and had even started to attend darshan, though she couldn't sit in the hall for more than about an hour as her back would begin to ache. Also, her son was due to arrive from England, so now that she was getting back on her feet and would have family support, it was the ideal time to move on.

Catherine was not happy with my decision.

"But we were supposed to be travelling together!"

"Catherine, I told you at the outset that I'm a very independent person who needs a lot of space and no plans were made. Nothing had been decided, merely a few ideas discussed."

"If it's energy work you're doing then I think we ought to do it together. I'll come with you."

I could see she was not happy about the situation. In the end we came to the agreement that we would travel together as far as the sacred mountain of Arunachala and then after a few weeks I would make my way to Pondicherry alone as Arunachala is en route to Pondicherry.

I was glad I had managed to get to see Sai Baba before he died, and I really felt that although he was surrounded by controversy he was an authentic spiritual master. "By their fruits shall you know them." Sathya Sai Baba had certainly left plenty of fruits on earth. Sathya Sai Baba's trust owns or manages colleges, schools, publication houses, hospitals, women's welfare, clean drinking water schemes and many social service organizations. The clear morning light I had experienced on my first day in Puttaparthi and the prolonged eye contact on first seeing him in the flesh were the confirmation signs for me.

Chapter 19

Arunachala: Ramana Maharshi

The express coach had been booked and paid for, the rooms at the ashram had been reserved and I had given notice on my lovely apartment in Puttaparthi. It was quite late in the evening the day before we were due to leave and I was dropping some of my belongings at Catherine's apartment so that I could travel light, carrying only the bare essentials. We were going to the Ramana Maharshi ashram in Tiruvannamalai. It would be an early start for us both as the coach left at 5am.

"I'm not going. I'm going to stay in Puttaparthi and have some healing. "

By now I was used to expecting the unexpected with Catherine, but that was both very last minute and unexpected. My normal reaction would have been anger. However, I accepted her decision without protest or reaction, a clear indication that my ego was losing its grip. So it was that I travelled alone to the town of Tiruvannamalai, home of the sacred mountain of Arunachala. The 5am coach was nowhere to be found so I ended up travelling by local bus, squashed in the middle of the front seat between a mother with a vomiting baby and an old woman with a live chicken. Whenever we stopped in a town (we passed through dozens of them) the bus was besieged by people selling their wares. They leaped on to the bus and thrust their hands through the open windows to try and sell their hot samosas, fresh bananas, tea, saris and more.

The drive was a hair-raising experience. The bus was ancient and I wish I hadn't looked at the tires before I boarded as they were completely bald. The bodywork was in a dreadful state, full of dents and scrapes. It was clear that the bus had already been involved in several collisions so I was feeling slightly vulnerable even before we set off. The roads were poor and there were lots of roadworks and sharp bends. The bus veered sharply from left to right as the driver struggled to steer using his one free hand. His other hand was occupied. He was having a long and loud conversation on his mobile phone. He sped around corners and people flew from their seats shouting at him to be more careful. On several occasions we were within a centimetre of a collision with oncoming vehicles. At one point we drove past a small crowd in the road who were gathering around a recently killed pedestrian. I saw the blood oozing out of the dead man's ear as he lay on the stony road.

Suddenly a lorry approached us, driving straight towards us completely on the wrong side of the road. Our bus swerved to avoid it and for a few moments we teetered on the edge of overbalancing. I leaned my body to the left as if my body weight would be enough to redress the balance, praying that we wouldn't topple over. We didn't, but the following week this very same bus on this route crashed. The entire side of the vehicle was ripped away, killing 7 people and injuring many more.

I took ill on the bus. By this point in time I had been in India for several months but this was my first illness. I began to feel clammy and sick shortly after leaving Bangalore. I had sharp, stabbing pains in my abdomen and I needed the toilet but the one toilet stop we made was so disgusting that I started to retch from the smell when I was within a few metres of the hut. I decided I would just have to wait. That 5 hour bus journey felt like the longest 5 hours of my life and arriving at my room in the ashram I headed straight for the toilet, a hole in the floor. I spent the next few days staggering between that hole and my bed in the ashram, not eating anything and waiting for the dreadful cramps to stop. I had heard that some of the ashram rooms were very nice, clean and modern. However, I was in an older block, built in 1942. I had a twin room to myself as Catherine and I had requested this. There was no shower, just the usual tin bucket and a tap for washing. I was so thankful that I was not in a dorm or a shared room because I was up and down all day and all night, emptying my bowels into the hole in the ground. After a few days everything calmed down and I was finally able to go out and explore and spend time at the shrine.

It would be many weeks later before I understood that this illness had been divinely planned, for it meant that when I first entered the shrine of Ramana Maharshi I was in a deeply fasted state. Fasting is a well documented discipline on the spiritual path and it was something I had tried quite a few times. I speak from direct experience when I say that an empty stomach empties the mind and fasting has been an enormous help to me on those occasions when I have felt stuck in my spiritual journey.

The resting place of Ramana was across the road from the accommodation block, situated at the base of the sacred mountain of Arunachala. I walked out of the gates. An orange-robed sadhu was leaning against the gate post smoking a cigarette. A middle-aged woman walked past leading a cow on a piece of string. Dozens of people were all heading in the same direction and I followed them into a hall. At the back was Ramana's shrine and devotees were walking round and round. Some were chanting, their malas slipping quickly through their fingers whilst others simply gazed at the tomb as they walked. Many people sat around the edge of the hall either meditating or soaking up the atmosphere. It was a wonderful place to sit. If places have consciousness then this was certainly a place of extremely high consciousness. I joined the people walking around the shrine; round and round I went, 111 times. Then I sat on the floor, resting my back against the wall with my eyes closed. I felt totally empty but it was not an emptiness of lack. It was a calm, still and fulfilling emptiness. I was bathed in peace.

Sri Ramana Maharshi taught enlightenment through the meditating on the phrase, 'Who am I?' Ramana saw the mind as a tool that could be used to illuminate the path but then once it has fulfilled this purpose it has to destroy itself. There was an excellent bookshop at the ashram and I was interested to read Ramana's thoughts on free will as I had been reviewing my beliefs on this subject following my transmission.

Free will and destiny are ever existent. Destiny is the result of past action; it concerns the body. Let the body act as may suit it. Why are you concerned about it? Why do you pay attention to it? Free will and destiny last as long as the body lasts. But jnana transcends both. The Self is beyond knowledge and ignorance. Whatever happens, happens as the result of one's past actions, of Divine Will and of other factors.

There are only two ways to conquer destiny or be independent of it. One is to enquire for whom is this destiny and discover that only the ego is bound by destiny and not the Self and that the ego is non-existent.

The other way is to kill the ego by completely surrendering to the Lord, by realizing one's helplessness and saying all the time, 'Not I, but Thou, oh Lord' and giving up all sense of 'I' and 'mine', and leaving it to the Lord to do what he likes with you. Complete effacement of the ego is necessary to conquer destiny, whether you achieve this effacement through Self-enquiry.

That's exactly what I was attempting to do, giving up the small self/the ego and allowing myself to be used as an instrument. It's all very well to say 'surrender to God' or 'follow God's will' or as Ramana says, "Leave it to the Lord to do what he likes with you," but how do you know what God's will is? I could ask questions like:

"Does God want me to write this book?"
"Does God want me to live in Devon?"
"Does God want me to take a job in the local hospital?"

How does God answer those questions? Maybe some people just guess what God might want. Personally I prefer to use numbers to guide me. Unlike feelings, impressions or thoughts, numbers appear in the physical universe in a way that can be seen by anyone. Using numbers as a guide is an unusual route to enlightenment but it seemed to be working for me. Am I the only person using numbers in this way? Quite possibly I am!

"We're going to go and see Mooji. Do you want to come?"

I was sitting in the German bakery under the shadow of the sacred mountain. There had been one of these cafés in Puttaparthi too and I had often eaten there as the food was prepared in a clean kitchen, washed with pure water and was quite delicious. I had heard of Mooji because Catherine had mentioned him. She had been on one of his silent retreats. I soon discovered that he was a very well-known spiritual teacher with a large following. He is a direct disciple of Sri Harilal Poonja (Papaji) who in turn is a direct disciple of Ramana Maharshi.

All that you are attached to, all that you love,
All that you know, someday will be gone.
Knowing this, and that the world is your mind
Which you create, play in, and suffer from,
Is known as discrimination.
Discriminate between the Real and the Unreal,
The known is unreal and will come and go
So stay with the Unknown, the Unchanging, the Truth.
Papaji

Mooji spent several months with Papaji. During satsang one day, Papaji told him: "If you desire to be one with truth, 'you' must completely disappear." When Mooji heard this he was really angry and he decided to leave Papaji for good, but later that day his anger suddenly lifted. His mind was in a state of such peace, emptiness and a love towards the master, that he knew he could not leave. Through Papaji's grace, his mind had been pushed back into the emptiness of source. Maybe that is what had happened to me on the first morning in Puttaparthi when I had woken up with a white light in my head. I had glimpsed that state of being, albeit only for a short time.

In 1994 Mooji travelled to Arunachala and stayed at the Ramana Maharshi ashram for 3 months. He now holds satsang and silent retreats near the sacred mountain. People come from all over the world to be in his presence. To get a message to Mooji you had to be amongst the first 50 or so people to arrive at the tent where he gave his discourses. I turned up early, slipped off my shoes and joined the dozens of other early risers sitting under the shade of the grass canopy. There were all ages and many nationalities. I sat cross-legged on the cotton mats, shaded from the already hot morning sun. A young fair-haired man to the right of me was standing on his head. Another one lay on the ground in an advanced yoga pose. 2 young barefooted children stood quietly, probably indigo or crystal children. A mother sat beside me and began to breastfeed her young baby. She spoke to him soothingly in an eastern European language.

The day that I arrived (January 29th) just happened to be Mooji's birthday but I was too late to get a message to Mooji as I was not amongst the first 50 people to arrive. Several times I aimed to be early enough to be taken upstairs to the room where Mooji held satsang but I never made it. I wasn't concerned about that because I knew that if I needed to get a direct message to Mooji it would happen. It obviously wasn't needed.

I was still able to sit under the shade of the grass canopy and listen to his discourses. They were filmed and were shown on a screen for all to see and hear. He had a soft, gentle, smiling face, full of warmth, love, patience and understanding. When he spoke, he spoke with the wisdom and truth that is only heard from an authentic teacher. Although I hadn't been able to ask him directly about the 11:11 phenomenon, he spoke about the subject of phenomena in general terms. Clearly I felt as though his words were directed at me.

"Don't attach to phenomena. Phenomena comes and goes. That is the truth about anything that comes and goes. Whatever comes... goes. It is not permanent. It is temporary."

Could he be talking about number signs? Number signs come and go.

"Perceive phenomenon but don't interpret," he continued. "Don't look for meaning."

I pondered for a while on that statement. I guessed that the appearance of numbers was a phenomenon. Did I interpret numbers or did I merely observe them? Did I look for meaning in the numbers? I did. I interpret numbers as signs that contain an energy according to the number. To me a number 5 is about change, an 8 is about the physical universe and so on. (See *Numerology Made Easy* by Hilary H. Carter.)

"Interpreting phenomena as having great significance will fall away."

Was he suggesting that I would gradually move beyond attaching significance to number signs? I think he was. That doesn't mean that my way of living was false. I believe that using numbers in conjunction with synchronicity is a way out of illusion but I was prepared to leave this way of living behind if I felt I needed to. I observe and follow numbers but I don't think I'm hopelessly attached to them... or maybe I am...!

"Don't identify yourself with anything temporary. And there is no higher power that can come in and take over. Pure, unassociated being is the only thing that is. Conscious presence is all there is."

One day he spoke about enlightenment. He said that somebody had asked him what happens when you become enlightened. He explained that it was not really possible to become enlightened because in reality there isn't a 'somebody' there to gain enlightenment.

He suggested 'self-enquiry' (who am I?) as an effective means of exposing the unreality of the ego. The true Self is formless and nameless presence which arises as peace, joy and happiness. It is felt as loving contentment. I would have liked to have asked Mooji if he had ever heard of my unique path of enlightenment using numbers but it was not to be.

Mooji's discourses are freely available on YouTube and I still access them from time to time. They are worth a listen.

I also took the opportunity to listen to Sri Vast whilst I was in Tiruvannamalai. "What happens when you become enlightened?" was the title of his talk.

Sri Vast was trying to explain the state of consciousness of an enlightened person. I thought that he summed it up perfectly when he said, "Stay in the space you were in before the question arose in your mind."

I know that place. I call it the place of being.

"The enlightened person is beyond all forms, religions, ideas, theories, the past and the future. The enlightened person experiences the totality of his existence in every moment on the ground where he stands at that moment. He is there totally. He is not waiting for something. He is not there to experience something. He has no intention, no purpose, he's just there. Life is happening to you right now in this moment. Enlightenment is what is happening to you right now. It's not in the future."

In other words he was talking about being in the moment. The path of number was teaching me that. Let's face it, if I wasn't totally in the moment I wouldn't be able to notice the number signs. It's a strange way of living a life. Maybe it's not leading anywhere but then maybe it's not meant to. Maybe my path is teaching me 2 of the main things that spiritual teachers teach: to be in the moment and to release the false construct of the ego. The numbers route was gradually peeling away my mind as the signs require that you act on faith and not on thought. I flow with the numbers. Where they lead I follow. I was certainly learning a lot from living in this way.

Liberate, totally liberate, until the question of liberation disappears within you. Flow, just flow with the life. In that flow you and me will disappear. The comparison of your inner and outer world will disappear. Without knowing you will realize you are already there.
Sri Vast

The holy mountain seemed to act like a magnet for spiritual seekers, therapists, gifted healers and a myriad of human beings of high consciousness. Every day there were so many interesting activities to choose from. There were yoga classes, therapies, meditation groups, spiritual film shows, talks, readings and more. One day I saw a poster inviting people along for a silent darshan. The literal translation of darshan is 'vision' or 'to see'. I turned up the following morning at the advertised location. I slipped my sandals off and entered the darshan hall. It was deathly quiet. About 40 or 50 people were sitting on mats on the wooden floor around 3 sides of the hall. They were mostly Westerners. Nobody spoke or moved. Some had their eyes open, some closed. The stillness was incredible. As I had never experienced silent darshan before I had no idea what to expect. After about 10 minutes of sitting on the hard wooden floor (I hadn't brought a mat along) hardly daring to move in case I broke the silence, the door opened and in walked a tiny Indian woman accompanied by a man. He escorted her to the front of the hall where she stood in silence. Then she began to look at us. That's all. She simply looked at us one at a time, staring deeply into each pair of eyes in turn. When she looked directly into my eyes I felt warmth and a love like a mother's love envelop my being. Then her eyes left mine and the sensation ended.

Eye contact carries a transmission of energy and that is why it is done. That is what had happened when Sai Baba had looked into my eyes. This silent darshan was given by Amma and she is from the Sri Siva Sakthi Ammaiyar ashram in Tiruvannamalai She is not to be confused with Amma the hugging mother.

Ramana's ashram was situated at the base of the holy mountain of Arunachala. I climbed up the side of the mountain to the meditation room, a peaceful place where it was possible to simply sit in silence. As I stood looking out over the magnificent view of the town of Tiruvannamalai, a huge sprawl of buildings lying on the flat plain below the mountain, I was approached by a young Indian man.

"Would you like to see the real meditation cave, the one where Ramana Maharshi spent much time alone?" he asked.

"Isn't this it?" I asked, indicating the meditation room. "I was told that there were 2 caves that he used, the Skandashram and Virupaksha caves."

"No. He did spend time in those but the one I know about is not known by the tourists. "

The ashram had warned everybody to be careful because of so-called unauthorized 'guides' on the hill but I was coming from a place of trust and not of fear. I accepted his invitation and we set off higher up the mountain. I enjoyed spontaneous adventures like this. I was reminded of the John the Baptist church that I had been taken to in Cappadocia, Turkey. I often find that offers and adventures that are presented to me rather than being sought out are usually more exciting and revealing. The guide and I set off together up the side of the mountain. Higher and higher we climbed. It was really hot and the climb was incredibly steep. I had to keep stopping to rest. There was no path. We were scrambling over rocks and rugged ground and I had to use a sturdy wooden stick to stop me from falling. I was only wearing sandals so I lost my footing several times. Twice I actually fell and grazed my legs on loose rocks. It was several hours before we reached the cave but it was worth it. From that height the view was incredible.

"This is where he sat," I was told. He pointed to a slightly raised platform inside the cave. When I put my hand on the place it began to vibrate strongly. I pulled my hand away and the sensation stopped. Then once more I touched the platform and again I felt this powerful vibration.

There was something incredibly pure and clear about Ramana's teachings that were reflected in the ashram.

Happiness is your nature.

It is not wrong to desire it.

What is wrong is seeking it outside when it is inside.

Nobody doubts that he exists, though he may doubt the existence of God. If he finds out the truth about himself and discovers his own source, this is all that is required.

Reality is simply the loss of ego. Destroy the ego by seeking its identity. Because the ego is no entity it will automatically vanish and reality will shine forth by itself.

– Be As You Are: The Teachings of Sri Ramana Maharshi

Walking around the base of the holy mountain is known as circumambulation. It is considered to be beneficial in all ways. Traditionally the walk is done in bare feet but I wore sandals. Having walked that sacred mountain I can say for sure that it is a major portal of light. Over the centuries, many saints and sages have been drawn to Arunachala and I am not surprised. There is a deep sense of spirituality on that mountain that cannot be explained. I have not felt it anywhere else. When Ramana Maharshi was asked about the special sanctity of Arunachala, he divulged that Arunachala is Lord Shiva himself. That would mean that Arunachala is nothing less than the secret dwelling place of God. It is this place that bestows Self-knowledge but because most people have so many other desires and do not truly want Self-knowledge, Arunachala has always remained comparatively little known. It is said that to those few who sincerely seek, Arunachala always makes itself known through some means or other.

I was reluctant to leave Arunachala. I could happily have spent months there. But I had work to do so I could not allow myself to get stuck anywhere. I was heading for the east coast of India to start my journey along the 11 degree line of latitude. However, part of me remains (and always will remain) on the sacred mountain of Arunachala.

Chapter 20

Pondicherry: Aurobindo and the Mother

As soon as I arrived in Pondicherry I found a room at the ashram of Sri Aurobindo and the Mother. I had not booked in advance so I was very lucky. Aurobindo was an Indian nationalist, freedom fighter, philosopher, yogi, guru, and poet and 'the Mother' was his spiritual collaborator, a Parisian born of Egyptian and Turkish parents. Over the years the town of Pondicherry had been in the hands of both the British and the French and it had a distinctly French flavour.

The ashram guesthouse was set in attractive gardens overlooking the Bay of Bengal. Unfortunately my room didn't have a sea view. Mine was at the back of the ashram and overlooked the petrol station, but at least I had a mosquito net on my bed. The Indian mosquitoes were vicious and I welcomed the protection.

There was a small café selling simple food and a tranquil meditation room with an uninterrupted sea view. Hot water was available twice a day and had to be collected in a metal bucket from the communal tap. There was no bath or hot shower. I had to sponge myself down using the bucket.

In the ashram, there were no obligatory practices, no rituals and no compulsory meditations. The general principle was simply the willingness to surrender to the Divine and open to the Divine Force so that it may work to transform one's being.

One day I took a trip out of Pondicherry to visit the experimental town of Auroville, founded in 1968 by The Mother.

Auroville wants to be a universal town where men and women of all countries are able to live in peace and progressive harmony above all creeds, all politics and all nationalities. The purpose of Auroville is to realize human unity.

Auroville belongs to nobody in particular. It belongs to humanity as a whole. However, to live in Auroville, one must be willing to serve as a channel of Divine Consciousness. It is a bold and exciting project and well ahead of its time. In the grounds is a massive golden dome known as the Matrimandir. This is a tranquil place of meditation. Inside, a spiralling ramp leads upwards to an air-conditioned chamber of polished white marble referred to as "a place to find one's consciousness". At the very centre is a 70 cm crystal ball in a gold mount which glows with a single ray of sunlight that is directed on the globe from the top of the structure.

A week after arriving, I had to leave the ashram guesthouse because it was fully booked. After the relative austerity of the ashram, I moved into a Heritage Hotel, an 18th century French Tamil house hidden away down a side street and built around a central courtyard. I had a room on the second floor, on the roof. I woke up on my first morning and when I opened the obscured glass windows I gasped, for my view was an uninterrupted view of the cathedral. That's all I could see, some palm trees and the towers of the cathedral. It was a pleasant shock. I had become accustomed to looking out on to the petrol station.

There were 3 other guests in the hotel when I arrived. One was called Pierre. He was a wine merchant from Bordeaux, not that far from the French convent. He was also a martial arts expert. He knew Montignac well. One night I was woken from a deep sleep by an urgent knocking at the door. I woke with a start and glanced at my watch. 1:11am exactly. I leaped out of bed.

"Who is it?" I whispered through the half-open window.

"It's me, it's Pierre. I have brought you some wine to try."

"Pierre, do you know what the time is?"

"Yes, I know it's late but today is the 11th so I thought you would be excited because 11 is your number. We can drink wine together to celebrate."

So it was the 11th day of the month and it was 1:11am, 2 reasonably strong signs. But I had already told him that I did not drink so he was a man that did not listen and he knew that I went to bed early yet he had no hesitation in waking me up. Despite the number signs, it simply did not feel right.

"I'm tired and I'm going back to sleep. Go away!"

This was a case of acknowledging the 11 sign, running it past my intuition and then choosing not to act on it. Young, fit, good looking and French, Pierre had a large ego and he was obviously not accustomed to rejection. His pride was hurt and he never spoke another word to me. A few days later he left the guesthouse.

In the past I have ignored my intuition and simply gone along with the signs. I remember advertising for someone to help me with some work on my house. A man responded to my advert at exactly 11:11am but it didn't feel right. As I was impatient to get the work done I convinced myself that the one sign was strong enough to ignore my gut feeling. He turned out to be a walking disaster and I learned the hard way what can happen by ignoring intuition.

By this time I had been in India for more than 4 months and the weather was becoming uncomfortably hot. I had 5 weeks left in India before my flight back to London. Before I left I needed to travel the 11 degree line of latitude from east coast to west coast yet I was finding it impossible to drag myself away. I felt a magnetic pull to Pondi (as it was affectionately known) and I just couldn't find the strength or willpower to move on.

The resistance that my ego managed to muster against the proposed 11 degrees of latitude trip was enormous. In a nutshell I had allowed myself to get stuck, the very thing I had vowed not to do. I came up with all sorts of reasons NOT to travel.

It would be **so** hot.

I would be constantly packing and unpacking. That would be

so unsettling.

Finding a reasonable place to stay off the beaten track would be **so** stressful.

The roads were **so** dangerous, with at least 250 people killed on Indian roads every day and many more injured.

My travel insurance had run out because I'd stayed longer than the 90 days permitted so I really ought not to risk an adventure way off the beaten track.

I realized that these thoughts were all projecting forward in time and that is something that my transmission had stressed that I needed to stop doing. Not only that, they were fear thought forms. I tried to nip them in the bud.

The sun was setting and the full moon was rising as I stood on my terrace watching the gathering crows darken the sky above me. I could hear the sound of music and singing coming from the nearby cathedral. When I lay on my bed, all I could see through the small open window were the white and yellow towers of the 18th century building. I wandered slowly down the stairs and round the corner, and entered the old iron gates which were normally closed when I walked past. Mass was being held. I waited in the courtyard, watching as the church filled up.

This was crazy. What was I doing in Pondicherry? Why did I feel unable to move on? Was I to travel the 11 degree line or not? I needed to know.

"Give me a sign," I demanded of the Universe. "If you really want me to go and travel it, I need a very clear sign. You know I'll do it if the sign is clear enough for me to read."

At that VERY SECOND, the garish neon lights on the large, painted cement statue of Mother Mary burst into life, making an explosive sound as they sprang into action. They buzzed loudly in the way that Indian electricity sometimes does.

"Holy shit!" I swore as I leaped backwards in alarm.

I honestly hadn't expected a sign as clear as that. It shocked me. I felt as though I had received an electrical charge myself, a bit like being hit by lightning. When I had recovered from the shock, my mind kicked in. There's 60 seconds in a minute, 60 minutes in an hour and 24 hours in a day. So the chances of those lights coming on at that very moment was one in 86,400. Yet I didn't need a number to demonstrate the odds. I knew that I had been given my sign.

I looked up at Mother Mary. "Thank you," I whispered humbly. "I'll go."

I wasn't sure how long the journey would take but I knew that the start date would need to be March 21st, the spring equinox. There are 4 days in the year that are of great significance that are beyond the man-made calendars. These are the shortest day, the longest day and the 2 days where day and night are of equal length. The shortest day is the winter solstice, the longest day is the summer solstice and the 2 days of equal length are the spring equinox and the autumn equinox.

I could understand my resistance to travelling the 11 degree line of latitude. Life was relatively calm and easy at the guesthouse in Pondicherry. I had the roof terrace to myself most days and I could practise my yoga undisturbed. I could wash my clothes in the bathroom and hang them outside where they would dry in minutes. There was an excellent vegetarian restaurant just around the corner. By this time I had been travelling and living out of a suitcase for months. For the first time since I had begun my travels I had felt settled enough to actually empty my bag and put my belongings into the cupboard and drawers. That made life so much easier. I could actually find what I needed without having to rummage through my luggage. The thought of packing up and being on the move again was not appealing.

To complicate matters even more, I had a strong feeling that for some reason I had to travel the line in 111 km lengths. That would mean having to stop every 111 kms. How would I know when I had travelled 111 kms? Even if I knew, how could I stop the bus? The 111 stops might be on a dangerous bend or somewhere where it was impossible to stop. Where had the idea of this way of travelling come from? Was it coming from my mind or from beyond my mind? Was I just making it up? Why would I make things so difficult for myself?

One thing I was learning in my personal search for answers to the 11:11 phenomenon was not to get caught in the mind. That meant I needed to stop all the questions and just follow my gut instinct, my intuition. "Stop asking why," I commanded myself. "Just do it! Like it or not you need to follow your destiny. Leap. It's the only way of staying on the 11:11 trail."

It was good advice. This 11:11 path involved taking huge leaps of faith. Pussyfooting around was the road to nowhere. I had a very strong intuitive knowing that, for some reason, this was how I had to travel so I had to trust that this would be possible. It would be a bit like sewing. Each time I stopped I would be anchoring the light, just as a sewing needle penetrates the cloth to anchor a stitch.

It's strange how I had the knowledge of what form the journey had to take. Fortunately I knew I did not have to travel by public transport this time, unlike my journey from Canada to Mexico, so I gradually came to the realization that the only way to travel would be by taxi. I would need to hire a car and a driver. I mentioned my idea to Sandeep who ran the travel desk in the guesthouse.

"Sandeep. I have an idea I'd like to run past you. I want to travel the 11 degrees line of latitude by car and I want to stop every 111 kms to take a photo," I said. I didn't mention anchoring the light, unblocking the grid and healing the planet. I thought my idea probably sounded weird enough without those added facts.

"I've never been asked to plan a journey like that before," he replied.

"No, and I doubt you'll ever have to plan another like that in the future. But if you could just give me an idea of the cost and how long it might take then I'll have a think about it."

"Where do you want to start?" he asked.

"I'll have to go south from here. Pondicherry is on the 11.56 degrees latitude so I really need to start at 11 or 11.11 degrees. I've had a look at the map and it looks like the nearest town might be Karaikal. I don't know how far that is though."

"It's not that far from here, 2 or 3 hours. Let me see."

Sandeep was sitting at the computer and he brought up a travel website that calculated the distance between Indian towns and cities.

He located Pondicherry and Karaikal in the drop down boxes.

"Here we go," he said, watching as the distance was calculated and displayed. He paused and looked closely at the computer screen. Then closer still. He looked puzzled and he didn't speak.

"What?" I asked. "What's the matter?"

"I don't believe it. Look at that," he said pointing to the screen. The distance was exactly 111 kms. The fact that Pondicherry and Karaikal were on the 11.56N latitude and the 10.56N latitude respectively demonstrated a remarkable fact. All the lines of latitude on the planet are exactly 111 kms apart. Earth herself had been measured in 111's!

At that point I knew that I had been given another confirmation sign and the trip was in the hands of the Divine. Sandeep was the person to arrange it for me. I gave him the go-ahead to make plans for me.

Later that day he handed me a sheet with my proposed itinerary. He had worked out the distances between locations 111 kms apart on or near the 11 line and he had discovered temples at almost every place. It was fortunate that the distance between Karaikal on the east coast and Kozhikode on the west coast was exactly 555 kilometres. That meant that by driving 111 kilometres each day, the trip would take 5 days plus one day to reach

Karaikal. The driver would be able to drop me in Mysore on his way back to Pondicherry on the 7th day.

"And the cost?" I asked. "I don't want to have to haggle with you so just give me your best price."

He spent a few minutes juggling some figures.

"The best I can do is 3,685 rupees a day. That'll include car, driver, hotels with breakfast for you, accommodation and food for the driver, all entrance fees and tolls. It'll be an air-conditioned car and nice, clean hotels. So 6 days... 6 times that... plus that... and that... total is..." He added it up and wrote the total. I looked over at the piece of paper. It came to 22,110 rupees. Twice 11, single 11 and a full circle. Those numbers looked good to me.

"Fine. We've got a deal."

And so it was that the journey took place. I have to say that it is very unlike me to hand over control to somebody else in that way. I had completely surrendered to whatever Sandeep had planned for me. Partly it was because I had discovered that he was on an 11 life path in this life. That was calculated by adding up the numbers in his date of birth, but partly because of the 11 suddenly making its appearance after a long spell of absence. Perhaps the Mother Mary incident had been a trigger for the reappearance of the numbers. It certainly seemed as if I had crossed a border in my life, stepped across a threshold, an invisible line that separated my old way of living and my new way of living. My feet were now firmly planted in the land of synchronistic miracles.

"You want to go tomorrow?" Sandeep asked.

"Yes, tomorrow will be fine."

"Okay, I will print you the details."

The printed sheet outlining my journey was sketchy to say the least but in a way that added to the sense of adventure. I was on my own personal magical mystery tour. "JOURNEY IN THE 11TH ATTITUDE" it confidently stated in capital letters across the top of the printed schedule. I liked that. It was accidently very accurate!

Chapter 21

11 Degrees of Latitude

The following morning my taxi turned up at the door. The driver had an alarming scar that gouged a deep scarlet channel in his dark skin, running from the front of his ear to the corner of his mouth. Worryingly it looked as if he had been through a windscreen. He didn't speak a single word of English but I didn't mind because that meant there wouldn't be any idle chit chat. I could keep myself focused on the purpose of this trip, which was to carry a thread of light from east coast to west coast. The car was a Tata Indigo with the number plate 2054. Ta is one of the 5 primal sounds in Sanskrit and it means 'life' so Tata is life/life. Indigo is a good colour as it's the colour of the third eye chakra. And 2+0+5+4=11.

Our first stop was Pichavaram Mangrove Forest. My driver stopped the car, opened my door for me and silently directed me towards a rowing boat. An old man was sitting in the boat waiting for me, dressed only in a dhoti, a white cloth tied loosely around his hips. Despite his age he was lean and muscular though somewhat scrawny. He silently rowed me across the calm backwaters in the scorching midday sun, watched by 2 lily-white storks. There were just the 2 of us in the boat, me and the boatman. He did not speak, nor did he smile. A kingfisher flew overhead, vivid and striking, the first kingfisher I had ever seen. I saw the way that the trees grew out of the water with massive twisting roots, like nothing I had ever seen before.

The crossing of the water was symbolic for it signifies a transition. As I travel in the way that I do, bringing light to the grid lines of the planet, it's not only the planet that is changed. I am changed too. It's a 2-way process for Earth itself is, like me, a living being. As I heal the earth, the earth heals me.

After my strange silent boat trip we continued towards Karaikal and the temple of Thirunallar. Now I was on the 11 degrees of latitude. Sandeep had told me that this was the only temple in the entire world that was dedicated to the planet Saturn. As an astrologer I was intrigued by this fact. The only Saturn temple in existence and it was on the 11 degrees line of latitude? As it turned out, there are a few other temples dedicated to Saturn but this one really was unique as it was the temple where Lord Saneeswara lost all his power to Lord Shiva which saved his devotee Nalan from Saturn's curse.

That night, after the temple visit, the driver pulled into the entrance of a hotel. As we stepped into the foyer I was amazed to be confronted with da Vinci's painting of the *Mona Lisa* hanging on the wall in reception. It just seemed so incongruous to find it in an Indian hotel. She watched me as I signed the register and ploughed through the reams of paperwork required to stay a single night in room 22. Maybe her appearance had something to do with the fact that the hotel was called the Hotel Paris.

The next day I was taken to a spectacular temple built right on top of an 83 metre high rock. Archaeologists say that the age of this rock is about 3800 million years, older than the Himalayas. As 3+8=11, I noted the appearance of a diluted double 11. The date was 23.3.2010 which adds up to 11. The 23rd is a pivotal date as 23 is the breakdown/breakthrough number. Thayumanaswamy temple is one of very few to have been built facing west. Although my driver drove me up the hill as far as he was able, I still had to walk up further, followed by an arduous climb of 300 steep stone steps. The 23 steps leading up to my French convent paled by comparison. It was extremely hot and I was exhausted by the time I reached the top. I stepped through the wooden doors.

"Stop!"

A Hindu priest came marching briskly towards me, naked from the waist up, his bulging belly hanging over the orange dhoti that was slung casually around his hips. I could see where the cloth was darkened and damp with perspiration.

"No foreigners!"

He spoke sharply.

"What?" I asked in disbelief.

"Foreigners are not allowed in here. Hindus only."

"But I bought a ticket at the bottom of the steps. They didn't say the temple was only for Hindus."

"Your ticket is for the hill, not for the temple. You can go through there," he said, indicating an archway off to the right towards the hill, "but you cannot come in the temple."

"Why not?"

"Because you're not a Hindu. Are you a Hindu?"

"I don't have a label like Hindu, Christian, Muslim or Jew," I replied. "I'm just a human being."

"The rule is Hindus only."

"I've come a long way to see this place. Please could you bend your rules and let me in?"

He hesitated. I stood in surrender. If I was needed in the temple, I knew I would be allowed in. I saw and felt him relent.

"Come."

He took me to a table and held out a metal pot of vibhuti in my direction. He dipped his finger in the pot and then changed his mind. Maybe he didn't want to touch the forehead of a non-Hindu. He indicated that I needed to put the ash on my forehead. I dipped my finger in the pot and drew 3 lines of this sacred ash across my forehead.

"Okay. Now you go."

So I was obviously needed in the temple. I stepped through the door into a huge hall of high, square pillars. The place was ancient. The now familiar feeling of being unable to breathe overcame me. I gasped, partly to get some air and partly because of the drama of being in such a powerful space. I looked at the carvings on the pillars and I could see that they were very like those in Chartres Cathedral. There were strange squatting figures and animals.

A middle-aged Indian woman approached me and smiled. Silently she indicated that I needed to follow her. She guided me in the direction of the Shiva temple. This was at the uppermost point of the hill and it was a lingam wrapped in a dark cloth. I stood there and anchored the light. As always, I was given a sign when the work had been done. In this case it was the sound of bells.

That night I had been booked into the Femina Hotel, a reminder that I was working with Divine feminine energy.

The next morning the driver set the trip meter and after exactly 111 kilometres he stopped. I looked around to see if there was anything of significance. We had stopped outside a Catholic Syrian bank though I had no idea whether that was significant or not. If it was, I didn't know what it meant. A few kilometres later we stopped for lunch. My bill was 1111 rupees. That night I went shopping. My bill came to 2211 rupees. I was taking note of the fact that the 22 was definitely making a regular appearance as well as the number 11.

The only stipulation I had made to Sandeep when I had handed him control over my 11 journey was that whatever happened I wanted to stop at Coimbatore on this journey. Sandeep was equally adamant that Coimbatore was bad news.

"You don't want to go there," he said. "It's an industrial town. There's nothing worth seeing."

"But I must go."

"Why? There are so many better places than that to visit."

"I must go because Coimbatore is situated at exactly 11 degrees and 11 minutes of latitude and it's the only town of any size at exactly 11.11."

"I know this place well. My family comes from near there. Don't waste time going there."

"I have to go. Please include it."

"There is nothing to see in Coimbatore. Really. If there was anything at all interesting I would include it."

"I must go Sandeep, even if there is nothing to see."

I have a stubborn streak in me. No way could I be dissuaded. Eventually Sandeep relented and Coimbatore was included. To his credit, he discovered that there was indeed a temple there, albeit slightly out of town, high on a hill overlooking the sprawling, polluted industrial city. My driver had great difficulty in finding this place. He had no satnav. He simply stopped at regular intervals to ask the locals for directions. The locals in Coimbatore had sent him on a wild goose chase and we circled the city several times, stuck in heavy traffic in the stifling summer heat, choked by the traffic fumes. At one point I almost told him to forget about visiting the temple, especially because Sandeep had been so reluctant to include it. Maybe all the delays and difficulties in finding it were a sign that I was not needed there and it was only my own personal stubbornness that was driving this. But just as I was about to tell him to give up, the driver saw a signpost and turned off the main road. Soon we were winding our way up a steep hill, one hairpin bend after another. Higher and higher we climbed, leaving the noise and pollution of the city behind us. I was glad we were driving. When I looked to my left I could see people climbing up a long flight of stone steps, dripping with perspiration. I don't think I could have managed that climb in the intense south Indian heat.

By the time we reached the top of the hill it was after 5pm and the sun was weakening. I still had steps to climb and I walked this last part of the journey alone, past the coconut sellers and the tea stalls. The driver stayed in the car. When I reached the top I could see a long queue of people to the left of the temple door. However, I was immediately approached by a temple 'official' who physically ushered me to the right-hand side. There was a booth where I had to pay 23 rupees. Number 23 again. This was obviously the fast-track line reserved for people who had 23 rupees to spare for I was the only person taking the right-hand route. I was shooed along like an animal and placed alone right in front of the altar. Everybody else was way behind me, standing behind the metal railings. By getting lost in Coimbatore I had arrived in the Marudhamalai Temple at 5:30pm, just in time for puja. Half an hour earlier or half an hour later I would have missed it. That's what I call divine perfection.

I sat down on the cool stone floor. Directly in front of me was a black curtain. I could see lights behind the cloth and shadowy figures were moving around purposefully. Suddenly the puja bells started ringing loudly and instantaneously I felt as though I was being filled with a charge. It was a bit disconcerting. Something was pouring down through me. I assume it was light. I was definitely being used as a transformer of some sort. I was having difficulty sitting upright as the charge was going through in massive waves which rocked my body. I was swaying.

'Breathe, breathe,' I directed myself.

Suddenly the curtain was swept aside with a flourish and there in all his glory was the God Murugan, son of Lord Shiva, the great destroyer.

The bells kept ringing, the puja fire was lit and I was told to stand. The fire was presented to me and I drew the flames towards me with my hands. Then my forehead was marked with ash by the priest. There was no ban on non-Hindus here. Incense was lit. This was thick, pungent incense smoke, much denser than any I had seen in any of the other temples. Then there was more bell ringing and I was told to sit down again. Once more the charge was put through me. It was like a rod of light that entered through the top of my head, as opposed to the threads of light that I had been accustomed to dealing with up until this point. The rod followed the line of my spine and entered the earth at the base of my spine. I just sat and focused on my breath, hoping I wouldn't fall over or spontaneously combust. I don't know how long I sat for, because it was pretty heady up there in that temple.

Gradually I could feel my body returning to normal. Once more I was told to stand and then I was given a teaspoon of milk, gently poured into my hand by the priest. Silently I blessed it and drank it. The priest's assistant pointed to the door. It was time for me to go. He then began blessing the dozens of people behind the metal railings.

Walking back down the long flight of stone steps towards the car I caught sight of the setting sun. As we drove back down the hill it was with the knowledge that there was now a rod of light deep into the earth at this point. Right there at the 11 degrees 11 minutes of latitude on the top of that steep hill is a rod of light so powerful that I can't imagine anything ever being able to dislodge it. My experience at that particular temple was so profound that I wondered whether that one incident alone was the whole reason for the Indian 11:11 journey.

But my trip was not finished. I looked at the printed sheet that Sandeep had given me to see what the next day had in store for me.

25ᵗʰ March
Coimbatore–Kottakkal–Calicut
After breakfast drive to Calicut through the paddy fields of Palakkad. Stop at Kottakkal to visit the famous Ayurveda Centre (111 kms). Afterwards visit of Kantarki Centre, interaction with Masters and students. Overnight stay at Calicut.

I couldn't find Calicut on the map but then I discovered that Calicut is the new name for Kozhikode. That would be the last stop on my journey. The new place names in India were confusing. For example Pondicherry was now Puducherry though everybody still called it Pondi.

Sandeep used to be a student at the Kantarki Centre. It's a temple, an Ayurvedic hospital and a school for martial arts, but not just any martial art. This is one of the last places on earth that teaches a very rare form called kalaripayattu.

I was invited to a demonstration that evening. It was taking place in a pit with an earth floor. This was newly constructed, with stone walls and a thatched roof. There were wide steps at one end and an altar in the corner. I sat on the deep steps, watching as the students entered the pit one by one. As they entered they knelt and touched the earth with reverence. This was sacred ground and they were honouring the earth. Then they approached the altar and bowed. Dressed only in a white cloth, naked from the waist up, the young men began their warm-ups. It looked to me as though these exercises had their roots in yoga and karate. Soon they were glistening with sweat, their beautiful slim dark long-limbed bodies toned to perfection. Then the main part of the demonstration started. The energy they created was tangible. At the end they chanted some mantras, touched the feet of the teacher with reverence and then left.

When I downloaded the photos I had taken, they were absolutely covered in orbs. Orbs are thought to be visible spiritual energy. The place was teeming with orbs. I have never seen a photo with so many. Then I took a photo of the room I was sleeping in. There were 3 orbs in my room, one of which was sitting on my bed.

Soon it was dinner time. At this small temple the food was all prepared by the women of the family. 3 generations lived together. There was the Master and his wife, the son of the Master with his wife and daughter, and the daughter's husband and son. Everybody who came and sat at the dinner table was fed, regardless of the time of day.

We had round-grained white rice which had been cooked outside on a wood fire. There was vegetable curry and chopped vegetables, a thin dhal and homemade samosas, all served on metal plates. We ate with our hands. All the food was cooked in accordance with Ayurvedic principles and the water that we drank was sweet and warm. It had been boiled with herbs and then strained ready for the table. The bananas were tiny and the watermelon was beautifully ripe and refreshing.

I was joined by 2 guests from Germany. We were the only people staying that week. One of them was a publisher.

"I don't publish a lot of books, only those that touch me in some way," he told me.

"I have written a book. It's about the number 11:11."

"11:11?"

"Yes. I think this is a special number. I think it's linked to the new consciousness that is arising on earth."

"You'll never believe it but that's my son's birthday. He was born on 11th November at 11am."

I could believe it. I silently thanked the Universe for this reassuring sign at the end of my trip. Undertaking the 11 degrees of latitude journey had not been easy. I had been reluctant to do it but I had seen the signs and had acted on them. Now, at the end of the journey, I had been given my confirmation that I had done the right thing. I had done what was needed.

"And what about you, Hendrich? Are you an 11 person?"

He told me his date of birth. Hendrich had incarnated on the earth less than 12 hours after my ex-husband! He told me that he was considering buying an old house at the foot of a Knights Templar church in Germany. I suggested that if the number 11 appeared in connection with the house that he could try just buying it without running it past his mind first. He e-mailed me a few weeks later to say that he had bought the house after discovering that it was number 11 in the street.

Until I met the German couple on the last day of my journey, I had not encountered a single foreigner as I crossed from coast to coast. Sandeep had sent me on a route that does not appear in any guidebooks. I had passed through towns and villages that were way off the beaten track. I had walked through tea plantations, and seen the rubber being tapped from the trees and the sheets of rubber being hung out to dry. I had walked alone through a jungle to bathe in a secluded pond fed by a waterfall. I had eaten delicious meals from banana leaves in local cafés and I had carried the thread of light from coast to coast. But more significantly I had anchored a massive rod of light in the temple near Coimbatore.

Now the trip was over and I was looking forward to spending a week or 2 exploring the famous city of Mysore. My driver dropped me at a hotel overlooking the magnificent palace and then he set off back to Pondicherry. I flopped down on the bed, exhausted by the heat. I was glad to be alone again and I was in a reflective mood, trying to make sense of everything that had happened as I had travelled the 11 degree line. Had the number 11:11 appeared in my everyday life more than usual during the journey? I thought it had, plus the synchronicity with the German publisher was quite a big one. And the 111 kms from Pondicherry to Karaikal was curious and very enlightening. Fancy the earth being inscribed with lines 111 kms apart!

The lines of latitude are neatly arranged around the earth at an equal distance from each other. That is not possible with the lines of longitude as they run from the North Pole to the South Pole. They are closest together at the poles and furthest apart at the equator. The circumference of the earth at its widest point (the equator) is about 40,000 kilometres. When that is divided by the 360 degrees in a circle the result is an astounding 111.111 recurring. Earth herself is definitely part of this 11:11 phenomenon!

I had been led to some incredible and very ancient temples. But I had not once been given a 111 hotel room. Still, I had completed the journey and now I could relax. My light work at this location on the earth was done. I casually flicked on the television and the voice I heard was English.

"I am the number 11."

I looked up in disbelief, just in time to see the actor on the television displaying the number 11 tattooed on to his upper arm.

"I need it more than you," said the second man.

Then all the players were shown wearing the number 11.

"Now we all get to wear it."

I tried to make sense of what I was seeing. I later discovered that it was a film called *The Fan* about American baseball and it had been halfway through when I had switched it on.

Assuming the film is a couple of hours long, the synchronicity of me putting the television on at the exact moment that those words "I AM THE NUMBER 11" are spoken was incredible, way beyond coincidence. But more than that, how many films have those words in the script in the first place? The chances of this event happening are incalculable. I was blown away and overawed by this piece of magic. Only on the path of number could this happen.

Chapter 22

Returning to the Convent

Catherine had been right when she had predicted "a lengthy journey". I could never have guessed that it would be almost 2 years before I would to return to France. Work commitments, my travels along the 111th longitude, a long trip to India plus my Indian 11th latitude journey followed by family issues in England that needed my attention had delayed my return to Montignac. Each time I attempted to return I was blocked. I was bemused. What was the point of being sent to Montignac by the number 11:11 and then being blocked so I couldn't spend any time there? Can you imagine being in that situation? I had followed the 11:11 sign, I'd taken a leap of faith and I'd bought the convent. I had no idea why I'd been guided to the convent and I didn't know how long it would be before I would discover the answer to my question. It could be one year or 20 years. It was all part of the non-attachment. I couldn't even be attached to knowing, or wanting to know. I had to completely surrender to the situation I was in. I could conjecture till the cows came home as to what the reasons were for me being there. Was it to heal past life stuff? Was it to help clear the earth grid or it could be that I had no particular reason for being there at all? Maybe I was being led to not even having a reason to attach to in order to teach me to just be in the moment with no reason, destination or purpose. How long? I allowed the question to arise but I didn't hold on to it. I regularly reminded myself to be in the moment.

In my attempts to return to France I once even got as far as the queue for the ferry before being called away by an urgent phone call. 'Everything happens for a purpose' became my catchphrase as I learned to accept what was happening without judgment and reasoning. My other favourite saying was 'There's always a big picture'. The delays didn't bother me that much. I was hardly desperate to rush back to the challenging and peculiar living conditions of the convent. Despite the fact that it had been upgraded by Mr Cook the convent still had an outside toilet and active insect life. In fact, as lovely as Montignac was, I really didn't want to return. I much preferred being in England amongst friends and family. The longer I left it, the more difficult the struggle became. It was a battle with my ego. "Oh please tell me what it is I have to do with this convent then I'll just do it then I can get out of there." But my calling to the Universe was a desire to get the work done and get out of France. I knew I needed to give up desire. My dread of going back was partly linked to attachment, the attachment to comfort. I wasn't keen on crawling back into that tent, cooking on a frustratingly slow 2-ring electric hob and using the outside toilet! It was also partly reluctance to drive 800 miles in my 14 year old car. The car was part of my 11:11 research. It was a Proton car and I had bought it during a week when earth was being bombarded with protons following some particularly large sun flares. The numbers on the number plate (272) added up to 11 and the letters to 33. The car was on the 11:11 journey with me and was destined to be a link with the world of numbers until it reached 111,111 miles on the milometer. Unfortunately the car had suffered a few mishaps. 3 people had driven into the back of me on 3 separate occasions (which I interpreted as a sign that I needed to get a move on, a literal kick up the arse) and the bumper was now held on by screws. A gang of drunken youths had jumped on the roof of the car on New Year's Eve leaving it badly dented. I had misjudged the width of a driveway and the passenger side was badly scratched all the way along, right down to the metal. The intense sunlight in France had caused the paint surface to bubble so it had dark bald patches. The bands inside the electric windows had snapped so I had siliconed them shut meaning that the windows would no longer open. People were beginning to comment.

"What on earth has happened to your car?"

"I know someone who is selling a car. Are you looking for a new car?"

"I see you're not into cars!"

I was starting to get embarrassed when people stared but I knew it was only the ego that could feel this way so I saw it as a test. Could I drive around in a wreck of a vehicle until I had moved beyond embarrassment? I was determined to keep my Proton until the milometer reached 111,111 miles. I had such insatiable curiosity. I just wanted to know where I would be at that moment. I knew it would be a meaningful place.

Eventually I resolved to stop projecting thought forms forward, to stop projecting this dread, stop assuming it was going to be so uncomfortable and difficult. I was going to be in each moment and just go. I was ready to continue on the path of my destiny.

As my diary freed up and the date of my inevitable return approached I began to experience regular flashbacks of the positive times that I had spent living in Montignac. Images of those beautiful medieval passages, the golden stone of the old houses, the fast flowing crystal clear waters of the fountains and the fantastic views of the Vézère valley from my garden would suddenly appear in my mind. I knew that the building was waiting for me and that I had a duty to return. I had to finish whatever it was I needed to do. It felt like I was being nudged in the ribs, reminding me that my work in France was not yet over. I was being shown that it wasn't all difficulty at the convent. As well as the hardships and frustrations, there was incredible beauty and magic. "In every grey cloud there is a touch of pink" was a favourite phrase of a friend of mine. I was being shown the pink.

I found myself reflecting on what had happened to me since I had become the owner of the convent. By the spring of 2011 I had owned the place for almost 3 and a half years yet I had a long list of unresolved questions floating around in my mind.

Was my home a former convent or not?

Yes, according to Bella who had been given that information by her father.

No, according to the local doctor who was a historian.

Yes, according to my next-door neighbour Alain who had been born in Montignac, had lived in the town all his life, had visited the original caves and who had done intensive research on the town.

No, according to the tourist information centre.

Yes, according to the neighbour with the ruined arch in his garden.

No, according to the letter from the historical society written to my friend Patricia.

My gut instinct told me that the answer was yes, but if I was right then I would like proof.

I also wanted to know if there anything I needed to find under the old cave floor. Or, as Catherine had said when she gave me a reading in India, I was to "render unto Caesar that which was Caesar's." In other words, just leave it be.

Overriding all of these niggling and possibly irrelevant questions was the one big question: 'Why had the 11:11 sent me to Montignac?' When the 11:11 sign had led me to the convent I had owned in Spain, it had taken less than a year to discover that I had been guided there to resolve some unresolved stuff from past lives, plus I was being used to co-ordinate the clearing of a massive amount of stagnant energy that had been blocking the earth's grid. But after 3 and a half years I still had no idea why I had been sent to the heart of prehistory in the Vézère valley. I was getting a bit worried. What if I couldn't find a reason? What if I never found out why I was there? What would I do then? Would I just stay for the rest of my life, waiting and waiting?

I have to tell you that there were great swathes of time when the number signs seemingly disappeared. At those times, when I looked at my life and the chaotic, exhausting, difficult and challenging things that I found myself having to deal with, I was tempted to doubt my whole way of living. My life had gone off at a sharp tangent to the norm and I knew that I lived in a very unusual and unique way. But then, after a period of number drought, along would come a number onslaught and all my doubts would disappear. The journey to France was one of those onslaughts.

It was May 23rd 2011. It started in the queue for the ferry. I was parked directly behind a car with 444 on its number plate. As I drove off the ferry and joined the queue for passport control I was adjacent to an estate car with the number '4' written on a card dangling from the windscreen.

As I joined the road out of Dieppe I got stuck behind a lorry with 44144 on the back. This was too short to be a phone number so I didn't know what it referred to. The number 4 doesn't often appear to me. The message of the 4 is linked to safety and security. Maybe I was being reassured that I was being looked after by the Universe? That night I was given room 204 in the hotel. The next day was May 24th 2011 and I realized that my milometer was about to reach 1044444. I watched it carefully so that I could take note of what was happening at the precise moment that those 5 x 4's lined up. That moment came at exactly 11:11 am. Of all the minutes in the day for it to happen! I just knew the Universe was talking to me. I was driving down the French Autoroute between Orleans and Limoges and what I did see blew me away, for at that moment I was behind a lorry, on the back of which written in massive letters was EGO.CO.AT.

Ego coat. One wears an ego in the same way as one wears a coat. It hides what is within the coat. Just as the coat hides the body, the ego hides our inner divinity. "It was just my imagination running away with me," by the Temptations was playing on the car radio. This was not my imagination. That is one of the best things about the 11:11 path. Number synchronicities can be seen in the physical universe by everybody and anybody. The repeated 4's linking to the 11:11 at the same time as ego coat appears in my universe? I thought that was incredible.

Within less than a minute the numbers had moved on to 104445. Only exactly 6666 miles to go before the car reached the magic 111111 miles.

I pulled into the now familiar town of Montignac and parked my car near Rue Creve Coeur (Rue=road. Creve=cut. Coeur=heart. Road of the cut heart?) and walked along the narrow medieval path towards my home. Nature had prepared a red carpet for my return. The path to the convent was strewn with bright red rose petals that had fallen from their bushes and their soft perfume was released as my steps crushed them underfoot. I felt blessed. This fragrant carpet was more beautiful than any man-made woven carpet or Turkish hand knotted carpet.

I stopped outside the double gates. The gates were criss-crossed with 2 years worth of fine cobwebs. Obviously nobody had opened them during my long absence. I cautiously brushed the webs away and unlocked the gates. They had become stiff with lack of use. Using my shoulder, and with all the strength I could muster, I threw myself against them and heaved them open. They creaked and then gave way. I was home.

The stone steps were shoulder high in weeds and alive with insects. Without human interruption, whole generations of bugs had enjoyed the freedom to multiply unhindered. I saw fat black spiders hanging from the webs and bright red crawling beetles scurrying to and fro along the stone. Several lizards darted away into cracks in the rocks. I couldn't walk through that amount of insect life so I closed the gate and walked around the corner to the other double gates. The cat was sitting on the stone pillar as usual as I approached. She watched me as I walked up the narrow passageway towards the entrance. These gates were even worse than the others. They were jammed solid. Then I remembered that as they would not lock I had wedged them shut so that they would withstand the winter storms. I had no choice but to climb over. I clambered up and dragged myself over the stone gatepost and jumped down on to the garden path. I paused as my feet landed on the hard, dry earth. The feeling was unmistakable. There was something magical and enchanting about this plot of land. It was as if I had stepped through the delicate skin of a bubble and now I stood inside that bubble. A tangible air of expectancy hung in the air like gossamer. I was back and the convent had been waiting for me.

Nature had reclaimed the garden with a vengeance. It was not only the steps that were overgrown. The garden was like a jungle. The rampant brambles had taken over again so it was back to square one. The winter had been particularly harsh and long. It had snowed twice and great chunks of stone had fallen from the walls, as had the cement under the roof tiles, leaving gaps in the fascias. Yet everything in the garden was exactly as I had left it all those months ago. There were piles of stuff waiting to go to the dump, the DIY equipment was lying on the path covered by a sheet of plastic and my garden swing was still tied to the hazelnut tree to stop it blowing away.

I wished I wasn't alone at that moment because if I had been with someone they could have walked ahead of me along the path to break the cobwebs. My life would be much easier if I wasn't afraid of spiders. I knew I needed to deal with my fear. I waved my hands in front of me as I struggled through the brambles. They clawed at my clothes and scratched my skin. By the time I had reached the front door my feet were bleeding. It felt peculiarly ritualistic watching my blood dripping on to the stone step at the entrance door, like some sort of ancient sacrificial blood ceremony. I made a mental note to wear proper shoes next time instead of my flimsy Indian sandals. I swept the cobwebs from the main door, turned the key and pushed it open.

It opened easily with a slight creaking noise.

Wow! The convent took my breath away. It was that same feeling every time I returned. I had forgotten how dramatic that room was with its high dark wood ceiling and imposing inglenook fireplace. I was momentarily wrapped with dense, intense silence. There was something incredible about the place, something really special. I'm not the only one that felt it. Other people had exactly the same reaction. I swear I could hear the convent breathing. A building of this age, especially if left undisturbed, was a living entity, nothing inanimate about it. Despite all my misgivings over this property, I had a very strong sense of belonging there at that particular time.

Entering the house I felt like an actor stepping into a part I was playing. The house was a stage set. It didn't feel real, yet it was my home. It didn't feel like my life. It was as if this life belonged to someone else. I felt as if I had stepped straight into the pages of a Dickens novel.

It was the smell that was the most overwhelming sensation. It hit me like a punch in the face and instantly brought forth a huge rush of memory and a plethora of mixed emotions. It was a familiar musty smell that spoke of ages past, of a rich tapestry of lives, of traumas and grief, of sadness and death, of joy and learning and of books and ink. This incredible building on this beautiful plot of land was my home, thanks to the 11:11 sign.

The ceiling was delicately laced with fine cobwebs, as were the windows. My clothes lay on the floor in plastic sacks. Opening them was like Christmas. I had been living out of a suitcase for over a year and had been wearing the same few clothes day in and day out. Suddenly I had a choice of things to wear. On the shelves were books I had forgotten about. There was my CD player and CDs I hadn't listened to for so long. My tent was dusty and dirty. There were water stains on the floor where the roof had been leaking. The old multi-paned window above the door had blown open and grit, leaves, insects and a dead bird had blown in. There was a new damp patch on the kitchen ceiling. Amongst the dust and grit on the floor was a worrying brown powder that looked suspiciously like wood rot. The eco woodworm killer obviously hadn't worked.

I needed to rest after my long journey. I lay down in my tent as I had done so many times before. I still carried the fear of the giant centipede reappearing but inside the tent I felt safe and protected, knowing that one of those ghastly creatures could not get at me through the insect screen. It was peaceful. The building creaked and groaned as the high temperature of the day changed to the cooler temp of night. The swallows quietened down soon after the sun had set and before long I was fast asleep.

Chapter 23

The Tower of Darkness

Quite a lot had changed in Montignac and the surrounding area since my last visit. Some nearby houses had changed hands and others were now empty. The Parisians next door to me had moved back to Paris so the ground outside my gate was no longer littered with cigarette ends and empty packets of Gauloises. Not that they ever stayed there for long. The street sweepers regularly swept the historic passageways. The town was very well kept.

Quite a few of the roads had been upgraded and even more of the houses had shed their 1960s cement render to reveal their original stonework. The whole area looked more beautiful than ever. The small supermarket on the edge of the town had moved to a much larger site and was now 10 times bigger. The fantastic little hardware shop on the high street had closed down and had become a bank. Bella looked more fragile than she usually did as she struggled to overcome a strange virus she had contracted. Alain looked more wizened and noticeably older. A small plaque had been erected on the house next door to mine directing tourists along the 'historic route' that led past my gate.

Other things remained the same. My Swiss friend still sat drinking coffee at the pavement café with his 5 little Yorkshire terriers, the diners at the excellent Italian restaurant still sat at the tables by the edge of the river and the ugly siren on the town hall still wailed at regular intervals.

As usual I spent a lot of time walking and exploring. It had been 2 years since I had spent time at the convent and on my return it was obvious that the energy of the entire area felt different. It felt lighter, less clogged and more welcoming. I definitely felt as if my travels along the various lines of longitude and latitude had somehow filtered back and cleared the place. The fact that I had been away from the convent for 2 years did not mean that I had not remained connected to it. Maybe the convent was reflecting the change in me too, for now I felt no fear being there alone in my tent. The most disturbing aspect of being there was the tower. Either the new lightness of the convent had brought the darkness of the tower into sharper contrast or the darkness in the one remaining castle tower had become more compressed.

Undeterred by this fact and refusing to come from fear, I walked up the road to the castle and stopped by the massive metal gates. I gazed through the rusty bars of the gate and I could see the door to the tower, an arched wooden door with studs. There was a distinct evil presence. As I stood there clutching the metal bars it suddenly dawned on me. As I had suspected, I was not in Montignac only to clear the convent but I was there to clear the tower too, that forbidding dark ruin. I'm not saying that my work clearing the convent at quantum level had been in vain, but as a storm has an eye, so does a vortex. Although the convent is in the eye because of its proximity to the tower, it was not in the very centre. The core of darkness was definitely inside the actual tower. The 11:11 had brought me to this point under its shadow, quite literally, in order to come to this realization. "Do not enter. Private." said the notice on the gate. I didn't want to enter! However, if it was to be cleared I needed to get into that tower although I had no idea how I could set about clearing it once I was inside.

I started work on my garden, clearing away the weeds by hand. I didn't want to put any chemicals down on this sacred ground so I pulled them up by the roots. Heavy winter rains had swept mounds of earth down the stone steps, burying the path. I scraped away at the earth, digging down to the level of stone. As I did so I revealed even more stone steps that had been hidden for decades. There was so much hidden in my garden. Every time I dug I found something of interest. I once found a massive stone dish that looked like a font or it could have been a basin for washing. Another time I found half a massive iron pot with a handle, the sort that would be hung over an open fire. I was with Bella that day. As we stood looking at my latest find a centipede scampered along the rim.

"Oh, watch out! It's one of those giant centipedes," she said. It was about a 20th of the size of the centipede I had seen shortly after moving into the convent. The centipedes that Bella had referred to as giant were the 'normal' centipedes that these cave houses were infested with. My centipede had been a one-off. I never saw another one and I never want to see another. I sometimes wonder whether the one I saw was the last of its species but as it could well still be alive, I also wondered whereabouts in the convent it might be hiding.

I filled my garden sack with the earth. It was beautiful compost so I was going to use it to create raised beds in the upper garden and grow my own vegetables. But the bag was too heavy to lift so I dragged it up the steps, one step at a time. 23 steps. Suddenly it wasn't a bag of earth that I was dragging up the steps. It was a body.

There were so many bodies to be retrieved. Some were headless, others without limbs. Some were crushed, others disembowelled. There were body parts still in their armour. I picked up heads inside helmets. I had to remove the piles of bodies from the base of the castle walls. They were really heavy. It was hard work. Some were to be taken to the sacred ground but the others could be put into the pit. I was the mover of the bodies. It was an awful job but I was paid by the body so a day like this was a blessing for me. It meant my family could eat well.

Was that a past life recall? Or did I momentarily enter the consciousness of the life of the mover of the bodies and experience his life? If we truly are One Consciousness then everything that I have seen, felt, tasted, touched and experienced has been seen felt, tasted, touched and experienced by the One

Consciousness. And this would be true for the experiences of every single person.

I have entered the consciousness of another life once before. My sister was living in a 16th century cottage within the walls of Salisbury Cathedral Close in Wiltshire, England. The house had recently been renovated as it had been allowed to fall into ruin. My sister told me that nobody had lived in the place for over 100 years. On my first visit I slept in the attic and I had a dreadful night. I experienced the trauma of trench warfare in the First World War, the sounds and smells of those God-forsaken alleys of death and suffering. I woke up calling out for help. When I relayed my experience to my sister she told me that she had forgotten to tell me that injured soldiers had been billeted in the attic during the First World War.

Research into the convent was top of my 'must do' list so I visited Périgueux and spent many hours in the strikingly modern building that housed the archives, poring over old books and maps in search of documented history of my convent. During one of these visits I found an early plan of my land and convent.

"What does it say here?" I asked the librarian, pointing to some obscure French writing on my plot of land.

"That's strange," he said. "I've never seen that before. It says the land is held in common."

"So it's common land?"

"Not really. If it was, it would just say common land. I honestly don't know what this means. It's not a regular garden. And it's closed land. Walled? I'm sorry I can't help you. I don't know why it should be described as closed land being held in common. These are very early texts and things aren't always described very well."

It was also during one of these visits that I met a writer. He helped me to translate some early texts that were held in the library. "What does this mean?" I asked, pointing to part of the text. "It looks like it says Benedictine."

He leaned over my shoulder, his cheek rather too close to mine for comfort.

"Ummm it says, 'and just outside the walls of Montignac was a Benedictine priory...'"

I was stunned. A priory! I simply couldn't understand how this priory had not been mentioned before that point in time.

"Where was it?"

"It doesn't say. It just says outside the walls."

"Outside what walls?"

"The castle walls."

"But it was on my side of the river?"

"Of course it was, because it says just outside the walls of the castle and the castle is near your house."

"The castle of Montignac?"

"Yes, yes. Montignac was a fortified town. It wasn't that big but it was a very important town in its day."

I was thrilled and excited. Armed with a photocopy of the relevant page of the book I returned to the tourist information office and asked for information about the Benedictine priory. Not unexpectedly, I was informed that there had never been a priory on my side of the river. I produced the photocopy as evidence of my statement. There was a great deal of hushed whispering and a flurry of phone calls were made. The atmosphere verged on panic. It took several days but I was eventually informed that there had indeed been a Benedictine priory on my side of the river. I was also told that the local bookshop had a book on the history of the town. I bought it.

The history book was enlightening. With the help of a translator I finally discovered a lot about the medieval history of the town of Montignac. There was written evidence of the Benedictine priory on my side of the river so I now had proof of that fact. It was called St Thomas. Was this the 'small chapel' that the doctor had told me about? I hardly think a priory could be referred to as a chapel. Why had he not mentioned the priory?

Surely he must have known about it? And why had the tourist information denied the existence of a priory on my side of the river? Now I understood why the adjacent road had been called 'road of the priory.' I could hardly believe it!

The first mention of this priory was in 1236 although the authors of the history book believed that St Thomas was founded earlier than the 10th century. It was demolished in 1573 and the stones were reused by the local people to modernise their houses. That would account for the uniform style of many of the houses and also for the beautiful mullioned windows that I had seen in a few properties. It also meant that St Thomas was in existence at the same time as the convent school.

I read that in 1719 the priory walls were still visible but nothing now remained of the priory, not a single trace. Nobody knew for sure exactly where it had been situated. According to tourist information it stood where the cemetery was but I was somewhat wary about trusting their facts.

Perhaps the upper parts of my convent had been built with the very stones of this old priory. No wonder my convent had such a special feel to it for the stones would have been imbued with centuries of prayer.

Obviously the tower was mentioned in the history book. In the 10th century the castle dominated the landscape. It used to have a moat and a drawbridge. Inside was a square Roman dungeon which was erected on a mound. There were 6 rooms in the castle plus a kitchen, basement, forge and little round tower where the money was kept. There were separate rooms for the army. The interior decor was not grand; in fact it was noted that the property suffered from a complete lack of care and by the early 15th century the castle was falling into ruins. There was, however, no direct reference to my 'école de bonnes soeurs.' Yet again I had drawn a blank. If only I could find Le Baron. He seemed to be the man with the answers.

Chapter 24

The Crystal Key

As I sat on my garden swing in the shadow of the hazelnut tree, less than a metre from the edge of the unfenced cliff, I knew I was sitting not far from the site of the former priory. Maybe that grey hooded ghost had been a Benedictine visitor? I could happily sit on my swing for hours, just gazing out at the hills and the passing clouds. I loved the stillness of the area. The swallows would swoop under the covered terrace to pick insects from the mosquito net. They were not afraid of me. In his e-mail more than 3 years earlier Andrew had said that the birds would visit my garden and he was right. They visited in their scores. The place was alive with birdsong. He had also said that I would be working on healing the 2nd chakra, and again he had been right because I felt I had come to terms with my dreadful hitchhiking experience at the age of 21. That trauma had been deeply buried within me, lodged deep in my 2nd chakra but I had finally let go of it and moved on.

Sometimes I lay flat on my back and watched the skies. I watched as the planes flew overhead, as many as 10 per hour. Occasionally a fighter jet shot past fast, low and very loud, ripping the valley apart with a deep roar. Now and then they broke the sound barrier and made the windows crack. Their roaring engines were in sharp contrast to the birds of prey that circled gracefully above me, their orange wings shining in the reflected sun.

Apart from summertime when the town was heaving with tourists, it could be unbelievably quiet in the convent and I spent most of my time there. The fact that I was landlocked and not accessible by car was both positive and negative. The negative was that everything had to be carried a long way from the car to the house: every piece of wood for the wood burner, every bag of cement or bag of vegetables. The positive was that I had no noise from passing cars. I was so glad that I was not isolated in an out of town area. In fact I was in the heart of the conservation area and the house was listed. The silence bounced off the walls. The 2 sets of double gates felt like a protection and I would leave them locked for days at a time. I was undisturbed by everyone and everything. No television or phone, no Internet or passing friends calling in for a cup, of tea and a chat. Time within the boundaries of my land was altered. Whole days would simply disappear. I would be in the convent, unaware of the passage of time and it was only hunger or some bodily discomfort that brought me back into the awareness of passing time. It was as if time was suspended. I don't know what happened during these periods. I didn't fall asleep. I was awake but I was not actually doing anything, just being. I think I might have been leaving my body during these periods. I know I must have spent long periods of time sitting very still because at one point I looked down and saw that a spider had spun a web between my leg and the side of the coffee table!

I seemed to be in a state of consciousness where either time didn't exist or it existed in a different form. I entered a realm beyond time. I was existing in a world within a world and it seemed to be bounded by the boundary walls of the convent. Maybe I had found a doorway into another dimension? Certainly I feel that the total lack of external stimulus allowed me to reach an altered state. I became very clear-headed at this time. I was aware that I was not alone but I was not afraid. I trusted that I was there for a purpose and that by being there I was in alignment with Divine Will. My lack of fear permeated the place and the 4 walls that had spooked me during the ghost and the centipede episodes now comforted me. I began to really love the convent. There was something very soft, feminine and gentle about the energy. It hadn't always felt like that. Those early days had been difficult. Things had begun to shift dramatically after I had played the quantum music, and the 2 year gap when I had been off gathering energetic keys seemed to have allowed a noticeable shift to have taken place.

Yet I could not even begin to imagine the horror and bloodshed that had taken place in Montignac over the centuries. How much blood had soaked into this earth beneath my feet? How many bodies had been thrown from the cliff by my garden swing? How many people had been left to rot in the maze of dungeons that were a stone's throw from my garden? Maybe my work on the energy lines had cleared the residue of those traumatic events. I hoped that was so.

It was during one of my timeless periods that I had a realization. I was sitting on the swing gazing out at the view and playing with my amethyst crystal. In a sudden flash a large piece of the puzzle fell into place. I had been asking for information for almost 4 years, asking why I was in Montignac and what I had to do and why had the 11:11 sent me there, and finally I was starting to get answers. The purpose and method of my work left me in awe of the incredible power and intelligence of the 11:11 sign. The date was June 1st 2011. An 11 day (6+1+2+0+1+1=11).

I was playing with the crystal when it suddenly came away from its silver mount and fell to the ground. My beautiful crystal. As I bent to pick it up I heard a voice. Clairaudience again, just like in Turkey!

You have the crystal key.

5 simple words yet they revealed so much. The moment I heard those few words I instantly understood what I needed to do. Catherine had already told me that by visiting the many sacred sites around the world I was clearing parts of the earth's grid that related directly to the convent. At each of these places I had been 'programmed'. I was the key. Not a metal key like the ones that opened the convent gates, but an energetic key. The energy had been spiralled into me, into my physical and non-

physical bodies using sound and geometric light. At each place I had been imbued with an energetic imprint so in a way I was a walking computer programme. Just as one would download a programme on to a computer, my new energetic blueprint would be downloaded into the crystal grid at the correct time and place in this physical dimension. This was necessary to aid the earth in her ascension.

My beautiful amethyst crystal had been with me on all of my travels. It was almost a part of me. I had owned it for years and I loved it very much. However, this crystal was part of the key. Because the crystal had been with me on all my travels it had been programmed in exactly the same way as me.

I was the key to unlock the crystal grid on the site of my old convent, but the crystal was the powerhouse and it needed to be placed inside the tower to allow the programme to be activated. Once this programme had been loaded into the tower, then the entire grid of light would be affected. There could be no going back. The light would stream through the grid, gradually at first and then in greater quantities, in much the same way that a sink unblocks.

The crystal had to be placed in the tower on the day of the sun, the longest day of the year that we call the summer solstice. No other date or time would do. This was a sophisticated time lock and numbers were a part of its mechanism. Once the crystal had been placed I had to wait 144 days because the only moment the energetic lock could be released through all dimensions was at 11:11am on 11/11/11 according to the local time on that particular longitude and latitude. At that moment I also understood why the 4 had appeared to me so often on my journey back to the convent, because it was exactly 144 days between the summer solstice on June 21st 2011 and the 11/11/11. 144 is 12x12. 12/12/12 will be the last of the triple dates before the 'official' earth ascension on 21/12/2012. The significant and transformational triple dates began on 01/01/01. Then we had 02/02/02, 03/03/03,

04/04/04, 05/05/05, 06/06/06, 07/07/07, 08/08/08, 09/09/09, 10/10/10, 11/11/11 and finally 12/12/12. The number 144 is not a mundane number as it is the number of ascension.

I realized that I needed to be at the convent to allow the connection of energy to take place on the physical plane as well as all the other planes of existence. I didn't know if I would need to just sit quietly in meditation and allow the key to unlock the grid, or whether I'd have to do something ceremonial. I wasn't concerned because I knew my exact role would be revealed to me when the time was right.

I thought about my programming and then compiled a list of the places where I remembered experiencing energy imprints.

1: The high altar at Glastonbury Abbey, Somerset, England, on the spring equinox, 2011
2: The watering hole, Medicine Hat, Alberta, Canada
3: Writing on Stone, Alberta, Canada
4: Sonora oasis, Mexico
5: Ground Zero, New York, USA
6: Ramana's meditation cave, Arunachala, Tiruvannamalai, India
7: High altar, John the Baptist cave church, Cappadocia, Turkey
8: Marudhamalai Murugan temple, Coimbatore, India
9: Meditation room, Sri Aurobindo ashram, Pondicherry, India
10: Thayumanavar Temple, Tiruchirappalli, India
11: Cholula, Mexico
12: Monte Albán (a sound key), Mexico
13: Teotihuacan pyramid of the moon, Mexico
14: Chichén Itzá, Mexico, autumn equinox, 2009

14 places. There was the number 4 again, although 15 would have been more meaningful because 15 as a binary number is

1111.

This was a time lock. As both the date and time were linked to the key, I had to get the crystal into the tower by June 21st. Surely that would be easy enough? It's not as if I had to go far to place it, as the tower was less than a 2 minutes' walk. I thought I'd go and see if there was any activity in the chateau and maybe sound out the owners. I knew that the owners lived in Paris and only occupied the building during the summer months. That was the case with many of the properties in Montignac. In August it was almost as if the town became an extension of Paris.

The chateau was in a dead end street, and even now in the 21st century it was not a welcoming place. Several more notices had been put up since my last visit.

"Private"
"No entry"
"Entry forbidden"
"No entry to the public."

The high metal gates that led to the tower were padlocked. I tried the chateau gates. They were locked too. There was no bell to ring and nowhere to knock, rather like my own house. There was no sign of any people and no cars were parked outside. I wrote a letter, though I did not know who to address it to because there was no nameplate on the mailbox.

Dear Madame et Monsieur,
I am a writer and I live here in Montignac, in Rue des Jardins. I am the author of *The 11:11 Code*. I am currently writing another book. This book concerns your tower.

I wonder if it would be possible to visit the tower and see inside? It would not have to be a long visit and I do not need to see inside the chateau, just the tower. Ideally I would like to visit on June 21st at 11am. Would this be a suitable time and date for you?

I do not have a telephone but you can e-mail me on the e-mail address on this envelope.

Kind Regards, Hilary Carter

I wrote "Le Chateau" on the envelope and put it in the box.

It began to rain as I walked away from the chateau. If Bella had been right about the 'ac' ending of a town meaning a link with water, Montignac was aptly named for the water did indeed flow down the hills. It flowed down the middle of the path, down the sides of the road and down the cliffs. The town was just one big waterfall and I was living in the middle of it. I was on the 1.1 line of longitude where it crossed the 45 degrees of latitude. 45 degrees is a renowned latitude because it is exactly halfway between the equator and the pole. It is a magical and mystical latitude because of that reason. That is probably why that there were so many Buddhist monasteries and retreats in the local area.

Following the 45 degree line of latitude due east from Montignac, the first city of any size that falls exactly on the 45 degree line is Turin. This latitude is sometimes referred to as the 45th parallel. There are known to be 2 triangles of magic on the earth, the white magic triangle and the black magic triangle. The black magic triangle is between San Francisco, London and Turin. The white magic is between Lyon, Prague and Turin. It was almost certain that my work at the convent was linked to the intersection of these triangles in Turin.

Chapter 25

Summer Solstice

It started off as an overcast morning. It was Midsummer's Day, one of the 4 most sacred days of the year. Today was the day that I somehow had to get into the tower to plant the crystal. As I sat in my small kitchenette eating toast and nut butter and drinking tea I noticed the reflection of the tower in the window watching me. At last, after almost 4 years of looking at the tower from the outside, I was going to see what it was like observing my convent from within the tower. Just as I was thinking that thought the lightning flashed and momentarily lit up the tower. That was followed by a sudden, massive crack of thunder. The windows rattled and the lights flickered. The thunder rumbled through the valley and I felt the earth tremble. Even my tea shook. It was as if the valley was being ripped apart.

The shock of the sudden, short storm (there was only the one crack and one flash) brought me out in goose bumps but I once again I refused to come from fear. Come hell or high water or even cracking thunder, I was going to plant that crystal in the tower. Nothing would stop me. However, I knew that at some deeper level my intentions for the day had been noted.

I sincerely hoped that the owners would permit me to enter. Although I had not received a reply to my letter and even though nobody had answered the chateau doors when I had stood outside and called out "Bonjour" on several occasions, I was heading out with positive intentions. I knew I needed to prepare myself well because I realized that entering the tower would be no walk in the park. I was going to be stepping into the tower of darkness and I wasn't going to take any chances. I needed to make use of every form of protection that I could. Although I wasn't afraid I certainly wasn't looking forward to this visit. I was doing this work alone on the physical plane but I was being used as an instrument by the forces of light from other levels. As usual I tried not to think ahead. If placing the crystal had to be done it had to be done and I was going to do it. End of story.

I showered in lavender soap then massaged my feet with sandalwood oil. I played the Quantum K music as I dressed in my white top and trousers then I sprayed my aura with protective spray, created in a quartz singing bowl and containing the essence of essential oils and crystals. I picked some dried sage and lavender from the garden and burned it in my Tibetan bowl. I smudged my aura with the smouldering smoke. Finally I anointed my chakras with clary sage.

I collected together the things I needed: my camera, the much loved amethyst crystal and a copy of my book *The 11:11 Code* as a gift for the owner of the chateau.

It was time to go and face the tower. I had written in the letter that I would arrive at 11am so I left my place at 2 minutes to 11, strolled slowly along the beautiful pedestrian street and crossed the road by the spring. I walked up Rue de la Tour (road of the Tower) towards the chateau. Yet another new notice had been put up.

"Visits to the chateau are not permitted."

I hoped that wasn't directed at me.

The gates that led to the tower were locked and padlocked. It was hardly very welcoming but then what would you expect from such a place? The bells on the church struck 11 as I approached the other set of gates that led to the front door of the chateau. There was a van parked immediately outside and I could hear voices through an open window on the first floor. Great! Someone was home. I knocked on the metal part at the bottom of the gate, called out, "Bonjour!" and waited.

As I stood there in the sun I observed an eagle circling

overhead, high in the sky directly above my head. Nobody answered my call so I knocked again. I saw a woman glance out of the window and I caught her eye. She couldn't pretend she had not seen me. "Bonjour!" I called up at the window. She ignored me, turned her back and disappeared out of sight.

Now that I knew that she knew I was there I waited. Maybe I was destined to be let me in at exactly 11:11 and that was why there was a delay...

11:11 came and went. 11:22 passed too. I could hear the woman talking to the man. He was delivering a washing machine and they were having difficulty getting it to fit in the kitchen. I could clearly hear the conversation. She knew I was coming to visit and she knew I was waiting but still she did not come to the gate. I called out again. Maybe she thought I would just give up and go away but I wouldn't. Personally I thought it was downright rude to treat another human being in this way. At the very least it was discourteous. Finally, at 11:33 she came to the entrance. Her appearance was very un-French. Her curly fair hair framed her face like a crumpled halo.

"Good morning, Madame," I said in my best French. "I am the writer who sent you a note asking to visit the tower. I have brought you a gift," I said, handing her a copy of my book. She took it from me. "It is very important for me to visit the tower to help me to write my next book so I do hope you will permit me to enter."

She glanced briefly at the cover of the book.

"It's in English," she announced and handed it straight back to me.

"And can you not read?" she continued. "Nobody is permitted to visit the tower. It is not open to the public."

"But, Madame, I am not just any member of the public. I'm not a tourist. I am a writer and I live in the next road to you. Your tower overshadows my house and it plays an important part in my next book."

"No visits are permitted."

"Madame, I realize you are probably very busy but all I ask is a quick 5 minute visit."

"There is no way you can visit my house."

"It's not your house I want to visit, it's the tower. Until I visit the tower I cannot finish the book. I only ask that…"

Despite the fact that I was mid-sentence she turned and walked off back into the chateau, leaving my words hanging in the air.

What was I to do? I had to get the crystal placed and it had to be on that day, summer solstice 2011. This day would not come again. Timing was crucial with work of this nature. Still the eagle circled above me. By now the sun had come out in full force and I was sweltering as I stood there. I sat down on the step and waited. I couldn't give up. I had to get that crystal into the tower. A second eagle joined the first one. Circling birds seemed to be a common theme on this 11:11 path. I felt a shift in the energy as the day reached noon on the longest day of the year. The midday bells tolled and still I waited. The overhead wires buzzed. Maybe I could try grovelling, getting on my hands and knees and begging?

Tourists walked past me at regular intervals. The chateau and the adjacent tower were on the same historic route as my place in Rue des Jardins. Still I sat on the steps of the chateau. 12:11. Then 12:22. Then 12:33. All the significant minutes were passing. By now I had been waiting for one and a half hours. Maybe this was just resistance from the forces of darkness. Maybe the woman was being unconsciously influenced. What she didn't know was just how stubborn I could be. What I didn't know was that she was just as stubborn as me! When stubbornness meets stubbornness, stalemate exists.

Suddenly the gate creaked and I stood up. It was the delivery man with the new washing machine. He wheeled it back to the van and drove off. They had obviously not managed to squeeze it in. Now the woman had no distractions. When she came to close the gate behind the delivery man I could see that she was genuinely surprised that I was still waiting there. She must have sensed my determination. Or maybe she was just curious to find out how someone could be so resilient and patient.

"Please, Madame, please just let me see inside the tower and I will never bother you again. I realize you are probably very busy and often get requests from the public to see your historic tower but I implore you, please permit me a quick visit."

"Why do you want to see inside?" she asked.

I hesitated. How could I answer? That I just wanted to plant a crystal in there as part of an energetic key that would aid the ascension of the earth? No. It sounded too way out.

"I need to write a description of the interior of the tower and to do that I need to see it." Not strictly true but not strictly a lie either.

"The entrance to the tower is through my house and you are not coming through my house. My house is private and not open to the public."

"But, Madame, I can close my eyes and not look at your house. And I'd like to tell you that you are very welcome to visit my home. It is a former 'école de bonne soeurs'. It was a convent school. You can come and have tea with me whenever you wish. My door is nearly always open. It is only closed if I am out or if I am working."

She wouldn't budge. There was no yielding. She was immovable. She would not let me in. By now I was getting desperate.

"Madame, I have to tell you that it would be best for you in the long run if you let me in. It would be wiser to allow me entry rather than refuse me. You might regret it if you don't let me in." I have to confess that I spoke the last sentence with a warning tone of voice. It seemed to help.

"You can't get in because the door to the tower is blocked."

"Blocked?"

"Yes, from the inside. I have closed it so the teenagers can't get in."

"How do you get in there then?" I asked.

"There is a passage from the house to the tower. I get in through that passage."

I realized that she was telling the truth and gradually our conversation softened and became more personal. We began to talk about our daughters and I discovered that like me she had struggled as a single parent. Not only that, she too was a Pisces sun sign. She owned the chateau, a woman alone, having inherited it through her mother's side of the family. It was when she revealed that her own mother was a 7th daughter that it dawned on me what was happening. She had a part to play in this drama. It was not me that had to place the crystal. It was her. Dare I ask her? Could I trust her? I mentally ran through my options. It was either ask her to plant it for me or I would have to clamber over the railings later that night and try and get it through one of the high unglazed windows. I had to go with my instinct and ask for her help.

I uncurled my fingers and revealed the amethyst. To anybody else it probably just looked like a nice crystal but to me it was much more than that. It had consciousness. It was beautifully cut. At the base the planes were 5-sided and there were 7 of them. At the pinnacle were 8 diamond shapes. Between the base and the pinnacle all the planes were 4-sided diamonds. This crystal had travelled thousands of miles with me and I loved it. My soul brother Will had given me the amethyst. Will, like me, had been born on the cusp of sensitivity which falls between February 19th and 23rd.

She gazed down at the crystal lying in the palm of my hand.

"This has been with me for over 15 years," I explained. "Please can you place it in the tower? It is very important that this is done today."

She looked at me with an odd expression. Doubtless she had never received a request quite like that before.

"You think I'm mad, don't you?" I asked.

"A little bit," she replied. Yet I sensed that she understood that she was being asked to do something that was beyond her understanding but that I was sincere in my request.

"I need to explain to you how important this work is for the future of the planet."

I tried to explain to her why it was so important but the subtleties were lost because of my lack of French esoteric vocabulary so I took her by the shoulders and looked directly into her eyes.

"Please, please," I pleaded with the soul language of my eyes. For a moment she hesitated, then she took the amethyst from my hand with a slightly amused expression on her face. Something happened when she took it. As she held it in her open palm one of the facets caught the sunlight and for a moment a ray of light reflected towards her face and hit her third eye. I saw the crystal rotate even though her hand was still. I immediately understood what had happened. Her energy was needed as the final imprint on the crystal key.

"It's broken," she said, pointing to the small hole at the top where the silver hook had come away.

"Yes, it fell."

"And I have important work to do, placing this crystal in the tower?"

She had no idea just how important her task was. And how important a role she would be playing in this drama. I was glad the amethyst was in feminine hands for I knew that the work being done was linked to the Divine feminine energy.

"Yes," I replied. "Could you do it as soon as possible? Now would be the best but whatever happens it must be today."

"I'll do it now before my lunch," she said and turned away, walking back to her gate. I looked at my phone. It was approaching 1:10pm. By the time it was placed it was likely to be 1:11pm. And so it was that the crystal was successfully placed in the tower on the summer solstice of 2011 by 1:11pm.

Chapter 26

Sabberan and the Golden Beings

The crystal was planted and the 144 day countdown to 11/11/11 had started so I knew that it was time to make contact with Sabberan. He was in his caravan in the Scottish highlands but luckily he had access to Skype.

"Hello, Hilary. I received your e-mail. What is it you need help with?" Sabberan asked.

It was good to hear his voice again. We had not spoken for several years, not since he had helped with the clearing of the Spanish convent I had once owned. My 11:11 journey could be quite lonely at times, with nobody to bounce ideas and feelings off of so I enjoyed the opportunity to talk to someone with Sabberan's depth of understanding and high level of consciousness. Sabberan is the keeper of the Keys of Creation and he is part of a soul energy that has been given the Keys of Creation to wield on behalf of Source.

"It's more of the same I think," I replied. "I have bought another convent, this time in France. I was led there by the number 11. The convent was haunted but now I have cleared it using quantum music. However, there is a tower nearby that emanates darkness. Whenever I am in the convent, in the garden or even in the town, I can literally feel the pressure of that tower. To say that it had a powerful dark presence would be a huge understatement. I can hardly put into words what I experience when I am within its shadow."

"Can you tell me a bit about it?"

"The tower is all that remains of the fortified town of Montignac. There were originally 12 towers but 11 towers have either fallen down or have been knocked down. Only this one remains. I'm sure you know how dark the history of this part of

France was, with the witch hunts, the hunting down of the Cathars, the wars between France and England and the dreadful animosity between the Huguenots and the Catholics. I read in the Cadogan Guide to the Dordogne that the counts of this particular fortified town were renowned for being the most evil in the whole of France. "

There was no response from Sabberan. I thought we'd been cut off. After all, he was in an isolated area. Maybe there was no signal. I waited. No sound.

"Hello. Are you there?" I eventually asked.

"Yes, yes, I'm just tuning in. I need to know where the tower is. Whereabouts in the south of France is it? Is it anywhere near Carcassonne?"

"Not that near, but it is in South West France, about 2 hours east of Bordeaux. It's in an area where the Cathars preached and it's also right in the heart of prehistoric France."

"And how old is it?"

"The tower is 10th century, but it's built on Roman foundations. There are loads of dungeons and a maze of tunnels dug out of the rock directly underneath it."

There was silence again, another very long silence. Again I waited. I could sense that he was working at another level.

"Okay that's good. I'm getting a connection here…"

Another pause. I could hear Sabberan sighing. Deep sighs.

"I know that you resonate with the number 11, but in this instance it is the 12 that is relevant. We are talking here of an octave. 12 is very relevant. Your consciousness is tuned to 11, but you are being guided to recognize the 12. On the spiritual path 12 indicates stable change. It is change that will hold. Although you can only see one tower, the other 11 exist in the non-physical. They are still there at the etheric level. When the 12 appears it indicates the completion of an octave. An octave has 12 notes, from middle C to 'middle' B. As we progress spiritually we progress through octaves."

I had been under the impression that an octave had 7 notes but my later research confirmed that Sabberan was correct. There was another long pause before Sabberan spoke again.

"I can feel the energy of the Counts. It's extremely negative energy, very dark." I heard him take a sharp intake of breath before he continued. Goodness knows what he was picking up now.

"There is something I need to tell you, Hilary. You have a past life connection to these Counts."

I wondered whether he was suggesting that I had been one of these evil counts in a previous life. I didn't ask him to clarify that point. All I can say is that to truly know the light one must also know the dark.

"Before we go on, there is a part of you that needs to be cleared. It is holding a shadowy energy. You know that when you do global work like this you are working on your own energy field at the same time, don't you? Clearing takes place on a personal level as well as a cosmic level."

That was exactly what Andrew had said in his e-mails 4 years earlier. He had told me that I was clearing second chakra stuff by being in France.

"Yes, I know it's the microcosm and the macrocosm. Can we clear that shadow that I am carrying?" I asked.

"Yes, we can do that now. But firstly I need to know, what is your intention regarding the convent?" he asked.

"I'm not sure that I know my intention yet. I had been considering using it as an individual retreat centre, a place where people can go to find their Divine feminine. But maybe I'll live there. I really don't know. I know that I was guided there originally to do this clearing and maybe when that's done things will become clearer."

"Important step needs to be taken here linked to the shift in 2012. Are you aware that the work you are doing is clearing work that is linked to the ascension process?"

"Yes."

I did realize that. I knew that my 11:11 journey was both a personal journey leading towards enlightenment, and as I worked on bringing more light to the earth, I was becoming more enlightened. I felt like an onion being peeled layer by layer. Sabberan explained enlightenment as happening in stages and there comes a point when you move up an octave that takes you across the threshold. At that point enlightenment is assured and there is no turning back. You just have to keep clearing and clearing until you reach the level that is the threshold of enlightenment. Then creation opens up to you.

Sabberan told me that enlightenment is possible for everyone as long as they are prepared to do the clearing work. He also told me that by undertaking my 11:11 journey I was clearing deep-rooted shadows of my consciousness. The earth too had the same shadows, pockets of dark energy and stuck stagnant negativity. Sabberan explained that there were thousands of lightworkers on the planet at this time whose specific purpose was to break through into the earth's dark energies, thereby allowing the darkness to release into the light.

He said that science has shown that electrons collapse 13 billion times a second. They disappear and then reappear. When they return they are complete. Nothing is lost as they come and go. They disappear into the void. Void is Source. Some people might refer to Source as God.

Our consciousness follows the same pattern. Every element of our consciousness returns to source 13 billion times a second. We are constantly travelling/vibrating between the physical and the non-physical. However, when we pass through these 'filters' we are not pure consciousness. We see and perceive according to our level of consciousness. The lower our level of consciousness, the more clogged up the filter. Our clarity is clouded by holding on to things. We can hold on to feelings, emotions, thoughts, people, possessions, beliefs, addictions and so on.

My own understanding of his explanation was that our light is blocked by any aspect of ourselves that is not vibrating at the level of Source. Our Divine Self does not hold on to anything. It just is. In each moment it exists in pure consciousness and does not react to anything. It acts from a space of no-thing-ness. When we have loosened the ego there is no filter which would mean that the filter Sabberan mentioned is what I call the ego. Sabberan refers to the coming and going as "passing through the gateways of translation."

"I am now in the presence of Supra consciousness which is at a higher level than super-consciousness. The reptilian consciousness has overlaid our true consciousness and programmed us to hold on to everything and not to release. That is the my/mine consciousness. Instead of being the light which is our true nature, we hold on to things from fear."

David Icke mentions this reptilian consciousness in his work so I was familiar with this term. I also realized why the great spiritual teachers drummed home the message of non-attachment. And non-attachment was a theme running through my 11:11 journey. I was constantly having to detach myself from things such as homes, possessions, people, ideas, thoughts, expectations and places.

"The Lords of karma are with me now," Sabberan continued.

I glanced at the time displayed in the corner of my laptop screen. 12:12 exactly.

"They are helping with this work… it's infiltrating as far as the Mediterranean… and more… further."

I could hear deep sighs from Sabberan as he was doing this work. There were even one or 2 groans. It was quite a while before he spoke again but I waited patiently, realizing that as we linked he was doing the necessary work.

"There was an ET portal between the towers. It's being closed down now. This was an entrance point for shadows."

There was another long pause whilst the ET portal was being

closed. Then I heard Sabberan gasping in wonder. At the same time I could feel my heart opening and expanding. I felt compelled to stretch out my arms and open my chest. What was happening? It was something vast. I'd never felt an energy like this before.

"Are you feeling the shift?" he asked. "This is incredible!"

So that's what it was! I could indeed feel the shift. I felt like a living star. It was if I had been touched by a magic wand and, just like in the cartoons I used to watch as a child, the touch of the wand had transformed me and I sparkled. My eyes were drawn to the picture of the Indian God Shiva on my living room wall. He looked straight into my eyes as I stood there in wonder.

"This is linking to the Mediterranean again. I remember this happened with the Spanish convent... it's affecting other places on earth too. There are 5 other points that link to the towers."

He did not state the places but I felt a very strong pull towards Malta and the adjoining island of Gozo. Gillian was spending the winter on those islands so I suspected she had been guided there to aid this planetary work.

"I'm remembering beyond time now. I had said to you to turn to me for help as you delve into the shadows." I glanced at the clock on my laptop. 12:22. I knew that he was speaking the truth. I love the reassurance of the language of numbers.

"This is incredible!" repeated Sabberan. "There has been a 7 octave shift in the earth's frequency. I have been waiting for this. I have been waiting so long. This is so powerful. I wonder if earth herself is crossing a threshold... Now a golden light pillar has been placed in the site of the tower and the Golden ones are taking their places."

"Golden ones? Who are they? Where are they? At the tower?" I asked.

"The golden pillar is at the tower. The golden beings are placed all around the earth, at strategic points on the grid. This is so beautiful." I could hear the emotion in his voice. I felt my heart respond at the thought of these golden beings and tears filled my eyes, a sure sign to me that my heart chakra was open.

"These new energies are being integrated into the world now. Higher frequency light grids are beginning to form around the earth as we speak… wait… no… it's earth's Merkaba field that is rising in frequency."

A Merkaba is an energy field. Every single thing in the universe including the earth has a Merkaba field around it.

"I have your Higher Self here with me, a body of radiant light. She is giving me your true name. She keeps repeating it to me. Do you want to know it?"

"Of course!"

"It's an unusual name. She is telling me that your star name is Cynkarta."

I thanked him for this information. I already had my spiritual name (Hari) but now that my light body was integrating I also had my star name. This confirmed what Catherine had told me in India when I had received my transmission in Palolem, India. "I am preparing for you a body of light," were the words that she had downloaded from Babaji. I was now stepping into that body.

"Is there anything else you need to ask?" asked Sabberan.

"You mentioned an ET portal. What is that?"

"Extra-terrestrial. A portal to allow extra-terrestrial energies through."

I was momentarily dumbfounded but I quickly moved on, taking this rare opportunity to get some answers. I had owned the convent for almost 4 years, 4 years wondering why I had been guided there by the 11:11 and at last I was beginning to get some answers.

"What are the 5 places you mentioned?"

"It is better they are not known."

I didn't need to know.

"How do you feel?" he asked.

I opened my eyes and glanced around my room. Everything

looked clear and light, as if my eyes were windows that had just been cleaned.

"I feel clear. Is the work done now? Do I need to do anything else?" I asked.

Again there was a pause.

"The clearing work is done. But you must run this past your own knowing. I am telling you that I perceive the work on the tower as being completed, but as an empowered being you need to run this past your own intuition. How does it feel to you? Does it feel finished?"

It did feel finished and I was relieved about that! I was now in my light body and the Golden Beings were in their locations to aid the transition of the earth. The earth had moved up 7 octaves and the time was now exactly 1:11pm. The date was 29/07/2011.

$$2+9=11$$
$$0+7=7$$
$$2+0+1+1=4$$
$$11+7+4=22$$

Twice 11. And 22 is the ultimate master number. Number underpins the Universe and the Universe operates according to mathematical Laws.

At last real progress had been made. Sabberan quietly and selflessly works for the benefit of all. We had agreed to do these clearings together before incarnating.

"Turn to me when you reach the point where you need help," he had said. "I will be there to help and support you with the work at the deepest level."

I was so grateful that he was there to turn to in my moment of need and I thank him for his help.

Chapter 27

Lifting the Veil

Shortly after the crystal was placed in the tower it was as if a veil was lifted, the veil between the past and present. A window through time opened for me and it wasn't an easy experience. My erstwhile pleasant wanderings along the numerous picturesque streets became challenging to say the least. I would be walking along a narrow passageway soaking in the beauty when suddenly and unexpectedly I would be transported back in time. I don't know why but it always seemed to happen at corners. Maybe that's where the energy congealed or maybe because that's where enemies met. The violence of those dark times was appalling. I glimpsed images of disembowelling and beheading, babies being sliced from limb to limb, body parts lying on the path (some still contained within armour), the grotesque dead bodies of mutilated women and children, pools of vomit and more. I saw blood literally running down the hills in the same way that the water runs down the hills after the rain.

Even worse than the sights were the sounds. On some occasions when the veil slipped I heard blood-curdling screams that churned my stomach. The terrified neighing of horses, desperate pleas of women being mercilessly raped, children calling out helplessly for their mothers, babies screaming, men groaning, thudding horses' hooves on the earth and other cruelties so horrific that I do not even want to mention them on these pages.

At times I really struggled to keep my consciousness in the 21st century. One day as I walked past my outbuilding that contained the medieval oven I realized why I had experienced such a strong reaction on the one and only time I had stepped over the threshold of that stone hut. I glimpsed some of the tortures that had happened within those stone walls. That historic medieval oven that Claude had been so keen to show me was being used as an instrument of torture. Red hot irons were on the fire and the cries of agony I heard were accompanied by the sound and smell of sizzling flesh. I once caught a glimpse of a man having a poker put into his eyes and another time a woman had been shoved into the flames and her hair was on fire. Each time the veil slipped and revealed the horrors of those dark times I chanted my mantra. "Om Namah Shiva," I repeated over and over again, erasing those ghastly events from the records of time.

Montignac had been occupied as recently as the Second World War. The residents of the town had gone to bed one Saturday night with the French flag flying on the town hall and had woken up on the Sunday morning to find the Nazi flag in its place. Resistance in this area of France had been particularly strong. So many brave souls had been prepared to risk their lives to fight the Germans. Plaques on remote road junctions marked the spots where many freedom fighters had been executed. Apparently there was a special branch of the SS in town. The local forests provided cover and a certain amount of protection for the resistance movement.

Life under Nazi rule was not easy. The farmers worked in their fields under armed guards and the majority of the crops had to be handed over to the occupying force. The residents had lived in fear for years. Some of the atrocities that took place were unbelievable. On the morning of June 10th, the SS entered the Dordogne village of Oradour-sur-Glane. The troops gathered all the people from nearby hamlets into Oradour and then they surrounded the village. Men and women were separated The men were herded into barns and garages. The women and children were crowded into the church. The slaughter began with a single pistol shot. Within minutes, the population of Oradour ceased to exist. 642 men, women, and children had been killed. After machine-gunning the helpless residents, the Germans burned many of the buildings down. The place has been left untouched as a memorial and a reminder.

A few kilometres from Montignac is the small hamlet of Fanlac. One day 2 old men who lived in the village took pity on a couple of young German soldiers and invited them into their home. They gave them fresh goat's cheese, freshly baked bread and wine. After enjoying this feast given in love, the soldiers then asked the brothers what they knew of the resistance movement in the area. When the brothers could not supply them with any information the soldiers took out their guns and shot them dead in cold blood.

Chapter 28

Church of Mary, Ephesus

One thing I can say with certainty is that you can always expect the unexpected on the 11:11 path. Out of nowhere the number 777 began to appear everywhere and I mean everywhere. 777? This had never happened before. I knew that 7 represented the spiritual and I knew I was on a spiritual journey, but what place did it have on my 11:11 journey? Along with the 777, the ancient city of Ephesus raised its profile. I recalled that Ephesus was one of the 7 churches mentioned in the book of Revelations. Was that why the 7 was appearing? 777? How did this link to 11:11? I turned to the book of Revelation. I didn't have to look far to find mention of the 7 churches for there it was in the first chapter. Chapter 1, verse 11. That's 1.11.

What thou seest, write in a book, and send it unto the 7 churches which are in Asia; unto Ephesus, and unto Smyrna, and unto Pergamos, and unto Sardis, and unto Philadelphia, and unto Laodicea.
King James Bible

Sometimes I don't understand the logic of the 11:11 signs. Actually, let me change that to: OFTEN I don't understand the logic of the 11:11 signs. Why could I not have been guided to visit Ephesus on my last visit to Turkey? My travels had taken me to Turkey several times already. I had spent the entire winter there not long before. As much as I liked the place, I simply didn't feel as if I had the energy to go all the way back there just to visit Ephesus. I knew I would return one day to walk in that ancient city but I imagined that day would be far in the future. I had tried to arrange a visit to Ephesus when I had been to

Cappadocia but it had not been possible, and when something doesn't flow I don't normally force the issue. Now I was wishing that I had been a bit more determined. Still, I may have my questions but by now I had learned that the questions were only arising from my mind and I needed to let go of them and just trust.

Ephesus... you have to go to Ephesus... you need to visit Ephesus.

The nagging voice wouldn't go away. It spoke to me with such insistence that in the end the urge to go back became so overpowering that I did indeed pack my bags and return to Turkey.

Although there were dozens of local companies in Izmir offering tours of the ancient ruined city of Ephesus, I decided to travel there by local bus. That way I would have the freedom to stay in the city for as long as I liked and I would be able to wander wherever I liked. As I knew this visit was being prompted largely by intuition, complete freedom to follow my inner urges, number signs, synchronicities and intuition was important.

The day I chose to go to Ephesus was the day I woke with dreadful toothache. It was so bad that I had no choice but to visit the local dentist and have my tooth taken out. As the tooth was a molar with 3 roots, the dentist had difficulty removing it. As he struggled to extract it the metal instrument he was using slipped and hit me sharply on the roof of my mouth, drawing blood and leaving me with a raised bruise and a deep cut. To most people this would have just been an unfortunate accident, but I happen to know that this point is a very significant point in the physical body. In many meditation practices the tip of the tongue is placed to the roof of mouth to connect the 2 main paths of the microcosmic orbit. How many people have injured this part of their body? How many people have drawn blood from that inaccessible point? I suspect the answer is 'very few'.

I knew that there must be a reason for this to happen on the day I was going to Ephesus. The fact that it bled was particularly interesting because blood follows energy. Where we bleed is a release of energy. I could only suppose that my presence at Ephesus would be releasing energy on a very significant part of the earth's energy system and my sore mouth was a case of the macrocosm being reflected in the microcosm.

I delayed my visit by one day whilst I recovered from my dental trauma. I finally arrived on a very hot September morning. The local bus dropped me on the main road and I walked the final 2 kilometres on foot, past the massive walls of the gymnasium.

As I entered through the turnstile at the entrance I glanced at my phone. It was exactly 11:11am. I was glad to see the 11:11 appearing especially as this particular trip had been purely inspired by gut feeling and the number 777 and no 11:11 signs whatsoever. The 11:11 signs had not started to appear until I set off for the airport, when I arrived at the check-in desk at exactly 1:11pm and was seated in row 11 on the plane.

My first stop at Ephesus was the massive amphitheatre. I sat for a while on the steps of this architectural masterpiece. It was a massive construction and despite the fact that September was not high season, it was busy.

Then I wandered around before heading for the church of Mary, which is also known as the council church. The church was packed with tourists, all listening to their guides. I stood on the edge of one of the English-speaking groups to eavesdrop and I heard how the Council of Nicaea had met in this very place in 431 AD to discuss the issue of Mary as mother of God. After a 10 minute lecture the English-speaking group moved on to the next site on their agenda. I was so thankful that I was not on an organized tour. I wanted to stay in this church and soak up the atmosphere. I wandered around the site and saw the baptism pool. I stepped down into the very space where the early Christians had been baptised with full immersion.

Gradually the other tour groups began to leave. It was lunch time and doubtless they would be going to eat in a local restaurant, followed by the compulsory visit to a carpet factory. Within 15 minutes all the groups had gone, leaving just a few stragglers. Soon they too left. I couldn't believe it. Less than 20 minutes after arriving at the Mary church, I was completely alone.

I sat on the high altar marvelling at the fact that I had the entire church to myself. Even the fact that there were no barriers preventing me from sitting on the altar was incredible. As I sat there I soon felt the now familiar feeling of an energetic interplay of cosmic energy with my energy field. I was having a download. I sat amidst a swirling and brilliant geometry of light. My third eye was dazzled with a webbing of diamond light. Then a tone began to surround me like a silver disc that hummed at the level of my ears. Light geometry and tone in the same download? This was a new experience for me. There was no personal message for me in this download. It was purely an imprint. All the other energy imprints had been received by both my own energy field and the amethyst crystal, but this one was different as the crystal was not involved. The last imprint into the crystal key had been from the chateau owner though her third eye point but the last imprint into my energy field was from the high altar at Ephesus. The key into my energy field was right there on the high altar, not in the baptism pool or the round stone font. And somehow my guides and helpers from other realms had completely cleared the entire church so that I could be imprinted in a clear and extremely powerful space. Miracles happen regularly in my life and this was one of them.

Later I realized why I had not been guided to Ephesus on one of my previous visits to Turkey. It was because I needed to collect the last imprint during the 144 day period between the summer solstice and 11/11/11. The date of collection of the final energetic imprint was a binary date: 01/10/11. It was the 15th imprint therefore had the link to 11:11 as the number 15 translates to 1111 in the binary system.

Chapter 29

Havan

After my trip to Ephesus I had time to return to Devon, England, to check on a building project I was involved in. Whilst I was there I saw a poster in the local shop. A nearby health centre was advertising an open day, giving everyone the opportunity to try all the different treatments that were on offer. There was only one therapy that I had never heard of and that was called BodyTalk. I had an amazing taster session, so much so that when the therapist told me that a training course was about to be happening in a nearby town, I expressed an interest in attending. My diary was quite full. I only had 2 free weekends before my return to France. They just happened to be the 2 weekends when the course was taking place. All I had to do now was to find the £550 I needed to pay for it.

I walked to the house where I was staying and opened the door to my bedroom. There was a brown envelope lying on the bed. It hadn't been there when I had left earlier that morning. It contained exactly £550 in cash, not a penny more nor a penny less.

Living life by numbers, signs and synchronicities makes decision making much easier. Of course I could have used this money to pay the electricity bill but because of the synchronicity of the amount it was clear to me that the money was intended as payment for the course.

How had that money got there? Somebody owed me quite a lot of money. He had fallen on difficult times so I hadn't pursued him. I knew the money would arrive when the time was right. Now was the time! He had found a new job and as he had just been paid he was able to pay me £550 towards his debt. Whilst I was out he had put the money on my bed to be sure it got to me.

Had he paid me £500 I would probably have used the money to pay bills, but to pay me the EXACT amount of the BodyTalk course was such a strong sign that I immediately booked my place on the course.

During the 4 day training, each participant was given one full BodyTalk session by the course instructor. This took place in front of the group as part of the learning process. When it was my turn to lie on the couch I was asked if there was anything I wanted to explore. I asked for help with my arachnophobia and my issue with insects in general. I also described my extreme reaction to the giant centipede at the French convent. That was my main concern. The instructor took my wrist and it felt as if she was wiggling it about, but I knew that she was accessing my subconscious or my energy field. I had never met this woman before and she knew nothing about my background. After a few minutes she spoke.

"I'm getting the word 'attack'."

What could she mean, attack? Maybe she was talking about an attack at the convent during the religious wars? Or picking up on the numerous times that the castle had been attacked?

"Well I'm sure that the convent must have been attacked at some point in its history," I replied.

"No. It's not the convent."

"Well maybe you mean the centipede. That wasn't attacking me. I don't think they even bite."

"No, that's not it. I'm getting attack," she repeated.

"Well even though I was frightened of it I wouldn't have done anything to hurt it. I wouldn't attack it or anything."

"No, that's not it."

There was a lengthy silence. Neither of us spoke. I was trolling through my memory bank, searching for clues. What could she be referring to? Attack? What attack? Panic attack?

Then suddenly the penny dropped. Of course! It was the attack that I had been lucky to survive, the fat, red-faced French man who had attempted to strangle me when I was 21! I let out an involuntary gasp of astonishment.

"What?" she asked.

"I know what attack you are referring to. It happened when I was 21. I had not been back to the south of France since that time. It was such a horrific experience that I vowed never to return to that area. And now I am actually living in the very area where I was attacked!"

She continued moving my wrist and then she spoke again.

"The centipede represents all that terror that you experienced when you were 21. It was a reaction on your part. You know in your mind that the centipede cannot kill you, but somehow you have linked that creature with that dreadful experience. Now we need to undo that connection and release the feelings of terror that you have been carrying round inside you all these years."

Thinking about it later, I could understand why I had unconsciously linked my attacker with the centipede. Both were threatening, dark, fat and hairy. I had found myself in an enclosed place (the convent) with the centipede just as I had found myself in an enclosed place (the car) with my attacker. The centipede had moved suddenly just as my attacker had pounced suddenly. I had run fast and far to escape my attacker just as I had run fast and as far as I could from the centipede in the convent. Now I understood why my response to the sight of the centipede had been so over the top.

She then started tapping my body in various places, asking me questions and giving me visualizations. After about 10 minutes she stopped and it was time to return to my seat. Following my attack I (Hilary) would have refused to go back to the Dordogne in this life. It was the 11:11 that had guided me back to there and had led me to this healing. I was so glad to have let go of the trauma of my attack at last.

Having completed the BodyTalk training I had one weekend more before my return to France. It was October 2011 and the full moon was in Aries. I was at the Babaji ashram near Exeter, Devon, for the full moon fire-ceremony known as Havan. I was sitting by the fire pit in the garden having showered and missed breakfast. It was necessary to be clean and fasted to attend Havan.

The fire pit is considered to be an altar and is treated accordingly. There are many aspects to a Havan. There are hundreds of little details in the preparations, the offerings, the decorations, and the performance, as well as the proper clean-up and handling of everything involved, even down to the ashes left afterwards. As one learns about all these details and surrenders to the beauty and holiness of it all, the ancient and all-pervading quality of the element of fire becomes something very special.

In almost every ancient religion on this earth, fire plays an important role. The smoke of the fire takes the prayers up into the ethers to where the Gods reside. The offerings are transmuted into a form that is ingestible, or digestible, to these Gods.

It can be compared to the way that we swallow food; and through the fire in our digestive tract, this food is made into energy usable by our bodies. Those with weak digestion have a cool-burning fire while those with strong digestion have a nice hot flame. By the same token, the fire ceremony takes the food offered, adds light to it in the form of fire, and makes it into energy to 'feed' the Gods. When honoured in this way, while reciting their names, it is their duty to offer blessings to us and to take care of us.

Once the ceremony begins, each of the words said is a Name of God. The different aspects are each called upon with reverence and given an offering. In another dimension, it is possible to see the named deity swoop in and take their offering as it is given to them. They are all lined up, waiting for their turn to partake. They, in turn, give of themselves: a blessing of assistance in life, a feeling of peace, an attitude of understanding or compassion.

That day the fire was particularly strong and fierce, probably because Aries is a fire sign and is ruled by Mars. Gayetri had to douse it several times to keep it under control. There were 6 of us attending Havan that day. We sat around the fire in a circle.

"Do you all know exactly how to offer?" asked Gayetri.

A couple of people looked blankly at her.

"You each have your bowl of offerings," she explained, holding up a stainless steel bowl that contained rice, raisins, nuts and flower petals. "Each time I say one of the 108 names of God then you pick up some food from the bowl and present it to the fire with an open palm. Don't just chuck it in the fire. Do it with care. You are offering this and as you do so, the Gods sweep down to take what is offered. In accepting the offering they enter into a contract with you. There is one very important rule. Under no circumstances must you use your index finger to pick up the offering."

I looked at her as she sat there with her index finger held high. It was exactly the same gesture that da Vinci has used in his paintings, his trademark pointing finger.

"Why not?" I asked.

"Because that is the finger that represents ego," she replied.

So that's what da Vinci was trying to tell us. In each of his paintings he is giving us a message in such a simple form. Ego. Plain and simple. That is what separates us from God.

Towards the end of the ceremony we stood up to receive aarti, which is when we draw the sacred flame towards us as a cleansing and a blessing. As we walked around the fire, each of us in turn drew from the flame. At one point I found myself directly behind the picture of Babaji. As I stood there I heard a voice. I had obviously developed the gift of clairaudience.

Don't be afraid of your power.

What? I didn't speak aloud but I questioned what that statement could mean and where that message had come from. It had come from outside me. It wasn't a thought. It was a statement.

Again the message came. "Don't be afraid of your power."

I still wasn't sure what was meant by that so I registered the fact that I had been sent this message and then I moved on. A few of us remained sitting by the fire pit at the end of Havan. I was sitting cross-legged with my hands in Gyan Mudra with the tip of my thumb in contact with the tip of my index finger, my spine upright and my eyes closed. As I sat there I realized that my body was rocking back and forth. It was a small movement, and much faster than I could do if I consciously tried to move my body. In fact the movement was so small it was probably imperceptible to the naked eye. I could clearly feel energy running through the 2 channels in my spine. I could also feel the places where energy was blocked and I felt the energy burning through the blocks with a tingling sensation. I realized I was having a kundalini experience. I sat there for quite a while, allowing the energy to do its work.

Eventually the movement stopped and I rose to leave, dipping my raw sapphire crystal necklace in the flames of the sacred fire just before I left. This was to cleanse it and transform it into an instrument of light. I had bought the sapphire from a Nepalese man in India who told me that it had been quarried in his country. It was a large, uncut stone suspended on a silver mount which I wore around my neck on a piece of string. I had started wearing it after my amethyst had been placed in the tower. I missed my amethyst in the same way that I sometimes missed my old friends. I placed the sapphire back around my neck knowing that this crystal had been sent to me to replace the amethyst.

Later I pondered on the message I had been given at the fire. Was I afraid of my own power? Was that because, like a lot of the lightworkers who had been alive in the times of Lemuria and Atlantis, we had misused our power in the past? This life I would use my power, the same power that we all have, in a different way, as a servant in the service of the light. I was determined not to go off track this time.

11/11/11 was fast approaching and events were happening all over the world, from Sedona in the United States to Badbury Rings in Dorset, England. Gatherings were taking place to mark this momentous day. A few 11:11 groups were going to the pyramids in Egypt and others would be holding ceremonies at Lake Titicaca in Peru. I wanted to be part of a gathering, joining with others on this once in a lifetime event. 11/11/11 wouldn't be happening again for 100 years! By this time I was aware enough to realize that when a sentence contained the 2 words I and want, it was the ego talking. Even though the 11/11/11 gatherings all around the world were linked to raising consciousness and the transition into the Aquarian Age, and even though it was a desire of mine to be part of one of them, I knew that I was needed at the convent on that day. So I made the necessary arrangements to be in France. I then pondered on what I was to do on 11/11/11. Maybe just being there was all that was needed, as I was part of the energy key and the opening would be happening on many levels of existence. I could just sit and hold a clear energetic space, secure in the knowledge that the crystal was in the tower. That was my understanding but I was about to find out that I had a role to play…

It happened in the forest. I was walking alone through a beautiful English woodland the following week. The leaves had started falling yet many remained, like fountains of colour adorning the branches. A beautiful red leaf drifted from the sky above me. I watched as it curled its way earthwards and landed softly at my feet without a sound. I was totally in the moment, engrossed in this graceful display, more artistic than any pre-planned and well thought through installation art that I might discover in an art gallery because of its spontaneity and naturalness.

'Now that the ET portal is closed you need to open up a portal of light on your land.'

I swung around. There was nobody there. Where did that come from? It wasn't a voice so it wasn't clairaudience, yet it wasn't a thought because it was it came from somewhere behind me. My normal thoughts come from inside me.

Open the portal in the shadow of the tower. Step up to your role. Thank you.

And it was gone, whatever 'it' was.

There are times when I wished my life was a bit more normal. Can you imagine being asked to "Open a portal of light on your land please"? What would you do? I had no idea how to go about it but what I did have was faith. Loads of faith. I knew I'd get the help I needed and I knew that I would step up because that's what happens when you surrender your ego. You become a physical instrument that is used by your higher power. I had to put Hilary and all her concerns, worries, lack of confidence, perceived lack of knowledge and fear of doing it wrong aside. That's what the voice had meant when it told me to "Step up" in a very firm but kindly way. I recalled the words of Babaji at the ashram. "Do not be afraid of your power." Did I have the power to open a portal? Yes, of course I did because it would not be Hilary who was opening it but Cynkarta. Hilary, my small self, was nothing! Cynkarta my Divine Self was powerful beyond measure.

Later that day I was reflecting on the clairaudient experience. I call it clairaudient but it wasn't. This message had been given to me like an imprint. You could compare it to writing. I could sit down at my laptop and write "EXPERIENCE" starting with the letter E and ending with E. Or I could buy a stamp pad embossed with that word and stamp the word so that the message would be received with no beginning and no end. Crop circles are transmitted rather like that. I could therefore call my clairaudient experience an imprinted message. Maybe the message had come from the same intelligence that created the crop circles. I was interested to see that some of the more recent crop circles contained the number 11:11.

I asked for a sign to confirm that I was indeed to open a portal. I did not have to wait long for confirmation; it happened that very night in the form of a dream.

I was standing in the lower ground floor room, the oldest part of the convent. The swallows came flying in. They welcomed me into 'their' territory. They flew round and round in circles above my head and I became aware that they were creating a vortex. I was caught in it and I couldn't move. This energy vortex had sound. It was a humming sound that created geometric patterns of light that rose out of the roof and up into infinity. I looked down on to the earth and on the flagstone floor I saw the same patterns imprinted into the earth.

When I woke up I was immediately struck by the similarity between that dream and the dream I had experienced when I had stayed at the Tibetan Buddhist centre on my first visit to the convent, with the 3 dark birds and the dark energetic trap. Unlike that earlier dream, I found this dream very easy to interpret. I knew that my sign had been sent. I was indeed to open an 11/11/11 portal at the convent. I normally like my signs to be in the physical universe but more and more I was learning to trust my intuition. However, just to drum the message home and to reassure me that I was being guided I was given another message of reinforcement. Checking my e-mails that morning I found one from a friend. She had sent me a picture of a tower in a beam of light!

Deep down I always knew that I would be at the convent on 11/11/11. It was Hilary who wanted to be at a group gathering for that special day but it was no longer Hilary in control of this vehicle I call a body. I was not in the driving seat. I was being led by a very wise presence rather like being guided by a bang up-to-date satnav that knew exactly where I was going, where I needed to go and how to get there in the easiest and most direct way. Not all the time, I hasten to add. Sometimes my 'satnav' couldn't get a signal and at those times I found myself being taken on strange detours as I temporarily wandered from the path!

I decided to advertise the portal opening ceremony and take it from there. Mindful of Babaji's advice about not projecting ahead I would simply set the ball rolling and see what happened. I brought up my Facebook page and was just about to post the details of my event when I noticed the time. 11:11 exactly. I gasped! After all these years the 11:11 can still take my breath away. It is the ultimate in confirmation signs. I needed to open this portal and my Higher Self was taking no chances with this one! I sent silent thanks for this extra sign of confirmation then I duly posted my event:

Join me on 11/11/11 in the historic town of Montignac, France, when a new portal will be opened in the heart of prehistory. Everyone is welcome to this free event. E-mail me for further details.

Then I posted my event and got ready to go out. Just as I was about to leave the house, the phone rang. It was my friend Kate.

"I just saw your event on Facebook."

"That's quick. I only posted it a few minutes ago," I replied. "Do you want to come?"

"Well, the strange thing is that I have taken the month of November off work and I've got nothing planned. I was thinking of going away but I had no idea where to go."

Kate was free from 3rd November onwards. I had booked the ferry from England to France for November 5th. Those dates were perfect and I could see the synchronicity of it, but could she see it?

I'm sure Kate won't mind me telling you that planning this trip was far from easy, mainly because her mind got far too involved. Despite the fact that she sent me her first e-mail at 11:11am she was still caught in a mind trap. It took quite some time, many more e-mails, a tremendous amount of synchronicity, number signs galore, complicated texts and phone calls but eventually she made the decision that she would be joining me, albeit that she would travel separately from me as she would be visiting a friend in Pau en route. She picked up her phone to text me and let me know that she had finally made her decision.

Dear Hilary, OMG it's 11:11. God Almighty! Picked up phone to say yes please and hope you will still have me... then I see the time... OMG!!!!! K

ANOTHER TEXT: *Still reeling from having sent text to you at 11:11! Had no idea what time it was! Reminded me of – Until one is committed there is hesitancy, the chance to draw back, always ineffectiveness... But NOW a whole stream of events issue from the decision. Lol.x*

Her quote was referring to:

Until one is committed, there is hesitancy, the chance to draw back. Concerning all acts of initiative (and creation), there is one elementary truth, the ignorance of which kills countless ideas and splendid plans: that the moment one definitely commits oneself, then Providence moves too. All sorts of things occur to help one that would never otherwise have occurred. A whole stream of events issues from the decision, raising in one's favour all manner of unforeseen incidents and meetings and material assistance, which no man could have dreamed would have come his way. Whatever you can do, or dream you can do, begin it. Boldness has genius, power, and magic in it. Begin it now."

I have it pinned on my wall.

Hi Kate, The fact that you are available to go to France for 11/11/11 and the fact that you were unaware that you sent me that first e-mail at 11.11 reminds us that this trip is part of The Journey Back to Source. They are also signs to me that you need to be there so of course I'll still have you!

Having made the commitment to go, you were given a confirmation sign when you saw that you were texting me at 11:11. Don't you just marvel at the magic of life beyond the ego?

I know your energy will greatly assist the opening of the portal. Look already what is manifesting by joining our energies. Hx

Chapter 30

Children of the Sun

The date was 1/11/11 and in an unusual and personal synchronistic twist it was exactly 111 days until my birthday on February 19th. This was the day that Catherine was moving to Glastonbury, the heart chakra of the world, to set up a spiritual retreat centre. She had bought a large house and would be running residential courses, workshops and retreats.

I was hoping that a neat date like 1/11/11 would reveal a bit of magic, a foretaste of what might be revealed on 11/11/11. I spent the day with my friend Will. He was checking my car over in preparation for my long drive from Devon, England to the Dordogne. To drive 1220 kilometres in an old and unusual car (no spare parts available) is a bit of a risky undertaking.

Nothing significant happened during the day. I took money from the cash point in town but there were no repeated digits. I heard no church bells chiming and nobody texted or called me. I was disappointed but I reminded myself that my disappointment was merely a result of having expectations of what could happen rather than living fully in the moment without projecting forward. I need not have been concerned though, because how was I to know that the 11:11 was about to make its most spectacular appearance to date? On the very significant date of 1/11/11, I was about to experience one of the greatest 11:11 synchronicities of my life.

It was late evening by the time I returned home from my friend's house and the long flight of outside steps leading up to the house where I was staying were unlit. As I had no torch I used my phone to light my way. I just kept pressing the buttons on the keypad to keep the screen lit, holding it away from me so the screen lit the steps. As I stepped through my front door into the light of the hallway I looked at the phone. It was exactly 11:11pm. Not only that, but it said "Message Sending". Message Sending? I must have accidently pressed some of the other phone keys by mistake. Somebody (I had no idea who) was about to receive a blank message from me. A message sent at 11:11pm on 1/11/11. There had been no number signs all day and then, at the 11th hour (quite literally!) I had this piece of number magic. This was utterly incredible. There is no way Hilary (my ego) could have dreamed up such a scenario. This was beyond any 11:11 appearance I had ever witnessed. It was even more magical than my original 11:11 wake-up call when I had simultaneously seen 11:11 on the clock, the car milometer and the trip meter on the 11th day of the 11th month.

2 minutes later I had a text from a friend. "Where is the sun?" it said. That's all. Not, "Why did you send me a blank text?" What did he mean by asking where the sun was? I rang him to ask what he meant and he told me that I had just sent him a photo from my media file. If you asked me how to do that intentionally I would have no idea how to do it. I'm not that techno savvy. The photo I had sent him was of the beach in the English seaside resort of Brighton. Because of the incredible synchronicity of the timing of this text exchange I knew that there was a very important message for me in those few words. I googled, "where is the sun 11.11". Like most people, I only look at the first page that Google throws up and on that first page there was only one website that contained the word sun. It was an organisation called the Children of the Sun. www.childrenofthesun.org.

11-11-11 Oracle Vision from Children of the Sun
The triple date portal of 11-11-11 is a cosmic trigger that launches all life into a simultaneous raising of vibrational frequency. This carries the potential to catalyze major impacts within the planetary grids, causing a very swift polarity reversal within our

consciousness. This keystone activation will launch the ascension process for all choosing humanity, triggering a powerful sequence of portal openings across the globe.

I know that happiness is part of the grand illusion of existence but at that moment I was so happy. I'm driven mostly by faith on the 11:11 path. I'm not aware of anyone else who follows this particular route towards dissolving the ego so when I see an unmistakable confirmation sign that I'm on track, I can't help but be affected by it. To read that portal openings were taking place across the globe on 11/11/11 was 100% confirmation that I had been right to follow my intuition and number signs. I didn't have any doubts whatsoever that by opening a portal at the convent on 11/11/11, I was acting in perfect alignment with Divine Will.

The Stargate is Inside Us

The inner 'Stargate' is already activating within each of us, as a whole new holographic reality. It is simply waiting to be acknowledged in order to anchor the created matrix of light into the core of our being as our new strands of DNA are fired through each burst of the greater collective awakening.

This rang true for me. I knew from my transmission in India that the number 11:11 appearing in our everyday life was linked to the reactivating of our so-called junk DNA.

When we speak of portals or stargates, we speak of these in context of a transition, from one dimensional perception to the next. This is occurring, first and foremost, within the inner realms of our consciousness. This is an inner event and one that connects the lifestream to the Soul, and more importantly, to the Group Soul. This is the key that unlocks the Seal to Divine Remembrance.

The Children of the Sun Foundation is a global platform of

planetary Light Servers who have come together without a
personal agenda to help and serve humanity as the new earth
(and the new human) is being birthed. They are helping to bring
in the Golden Age, an age of peace and co-operation. It was clear
to me that I was part of this group soul.

Our charity to Earth is in ensuring we form global Group Avatar...
empty of self and one with coherently connected, ascended and free
Unity Consciousness.

Individuals from all corners of the globe are offering themselves
in service as conduits through which the energies of manipulation, resistance and untruths are purged from both the self and
the collective whole. The group comes together by connecting
via the crystal grid. The crystal grid is part of the template for the
new earth, rather like an underlying framework. It's made of
crystal light, much less dense than the existing earth. Already
some of the crystal cities are forming in the 5th dimension.

This grid of light is also referred to as the Grid of Love, Unity
Grid, the Ascension Grid or the Christ Consciousness Grid. It is
a higher dimensional structure that has always existed around
the entire planet for its use by humanity. Some people say it was
previously used during the time of Atlantis to support its higher
dimensional existence. This grid is increasingly charged as more
of us connect to and merge into its multidimensional expansive
energy.

The grid is like a spiritual telecommunications system and
through it we can connect to the higher consciousness of humans
all over the planet. At the highest level of consciousness we are
One. When we connect to the grid we each have access to the
same information. It's open to each and every one of us, not just
a chosen few.

If we choose to connect to the grid regularly, we strengthen
our ability to receive and transmit these really high energies. It

also enables us to expand our consciousness and develop skills such as telepathy, clairaudience and multidimensional communications.

Thousands of people all over the planet unite via the grid twice a month, once on the new moon and again on the full moon to focus on healing and world peace. By doing this the new consciousness matrix is strengthened. The goal is a shift in frequency that will end all major conflict and destructive energy between humans.

You can connect to the grid wherever you are of course, but you'll probably find it easier to tune in at one of the crossing points. You'll find that the crossing points are usually located at sacred and mystical sites such as prehistoric earthworks and megalithic sites. That's because the grid was known to the ancient peoples. No wonder that there is a portal in the cradle of civilization in Montignac!

The grid connects to all of the crystals in the Earth and it crosses major portals, vortexes and dimensional doorways that connect the Earth to cosmic forces and other dimensional worlds. That's why my crystal had needed to be planted in the tower. I didn't know at the time why it needed to be there but now I understood.

I read that the planetary grid project was initiated on September 11th 2007. Less than 8 weeks after this project was started I became the owner of the convent. September 11th 2007 is a master number day.

September=9th month
11th day
2+0+0+7=9
9+11+9=29
2+9=11.

11 and 22 are the 2 master numbers.

There are points on the earth, both old and new, that can hold particularly massive amounts of energy. On their website the Children of the Sun gave details of 4 of these sites: Mount Kailash in Tibet; Sedona in USA; Lake Titicaca in Peru and Bolivia; and Arunachala in India. That explained why Arunachala felt so special and so sacred to me and why I had needed to pick up an energetic key from the cave on that sacred mountain.

There it was. There was my message. I had really wanted to be part of a group gathering on 11/11/11, but I had followed my heart, the number signs and my intuition in deciding to be at the convent. Yet I was going to be part of a group after all, a group of thousands, just not in the way I had imagined! Thanks to the existence of the crystal grid I would be connected via the grid to my group Avatar on 11/11/11. Although the group would be located in various physical locations on the planet on 11/11/11, at the level of the crystal grid we would be connected as One.

Through group work we can literally stop storms, prevent earthquakes and bring greater ease to unfolding events. In so doing, we first qualify every request to be in alignment to God's Will and the highest good of all to make sure that no mistake is ever made.

If you feel inspired to establish a Children of the Sun GEO Light Team to serve your own community, geo-region or country... please link here for more details.

Did I feel inspired? After witnessing that piece of 11:11 magic I was 100% inspired. Without any hesitation I stepped up to the role and signed up to become a co-ordinator for my area of France. How fitting that in the last few minutes of 1/11/11, a repeated digit date only second to the 11/11/11 date and definitely a once in a lifetime day, I was led to my soul group and to my humanitarian work as a servant of the light.

Transcending the Concept of Free Will

We are releasing our human operating system including the idea of having personal free will. This is the illusion that keeps the ego masked in its controlling dance of mind controlled manipulation. Free will is clearly a very outdated concept to where we are evolving as a planet and a race.

At last I had a satisfactory answer to my free will dilemma. Free will was an illusion. The only will is Divine Will. Although we appear to have free will within the play of consciousness, the play is already written. The final act involves us surrendering the ego. We can ad-lib within the play (that's what we think of as free will) but eventually we will reach the last act. In the end scene we come to the realization that free will is an illusion, thus fulfilling our role as actors on the stage of life.

And I believe that the 11:11 time prompt is the sign to show you how to get in line (or could that be line, line, line, line?) with Divine Will. You can fast forward to the final scene whenever you want. There are many routes to enlightenment. My 11:11 path is just one of them. I believe that anybody who chooses to can follow the 11:11 path. All you need to do is stop ad-libbing, put out the intent that you are ready to follow the 11:11, hand over the ego and be alert to the appearance of numbers in your everyday life.

Chapter 31

The Portal

I started to get organized for my trip to France. I exchanged some British pounds for euros at the Post Office to use on the journey. It was November 2011 and the exchange rate was 1.111. Then I looked for my European health insurance card known as the E111 and wrote down my ferry booking reference number which added up to 11. I knew I was on track.

I had started preparing my body for the 11/11/11 portal opening which meant eating a particularly strict vegetarian diet with no additives or processed foods. I needed my physical body to be at the right vibration to be able to take the force that I knew would be put through me. My blood composition needed to be PH balanced and my bowels and stomach clear. What you put into your body (your physical instrument) is important. When my resolve weakened during these days I reminded myself that an average life of 75 years is about 28,000 days. All 'Cynkarta' was asking of 'Hilary' was 11 days of particularly careful eating. It goes without saying that tea, coffee, meat, fish, any form of processed food, eggs, alcohol and any type of drug was forbidden.

I set off on November 5th which is Guy Fawkes Night in England. The skies were ablaze with firework displays. The 8 hour night crossing from Portsmouth to Dieppe was stormy. November isn't the best month to travel by sea in northern Europe. As I started my journey I checked the car milometer. 108,444.4. The trip meter was on 48. The number 4 is about safety and security so I was quietly confident that I was being looked after and that, despite my car being 14 years old, it would get me there. 4 years earlier as I had set off at the beginning of my journey with the French convent the milometer had read

87,777.7. That meant I had driven exactly 20,222.2 miles in the previous 4 years. That averages out at 5,055.55 per year. A recurring 5! 5 is the number of freedom and it is my own life path number. Do you see the magic in those numbers? Maybe these incredible synchronicities around number are happening to other people but if they do not have the same obsession with numbers that I have then maybe they are going unnoticed. I need to stress that unless you living are in the moment, the language of numbers cannot be read. Massive number signs might be right there in front of your eyes but if you're thinking about something that happened in the past or if you're projecting thoughts forward by using your power of imagination, then you're lost in thought and therefore you're effectively deaf to the message that numbers might be screaming at you.

It was a long drive down from the northern coast of France at Le Havre to the town of Montignac. As usual I stopped off at Chartres to visit the 11 circuit labyrinth. It always drew me like a magnet. I marvelled at the similarity between the wall carvings in Chartres Cathedral and those in some of the Indian temples I had visited.

Joining the main road south of Orleans the satnav stated "continue for 164 miles" so I knew that there was a long, straight drive ahead. Eventually at Brive I came off the Autoroute. I drove slowly along the beautiful winding country road between Terrasson and Montignac. Hundreds of autumnal trees lined the road, dripping with coloured leaves. Suddenly a massive hawk flew down directly towards my car and its wing actually touched my windscreen. It was so close to me that I saw its eyes clearly. I gasped in wonder! To look a hawk in the eye was a first for me. I was utterly thrilled by that event but before I could fully take in what had just happened, another hawk flew down almost as close. I have never been so near one of these beautiful birds of prey and this felt like a blessing. To me a hawk represents the element of air. I remembered seeing the circling hawks at Writing on Stone when I was performing a ceremony to the 4 directions. Birds had been appearing in my dreams too.

Immediately after my eye to eye contact with the hawk I experienced a strange visual disturbance. Everything I looked at was surrounded by geometric light rather as if I was looking through a kaleidoscope. The centre of my vision was normal but everything had this halo around it. Before I had time to become worried about why this had happened, 3 jets of water appeared directly in front of the car. 2 sprung up from one side of the road and one from the other, forming an arc of water. I drove through this liquid archway laughing at the unexpected appearance of this watery portal. I was being welcomed back home, of that I had no doubt. I felt like royalty!

I expect you are wondering why and how this water appeared. I had been approaching the dusty stone quarry on the edge of the famous papermaking town of Condat and the water was obviously intended to clean passing vehicles. Even so, the way the water had suddenly sprung up at the very moment I was passing was amusing and significant.

When I arrived at the convent a praying mantis was waiting on my door step. That insect stayed in my porch for the 3 days leading up to the portal ceremony. I opened the main door into the house and was shocked to see that the floor was littered with dead centipedes. They were everywhere in the house: on the towel in the bathroom, in the kitchen sink, on the floor, in the shower tray and on the steps. I could only assume that a massive nest of them had hatched out though I had no idea why they were all dead. Maybe they were symbolic of the letting go of my attack thanks to the BodyTalk session.

It was lovely to be back within those peaceful stone walls. Arriving back at the convent was like coming home. You know that peace that you get when your mind and emotions are still? That is what it was like at the convent. I was enveloped in an aura of peace. Life in 21st century Montignac was quiet and slow.

Because of the lack of stimulation from television, social interactions, telephone, Internet access, supermarkets and so on in the convent, I was often completely in the moment. I would notice little things like the way the way tea moved in my cup, the sound of the wooden beams as they creaked, the scent of a flower in the breeze or the sound that the water made as it dripped from the roof.

Within the walls I found it so easy to meditate. Of course it smelt of damp earth and bird droppings but in a way that was quite grounding. This was the first time I had been back since the tower was cleared. That night when I lay my head down inside the tent I noticed that when I closed my eyes I could see light, in exactly the same as in India when I had slept just outside the walls of the Sai Baba ashram. Normally when I close my eyes it is dark. That night I had another significant dream.

I was standing on the upper floor of a building when I looked and saw a tidal wave coming. I was with somebody and I asked them to hold my hand. Then the huge wave came and I felt a massive adjustment in my 7 bodies, as if I had transformed. I had experienced a personal shift in my energy field.

I woke just as the sun was rising. It was cold and wet and the dampness had permeated my body so I didn't feel great. My body likes dry heat, not damp cold. The first thing I saw when I opened my eyes was a spider. It was inside the tent looking down at me. My panic to get out demonstrated to me just how alive and kicking my arachnophobia was. I screamed and fumbled for the zip to release me from the hell of being confined in a small space with a massive spider. How long had that been there? Had it been crawling over me? I felt queasy just thinking of it. Yet I also knew that the spider was afraid of me. I could sense its panic and helplessness. It was not intending to harm me in any way and its life was in my hands. 'Just get a jar and put it in the garden,' I instructed myself. 'Don't panic. Panic is just a reaction. Act rather than react. Your mind has created this fear and your mind can undo this fear.'

The soothing voice inside me helped to calm me and I went to find a jar. By the time I got back the spider had disappeared. Moving the duvet carefully to one side I found it and tried to place the jar over its legs. The jar was too small. This was a massive spider. I found a larger jar and covered the spider completely then I slipped a card under the jar and released the poor creature into the garden. Panic over. I calmed down. The thought of the spider being afraid of me was quite helpful. I'm not saying that I have recovered from my spider phobia but I have moved on a little. I realize that my fear comes from something much deeper that I have not yet been able to contact.

Despite the fact that more than a dozen people had enquired about the portal opening event, only Kate had committed to join me but I must admit I was relieved that I was not going to have to co-ordinate dozens of people. I think I was being initiated into my role gently. The fact that one person had committed to attending and had made and paid for all her travel arrangements was enough to prevent me backing out. I was committed because she was committed and I thank her for that.

I had arrived in Montignac before Kate. She kept in touch with me by text and it was clear that she was continuing to experience a blitz of 11:11's. She was being shaken to the core by the dawning realization that what she was experiencing was unprecedented and very real. Her shock at the repeated appearance of the 11:11 left her reeling. I was able to support and comfort her because I had trodden the path before her.

It was interesting for me to witness someone else's 11:11 wake-up call at such close quarters. I had only once witnessed somebody freaking out because of the 11:11. It happened at Gaunts House Summer Gathering. Gaunts House is a spiritual community in the Dorset countryside in England. It is home to a Community of Profound Learning (CPL) – a spiritually-based and holistic-minded group of free thinkers committed to exploring and supporting the evolution of consciousness. I had just given a talk on the 11:11 phenomenon and was leaving the site when I bumped into Craig. He was in a hurry.

"Oh no, have I missed your talk about the number 11:11?" he asked. "I was stuck in traffic so I'm late. But I'm glad I caught you because I wanted to show you this."

He pulled a car park ticket from his back pocket and handed it to me. The time 11:11 was clearly displayed in black numerals.

"This is today's car parking ticket. It's about the 10th time the 11:11 has appeared this week. It's starting to freak me out, Hilary. The number 11:11 is appearing everywhere and I just don't know what it means. That's why I wanted to listen to your talk. I thought that maybe you had some answers to this."

"Craig, I can't stay and chat. I'm off to teach a yoga class. Did you read my book *The 11:11 Code*? That might help you to understand what's happening to you."

"Is it out? I need a copy. Do you have one on you?"

"There'll be a few copies in the house," I said. "Read it and then get back to me if you want to chat about anything."

A couple of days later I received an e-mail from him.

Hilary, I was reading your book and I came to the bit where your milometer and trip meter both read 1111. Out of curiosity I felt compelled to go and check my own car milometer. When I looked I saw it was 1111. I simply couldn't believe my eyes. I was stunned, shocked, worried, frightened, amazed, gobsmacked, awed and incredulous. I feel that was a defining moment on my 11:11 journey. I now know for certain that the 11:11 phenomenon exists and I know I will never be the same again. There is something happening that is beyond me, beyond my control and beyond my understanding. It is both exciting and scary. I don't know where it will lead me but I'll keep you posted.

Chapter 32

The Obelisk

The town of Montignac woke slowly, rousing itself somewhat reluctantly into another day. Unlike the lively summer mornings when everything sprang into life in the way that a young child greets the morning, in winter everything was much slower. The wood smoke from the chimneys of the occupied houses curled lazily upwards and a soft haze hung over the river valley. The smell was comforting and evoked memories of winter days from my northern England childhood. Many of the nearby houses were empty, second homes belonging to wealthy families. The businesses that relied on tourism, such as the antique shop and the boutique, closed down for winter and only one of the bars opened every evening. Sometimes the intense cold and persistent rain hung around for days at a time so people retreated behind closed doors and bolted window shutters. What a contrast to the summer! I was thankful for my wood burner but even a blazing fire needed the backup of electric fan heaters to stop me shivering. Having the wood burner lit brought warmth to the heart of the house and made me wonder how long it had been since a fire had been lit in the house. I reckon I must have been at least 6 decades.

Kate was preparing for her late autumnal visit to this lovely little town. She was still experiencing her world being rocked by numbers. As she was discovering, if you had any unhealed or unresolved fears and issues, the 11:11 sign would bring them to your attention. It seems to me that is what the 11:11 does. It brings up the residue of our stuff. Just like the dregs at the bottom of a cup of coffee are the gungiest part, so our unresolved issues are the deepest stuff in our psyche, the stuff that we have pushed as far down as we could in the hope that it would go away, the stuff that we dislike the most, that's the most difficult to face. On the 11:11 path it's normally the issues we would rather not deal with that come up. My attack in the Dordogne at the age of 21 is a perfect example. I had never spoken about it to anyone. I had put a big heavy lid on it in order to try and forget about it. But doing that did not get rid of it. All it did was to lie there inside me as a festering and unresolved wound. Bringing it up from my subconscious and out into the open was uncomfortable and challenging but once it was out, it lost its power.

I had to deal with many other things that were brought up by the 11:11 including my fear of ghosts, fear of spiders, fear of returning to the place in France where I had been attacked, fear of public speaking and fear of power to name just a few.

The French trip brought up a lot of issues for Kate. She had to deal with being too much in her head, fear of being alone and a tendency to plan in too much detail that left little room for spontaneity. She had yet to deal with her greatest fear of all, that of the unseen worlds. She was a natural mystic and had chosen a 22 life path, the highest and most difficult of all 11 life paths. There are 11 possible paths for the incarnating soul to choose from, 1–9, 11 and 22. 11 and 22 are the master life paths and anyone on a master path carries huge potential and extra charge. (*See *Numerology Made Easy* by Hilary H. Carter)

It said on the Children of the Sun website that we would just know what was to be done on 11/11/11 and they were right. I knew where the portal needed to be opened, in the cave. As soon as I stepped into that ancient room, I felt the difference. It was much clearer than before Sabberan's work on the tower. From the channellings that Catherine had given me I also knew that my travels had cleared the parts of the grid that had prevented the crystal light from penetrating this part of the earth. It even smelt different. I can't begin to describe how ancient it felt. I'm not talking of centuries, I'm talking of millenniums, right back to the very formation of the earth. That entity that I had recognized as being here so early on in my French adventure was the Guardian of this site. I was finally ready to work with it and in doing so I would fulfil my purpose in France.

It was a beautiful autumn day and I walked into town in search of a broom to sweep the cave floor. I was casually looking in the shop windows as I walked along the main street. Suddenly a picture in the estate agents' window leaped out at me. It was a photo of the interior of a house and it had exactly the same fireplace as the one in my cave. I went in and enquired about the property that was for sale.

"Where is it?" I asked.

"In Rue des Jardins," replied the estate agent. "It's a small property in the heart of the historic area and it's very, very old."

"I was just curious about the fireplace. I have an identical one in my home. It seems to be rather a grand fireplace for such a humble property."

"Ah yes, but all those old places up on the hill by the tower have been built from the original stones of the old fortified castle of Montignac. I have come across several properties like that one in the window that have the finest quality stone fixtures and fittings. Even the walls of those houses have been built from the stones of the castle. Have you not seen some of the carvings on these old houses? There is one with crossed keys and another with a coat of arms. They're all from the castle! You probably know that the castle dates back to the 10th century so these stone fireplaces, sinks, steps and doorways are ancient. Not only that, they're top quality. I'm talking royal quality here."

"I thought the houses in Beynaguet had been built from the stones of the old priory."

Needless to say he had not heard of the secret and mysterious priory so I enlightened him.

"Then maybe the priory stones have been reused in that area too," he continued. "Although it is also possible that the priory stones were used to rebuild the castle after one of its earlier attacks meaning that the castle stone originally came from the priory. All I can say is that the properties in your area are really beautiful and very old."

Now I understood why my fireplace was so fine. It could have come from either the castle or the priory. Or both! Although I would never be able to confirm its origin with 100% certainty I feel that the lower ground floor is built from priory stones and the upper floors from the castle stones. I then described the sink/font that I had recently uncovered.

"That's exactly the sort of thing I'm talking about. This area has been at the centre of so many wars and revolutions that the castle has been destroyed many times. You do know that at times the border between the English and the French ran virtually down your street, don't you?"

I did know and that is probably why I had experienced visions of such violence and bloodshed. If, as Sabberan had hinted, I had once lived in the castle, it was disconcerting to think that I was now actually living within the same stone walls, albeit they had been moved 100 metres or so from their original location. I was glad that some of the convent stones were imbued with prayer from their time in the priory. God alone knows what terrors the castle stones were imbued with.

Kate had arrived in town a few days before the ceremony and I was so pleased to be able to show her around. I took her to the bubbling springs at the foot of the Lascaux hill where we sampled the water. We gazed through the solid iron gates leading to the tower and toured the medieval wash houses. We saw the old Clarisses convent and stood poignantly by the ruined church arch. We walked the cobbled passageways, saw the old mill and tannery and the graceful 16th century hospital of 'Saint Jean l'Evangeliste' that now housed the tourist information office.

Further afield I took her to the dramatic fortified town of Domme, once home to the Templars. We went to Sarlat and visited the artist in his tower, marvelling at the interior view of his round stone roof as well as his interesting collages and paintings. The 16th century roof was original and it was miraculous that it had remained intact for so many hundreds of years.

We also went to the fortified church at St-Amand-de-Coly, once an Augustinian monastery that had been built on the site of a hermit's cave. It still bears the damage inflicted during the many religious wars.

We were brave enough to visit most of the 'Maison Forte de Reignac', the strangest and most secret castle of the Périgord Noir. The memory of the torture room with its display of genuine instruments of torture still haunts me.

The old Templar church in Condat-le-Lardin greeted us with loud chiming bells that made us jump out of our skins but also acted as a sign of connection to former days. In a display of synchronicity we had arrived at the church door at exactly noon. Many lives ago Kate and I had both been Templars in the area. At one point we met an English man and he remembered being a Cathar in this area. As is often the case, a group of us were being drawn to the location of a past life trauma to heal the past.

"If you come back in the summer we can take a kayak down the river and see the chateaus. Then we can swim in Tamniés lake or spend the day at one of the outdoor pools," I enthused.

The list of 'must see' places to show Kate was endless. It made me realize I had done an about-turn. From those early days when I so reluctantly found myself back in the Dordogne with its unpleasant and disturbing memories to this point in time 4 years later, when it dawned on me that I had become an ardent Francophile!

Kate was coming to help me to clean up the portal room the day before the opening. It was 10/11/11 and it was also the day of the full moon in Taurus. That morning I woke from a very deep sleep with the phrase 'leave no stone unturned' in my mind. That's all. It must have been the residue from a forgotten dream as I had slept so deeply that I couldn't remember dreaming. My immediate thought was that I needed to look under the large stone on the cave floor before the 11:11:11 ceremony tomorrow.

When Kate arrived we spent time in meditation because it was the full moon and we knew that at full moon and new moon we were connecting via the crystal grid to the Children of the Sun group Avatar. Sometimes deep meditation brings me significant information or useful insights. That day I was shown that the convent was part of a complex grid of ley lines that formed, through sacred geometry, the exact pattern of the flower of life.

After the meditation we had work to do. The cave badly needed cleaning. I imagine that it had not been inhabited for centuries. It was dark and damp and full of cobwebs. Thank goodness that Kate was there to help. It felt nice to have some support on the physical level for a change.

We started by cleaning the walls. This wasn't an easy task as each bucket of hot water had to be carefully carried down the 23 steps and then through a narrow, overgrown steep pathway to the door of the cave. This door was 13th or 14th century, studded with old metal nails and made from ancient hand-cut wood. Kate cleaned the altar. We were using the stone arched recess as the altar. This was the arch where several people had seen the ghost of a robed figure sitting.

The portal was to be on the ground in front of the altar. As I swept the convent floor I had the realization that the ET portal had needed to be closed before the portal of light could be opened. The time lapse of 144 days between Midsummer Day and 11/11/11 had been necessary for the crystal to work on transforming the stagnant energy that had accrued in the tower over the centuries.

I removed bucket loads of earth from the floor. I had thought that the floor was stone slabs and earth but as I swept away the earth to try and level it out a bit I made a startling discovery. Under the earth were stones about the size of my hand, carefully arranged in patterns. They were long deep stones that were planted into the earth in the same way that teeth are planted in the gums, with deep roots and only a small amount showing. These floors are known as pise floors and indicate that the room was intended for human habitation and not for animals. This floor was a rare find as most of these pise floors have been cemented over or dismantled. This one had not been touched for centuries. I knew it must have been at least 600 years old and possibly as old as 1000 years.

There were a few larger slabs on the floor and my waking thought about upturned stones was my message that I needed to lift the largest of these for this was to form the centre of the portal. My intention was to lift the stone just high enough to slip a carnelian crystal underneath. This would enable the healing of the second chakra of the land as Andrew had suggested in his e-mail almost 4 years earlier. Each chakra is linked to certain crystals or gemstones and carnelian is linked to the second chakra. There was no way that I could lift it on my own. Using a metal bar and a strong garden fork, Kate and I started to heave the stone out of the ground. As we did this a memory flashed through my mind, the memory of Claude pretending to lift this very stone as he joked that there might be hidden treasure under-neath. That day, the first time I had visited the convent seemed so long ago. It was almost exactly 4 years. The number 4 again. Claude had been right. There was indeed hidden treasure at this point, a treasure more valuable that any gold coins or gemstones. Under this stone was a physical access point to the crystal grid of light.

Moving the stone was no easy task. It was unexpectedly heavy. I had imagined it to be quite slim and flat, but as Kate and I prised it up with metal bars and a garden fork we were taken aback to discover that it was in fact an obelisk. No wonder it was so heavy! We could clearly see that the stone had been carved and fashioned into a pillar. Doubtless this had been taken from the castle at some point in the past. We lifted it right up so we could take a good look at it. We leaned it against the floor and it fixed itself on to the earth. It stood there solid and immovable, standing upright at a slight angle. No way was that stone going to be replaced into the hole that it had vacated! I looked at the hole that had been left in the floor. It was the perfect size for a fire pit. It was almost as if the portal was creating itself.

I would be working mainly on an energetic level, simply opening the portal to allow the crystal grid to find a clear and sacred place of the highest vibration possible to anchor. Once anchored, the portal would be connected to the rest of the grid and would gradually increase in strength and intensity over the following months and years.

"Let's take some before and after photos," suggested Kate. "I can use my iPhone."

Kate took a few photos and then paused.

"That's strange."

"What?" I asked.

"Come and have a look at this."

I looked over her shoulder at the iPhone screen. The area around the portal was bathed in a soft, silver glow.

"What's that light?" she asked.

"I've no idea. Take a few more and see what happens," I suggested.

She took some more and they came out exactly the same. The portal was glowing! I'd never seen anything like that before so I asked her to take some photos of another part of the room, away from the portal. There was no glow. It was only the portal that glowed. I can only assume it was bathed in astral light.

Chapter 33

The Opening

At last the big day had arrived. I had been waiting many years for the date 11/11/11 and I had no idea what to expect. Surely something memorable would happen. Today was the day of the portal opening and I didn't know how many people would be turning up to join in with this momentous event. About a dozen people had responded to the online invitation to come along to this once in a lifetime and completely free happening. I had even had a journalist from Le Parisien asking if it would be all right to come along and video the event. I had responded to all their e-mails but nobody had confirmed that they would be attending. I was prepared to go with the flow and if loads of people turned up, so be it. If it was to be filmed, so be it. And if nobody turned up, so be it. I was thankful that I had Kate coming along to help and support me as I had never opened a portal before. It was dark and intense in that cave and I would be glad of her company!

"What time should I come?" she had asked the day before. Kate wasn't staying with me. She was staying in a local bed and breakfast. I had offered her a bed in my room but as living conditions at the convent were so basic she had wisely opted for a warm, comfortable en-suite bedroom at the 'chambre d'hote' at the bottom of the hill instead.

"10am would be great but certainly no later than 10:15 as there is so much to prepare," I replied.

I rose early and started preparations while I waited for Kate. 10:00am passed and so did 10:15. 10:30 came and went and there was still no sign of Kate. Eventually, at about 20 to 11 she came through the gate. I was still in the portal room getting things ready.

"In here!" I called out when I heard her, but she didn't come and join me. I went out to see what was happening. As soon as I saw her face I knew there was something wrong. She looked pale and drawn and she had obviously been crying.

"What's the matter?" I asked. "Are you not well?"

"I had a dreadful night."

"Why? What happened?"

I could see that she was shaking. Whatever it was that she had experienced had obviously affected her deeply.

"You have no idea what an awful time I have had. It happened in the middle of the night. I didn't know where I was. I didn't even know what planet I was on. Then I felt as if I was being divided into 2 people, me and someone else. Yet I didn't know who that 'me' I am referring to was. Do you understand what I'm saying? It was such a frightening experience. I couldn't sleep. There was nobody I could call on. I didn't want to wake you up because I knew you needed your sleep in preparation for today. I felt so far away from home and it was just one of the worst things I have ever experienced, not knowing who I was or where I was."

She began to cry. It crossed my mind that maybe she had started experiencing a past life or that she was entering the consciousness of a soul who had lived in Montignac centuries earlier in the same way that I had been doing. Maybe that is why she felt like 2 people. Or maybe she was moving through a dimension. But there was no time to start discussing possibilities. The portal had to be opened in 20 minutes and it had to be done on time. Late was not an option. 11:11:11am on 11/11/11 would not be happening again in my lifetime.

"I need a hug," she sobbed. I hugged her to me. She felt frail, fearful and vulnerable. "I need a channelling. Can you give me a channelling?"

Channelling was fairly new to me and I had no idea whether I could just channel on command or not. And time was marching on. People could be arriving for the ceremony at any moment, but she continued to shake and cry and I knew I had to help her.

"Come upstairs. Sit down and collect yourself."

We sat on the covered terrace, still open to the elements because the sliding door had not yet been fitted. Getting the frame perfectly square had proved too big a challenge to me so I was looking out for a builder to finish the job. I pulled up a chair for Kate and we sat quietly for a few moments. Then I was enveloped in a feeling, a knowing.

I get the distinct feeling that you'll not be joining me at the portal, Kate.

Suddenly it wasn't me talking. Well, it was my voice but the words were not mine.

No, you will not be joining Hilary at the portal. Your work in the portal room is done, Kate. You have helped with the preparation and we thank you for that. Now you must place yourself in the light of the sun on the top of the cliff. Hilary will be in the dark and you will be in the light. Do not underestimate your role in this, Kate. You are needed as the kingpin. Just as a tarpaulin will blow away in the wind if it is not held down, so you need to place your feet firmly on the ground and hold the light for Hilary as she opens the portal. You must sit with your feet placed firmly on this sacred land and hold thoughts of peace and beauty. You are the intermediary between the crystal key in the tower and the energy key in the form of Hilary. We need you just as much as we need Hilary. In fact this work would not be possible without you. You will hold the tarpaulin of protection for Hilary whilst the delicate work of opening is undertaken. You are not to move from the place on the high point for 33 minutes. We ask that you stay focused and positive. You are the positive polarity and Hilary is holding the negative polarity for the work is magnetic in nature. We were working on your energy field last night in preparation for this event. We had to make massive adjustments in a short time and this accounts for your strange experiences. You need not fear. We are protecting you. The portal will be opened with our help. Hilary knows that she is working with the Guardian of this site who has held it in trust until this moment in the space/time dimension. There will be no other physical body on the site of the portal. Just Hilary. We thank you both.

The voice left just as suddenly as it had come.

"God, that was a channelling. That was amazing," I said. "I've never had it coming through as clearly as that. It was like I was overshadowed by another being."

"Oh and that feels so right," said Kate. I sensed relief in her voice.

"Hmm, from what was said it sounds like there is nobody else coming. I need to get down there and get started. It's nearly 11am and I know that time is crucial with this opening."

The channelling was correct. Nobody else turned up. And so it was that I found myself alone in the cave at 11:11:11 on 11/11/11. This seemed to be a recurring theme in my life. I was always being thrown back on myself and my own resources. Yet I wasn't alone because Kate was keeping the magnetism in balance and we were joining in consciousness with thousands of other people all over the earth through the crystal grid. I knew that the Guardian was there with me too.

Opening the portal was simple and straightforward. Everything came so naturally and the ceremony flowed beautifully. I guess I must have done this work before in Lemuria or Atlantis, before those great civilizations were submerged under the waters of the sea and destroyed. I used the 4 directions and 5 elements. Fire, earth, air, water and metal. I used chants, mantras and the clearing and healing sounds of my Tibetan bowls. I burned lots of incense. I lit the fire in the newly created fire pit and it burned well. I offered incense grains to the fire and surrounded it with orange candles as I knew that this portal was linked to the second chakra and orange is the colour of that chakra. I planted the relevant crystals in the correct places and aligned one of them with the tower. Part of the way through I opened my Penguin Classics book on the teachings of the Buddha to select a reading. I opened it at random on page 64 and read the following:

326. In days gone by this mind of mine used to stray wherever selfish desire or lust or pleasure would lead it. Today this mind does not stray and is under the harmony of control, even as a wild elephant is controlled by the trainer.

327. Find joy in watchfulness. Guard well your mind. Uplift yourself from your lower self, even as an elephant draws himself out of a muddy swamp.

328. If on the journey of life a man can find a wise and intelligent friend who is good and self-controlled, let him go with that traveller and in joy and recollection let them overcome the dangers of the journey.

329. But if on the journey of life a man cannot find a friend who is good and self-controlled, let him then travel alone like a king who has left his country, or like a great elephant alone in the forest.

330. For it is better to go alone on the path of life rather than have a fool for a companion. With few wishes and few cares and leaving all sins behind let a man travel alone like a great elephant alone in the forest.

As I stood at the new portal I heard my neighbours sitting chatting on their terrace and children playing on a nearby balcony. Other people were down at the war memorial laying wreaths to remember the war dead as 11/11 is Armistice Day and it's a national holiday in France. And there I was all alone in a damp, dark, uninhabited cave opening a multidimensional doorway to allow the crystal grid to anchor into the physical earth at this place. I try not to test the Universe, but that day I did. I asked for a confirmation sign that I was working multidimensionally, that I was not going crazy and that I was right in following the signs that had led me to this point. It was Kate who gave me the sign. I had gone to lie down for an hour after the ceremony. Kate had been taking photos of the surroundings while I rested.

"Look at this!" she exclaimed when I emerged from my tent an hour later, thrusting her camera in front of me. There was my house, the dear little convent, and above it was a massive violet ray in the shape of a pyramid. It covered the entire roof and half the stonework. Below the violet colour were 2 bands of white light. We both looked at the picture in disbelief. It was indisputable that the image showed a down-pouring of light from above the house.

"It's nothing like the photos I took yesterday," she said and it was true. "When I saw the shower of violet light rays I clearly heard that this was to thank you for your work."

This was indeed the sign I had asked for. Many weeks later I was looking at the 'properties' for the photo, checking the pixels as I thought it might be suitable to use as the cover for this book. It was then that I saw the time that the photo had been taken: exactly 1:11pm.

As usual there was more magic to come on that day. I don't look for rewards for doing the work that I do but the Law of the Universe works in such a way that I am rewarded. That day I received quite a few texts from friends who knew about my 11:11 obsession. They were all full of numerological significance. One was sent at 10:55:55, one at 12:22:22 and another at 12:44:44.

Much later that afternoon Kate and I were sitting in the garden amongst the piles of garden debris, trimmings from the many trees that had been pruned on my last visit in June.

"Should we have a fire to get rid of it? It'll be nice and dry so it should burn well," I said. "It would be a lovely ending to the day. It's such a beautiful evening it would be good to be outside." Despite the fact that it was November the weather during the day had been unseasonably warm. The days were very warm, too hot for a coat. But in the evening the temperature dropped sharply and the nights were cold. Kate agreed with my idea. As I walked towards the house to get the gloves, rake and matches, I heard a strange sound. It was a sort of crackling. I walked back towards Kate, trying to trace the source of the sound. I could only hear it when I was in the upper part of the garden, not on the middle path.

"What's that? Can you hear it? A crackling sound..."

We stood in silence and tried to identify the source of the sound. It was coming from the direction of the tower. We looked over and there at the base of the tower was a smoking fire. The twigs and leaves were crackling in the intense heat. How perfect. On the land next to the new portal our fire was about to be lit and on the land next to the tower containing the amethyst a fire had already been lit. By now I understood that the crystal had absorbed my change of energetic patterning as it had been with me at every key collection point and at the Template Ceremonies. What I hadn't realized at the time was the link between the tower and the convent.

The fires felt very symbolic. The fires felt like beacons that connected the 2 plots of land. And those fires symbolized the burning away of centuries of darkness and ignorance.

What was the owner doing in the grounds of her chateau in November? She was never there in the winter. She spent summers in Montignac and winters in Paris. She was, of course, completely unaware that she was being prompted by the Universe and that her 11/11/11 fire was part of a grand cosmic plan.

Our fire was big and the heat was intense. We could throw

anything on it and it burned in minutes. Even the damp wood was soon reduced to ash. It felt very witchy, the 2 of us feeding this beautiful and perfectly round bonfire. That heat must have penetrated deep into the earth. I could hardly begin to imagine how many fires had been lit on that ground before. Momentarily we paused from our work and we were just in time to see a massive orange moon rising to the right of the tower. It was a fitting end to a memorable day.

Once the portal was open it was as if a block had been lifted. The very next day, things began to flow. On 12th November Kate moved from the bed and breakfast into a nearby cottage. The owner's partner was a builder and 2 days later he came round and started work on my house. He closed in my terrace so I now had an inside toilet, doors were put on the kitchen cabinets and worktops were put in place. The shower screen was fitted and my gate was mended so that it now could be opened and closed. Although I still had very basic living conditions, to me it was pure luxury not having to venture outside to access the kitchen and bathroom.

My search for the elusive Baron finally bore fruit. I had managed to find out which road he lived in and as I wandered along his street wondering which door to knock on I saw a group of people standing chatting. I walked up to them.

"Excuse me, I'm looking for Le Baron," I said.

"Le Baron?" replied a striking looking man with a large belly and a flamboyant handlebar moustache. "That's me."

I could see why he was so named as he was a handsome man with a powerful presence that certain people carry. It was a light that came from a well-developed aura and a sharp intelligence. I was so glad I had found him as he was about to leave town along with his 85 year old mother. A few weeks later and I would have missed them both! They were off to live in Spain. Although it was Le Baron who had the information I was seeking, everything he knew had been handed down to him by his mother. She was the holder of the folk knowledge of the town, the stories and legends that are held by and passed down through word of mouth amongst the people. Her family had lived in Montignac for centuries and she carried the thread of knowledge that had been carried through the generations, a thread that could easily snap. There is written history and there is oral history. Oral history tends to focus on the human stories rather than on dates, facts and figures.

As I had suspected, knowledge of the convent school was deeply ingrained in local legend but it was not in any written texts. I reminded myself that even the origins of the Benedictine priory were not written because it had been established so early on.

"So was my house a convent school?" I asked her.

"Yes it was."

"Do you know who ran it, which religious order?"

"It was Catholic. It was a closed order of nuns. They took the girls in at the age of 12 or 13, just after their communion. The mothers put their daughters into the convent because they thought they would be safe there. They often did this against the wishes of their fathers. In fact it is said that many fathers turned up at the convent to claim their daughters but they were sent away by the nuns."

"Could the mothers visit their daughters?"

"Oh no. Never. It was a closed order so once the girls were behind those gates that was it for life. Their mother would kiss them goodbye at the gates and never see them again."

"How many nuns were there?"

"I don't know that. And not all the girls of the town were put in the convent, just some."

"What colour robes did the nuns wear?"

"I'm not sure. But I do know that the convent belonged to the Carmelites."

I later discovered that the Carmelites wore grey robes. Grey robes, like the ghost that I saw walking through the wall.

"I have been told it was an école de bonne soeurs."

"School of the good sisters? Strictly speaking yes, that's true because the nuns taught the girls to read and write. But as I said it was a closed order so the girls and women lived within the walls. They prayed and learned and read the scriptures. In fact there is a little prayer hut in your garden where the nuns could retreat and pray alone."

My wood shed! The little stone building with the medieval oven...

"Your garden is the original garden that belonged to the convent."

"Can you tell me what century this convent was founded?"

"Oh it's really, really old. At a guess I'd say it was 12th century but it could well be older than that."

"And how long was it in existence for?"

"I don't know."

"Why do so many people refuse to acknowledge that my convent ever existed? I'm talking about the local historians and the tourist information centre."

"It could be because of the scandals that grew up around the place. Many of those girls were held against their will and it is known that sometimes they managed to get out. There was an underground route. You probably already know that this area is laced with tunnels and the local people all knew where the tunnels were."

"So you're saying there was an entrance to a tunnel on my land?"

"Yes. If you look carefully you might even find it."

I think I had already found it. At the bottom of my cliff wall was a deep cleft in the cliff that had been blocked in with cement. I imagined that had been done to prevent children and animals crawling inside and getting lost. I was certain that must be the tunnel entrance she was talking about.

"If any of the girls gave birth, which they sometimes did, the babies were killed and buried in the walls or in the garden. They sliced the babies in 2 with a sword. That's how they killed them. Everybody knew that's what happened."

I tried to imagine what it must have been like to be a young girl within the walls of my home hundreds of years ago, locked away forever. I know for certain that I would have been one of the escapees!

"When was it closed down?"

"I can't say. Your place is so ancient that it has passed through various hands over the centuries. I knew the old woman who lived there before the war. Much of the convent had virtually fallen into ruin by then and some has been lost forever but recently a builder renovated part of it."

The building behind mine, the one with a lovely stone arched doorway, had been brought up to a habitable standard. Like Alain's house an extra storey had been added so the ceilings were not high and like Alain's house it had no garden. I was the person fortunate enough to have become guardian of the sacred land thanks to the number signs that had led me to France.

Was the information that Le Baron's mother gave me accurate? I don't know for certain. It would certainly explain why my land was marked as "closed land in common" in the archives. Is oral history less accurate than written history? Not necessarily. Truth exists in the stories that are passed down through the generations. Sometimes this truth can be more accurate than the written word. Even Lascaux itself, one of the most important prehistoric sites in the whole of Europe, was known about long before it was discovered. For years the local people had talked about a secret underground passage on the outskirts of Montignac. It was rumoured that the passage led to hidden treasure. In exactly the same way, my neighbours all spoke of the old convent school that was so old that all records of its existence were lost. The oldest houses in the area were said to be 13th century. That referred to the standing structures. However, houses like mine that had been built directly into the cliff or the caves had probably been built and rebuilt many times during the frequent wars in this troubled part of France. It was clear that any religious institutions would have been the target for much violence during the many religious wars. The foundations of places such as mine could have been Roman or even older. As a cave house, it is possible that my ground floor room was as old as Lascaux!

In the end I just had to let go of the need to find written proof as the deepest origins of my convent school did not exist in writing. The full and detailed history of my convent will never be known but that doesn't matter. My heart knows the truth.

Leaving the secluded courtyard of Le Baron's 450 year old house, I headed up the steep hill towards the chateau. I had written a letter to the owner.

Dear Madame, Thank you for your help with the 11/11/11 work. It is now finished and the portal is open. You are welcome to come and visit whenever you wish. Kind Regards, Hilary Carter.

That night I dreamed of a door. In the keyhole was a brand new shiny golden key. I had never seen this key before. The top was perfectly round, like a solar disc. I turned the key and stepped through the door.

Like the pieces of a huge jigsaw puzzle I looked back and saw clearly the perfection of what had unfolded over the previous few years. The journey had started when I saw the convent advertised on the Internet. That was my first connection. It was 6 months before I visited the place for the first time. During those months an energetic shift was taking place within me and then also within the convent. The process moved up a gear after my first visit when I made a connection with the land on which the convent sat. Once my name was on the deeds I became the official

Guardian and from that point in time onwards my work inten-sified. My travels to the pyramids of Mexico, the sacred sites of the indigenous peoples of Canada and the USA, the early Christian churches and Sufi shrines in Turkey and the temples and ashrams in India had been necessary for me to collect keys of energy and to clear the ley lines that were blocking the flow of energy to Montignac.

I had been working on the second chakra of both the land on which the convent sat and within my own chakra system. Sexual abuse is held in the second chakra and I had needed healing in the second chakra because of the sexual attacks that I had experi-enced in the Dordogne earlier in my life.

When I reflect on the life I am now living I am filled with a sense of wonder. 'Hilary' could never have created such a life using thought forms. She simply does not possess the degree of imagination needed to manifest such a unique and miraculous existence. My life is a magical adventure of signs and synchronicities. I am constantly amazed at the way that numbers continue to communicate with me by appearing in my everyday world.

The ego is limitation whereas the Divine Self is limitless. When I first bought the convent I had felt a desire to name the property. I felt uncomfortable with the fact that it had no name and no number, as if it lacked an identity because of this. Yet in a way this very thought reflected a much deeper concept, namely that of having an identity because having a separate identity is the first step towards having an ego.

I have gone out on a limb by deciding to live my life according to the number 11:11 but I don't regret having chosen to live in this way. That's partly because I feel I have gained so much on a spiritual level but mainly because it has led me to see where Humanity is heading and it is a wonderful place.

Axis Mundi Books provide the most revealing and coherent
explorations and investigations of the world of hidden or
forbidden knowledge. Take a fascinating journey into the realm
of Esoteric Mysteries, Magic, Mysticism, Angels, Cosmology,
Alchemy, Gnosticism, Theosophy, Kabbalah, Secret Societies and
Religions, Symbolism, Quantum Theory, Apocalyptic
Mythology, Holy Grail and Alternative Views of Mainstream
Religion.